**Using Social Research in
Public Policy Making**

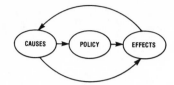

Policy Studies Organization Series

Using Social Research in Public Policy Making

Edited by
Carol H. Weiss
Columbia University

Lexington Books
D.C. Heath and Company
Lexington, Massachusetts
Toronto

Library of Congress Cataloging in Publication Data

Main entry under title:
  Using social research in public policy-making.

  (Policy Studies Organization series; 11)
  1. Policy sciences—Addresses, essays, lectures. 2. Social sciences and state—United States—Addresses, essays, lectures. I. Weiss, Carol H. II. Series: Policy Studies Organization. Policy Studies Organization series ; 11.
  H61.U65   1977   309.2'12   75-42954
  ISBN 0-669-00498-7

Second printing August 1978.

Published simultaneously in Canada.

Printed in the United States of America.

International Standard Book Number: 0-669-00498-7

Library of Congress Catalog Card Number: 75-42954

To Amitai Etzioni

Contents

Acknowledgments

The Policy Studies Organization gratefully thanks the Office of Intergovernmental Science and Research Utilization within the National Science Foundation for its aid to the symposium on which this book is based. Thanks are particularly owed to Frank Hersman, Louis Higgs, John McGwire, and David Richtmann of that office.

I would like to thank Howard Davis and Susan Salasin of the National Institute of Mental Health, and the Institute, for their support of my research on social research and government policy. Stuart Nagel of the Policy Studies Organization stimulated this collection of papers, Janet Weiss gave cogent advice, and Herbert Gans made helpful suggestions on the Introduction. Sara Tollstrup handled the organizational tasks and typed the manuscripts. I thank them all.

Above all, I would like to express my appreciation to the authors who contributed their time and talents and to my family who contributed what they thought of as encouragement.

Carol H. Weiss

1 Introduction

Carol H. Weiss

As the title of the book descriptively if not mellifluously indicates, the substance of the discussion within its covers is the use of social science in decision making. The decision making under review has two special features. It is decision making by governments and governmental units. And it is of sufficient scope and importance to merit the term *policy making*. Although none of the authors ventures a formal definition of policy, we are clearly concerned here with matters of moment, with decisions that go beyond the routine, and therefore with the use of social science research under conditions of complexity and uncertainty.

The imagery underlying the chapters in this volume is that of social science research entering an arena that is crowded: with people, agencies, missions, goals, interests, advocates, information, experience. The policy world is a busy place. Social science research does not rise up and carry all before it. Neither is it totally irrelevant. What happens between these extremes—when, how, and where social research has effects, and what kinds of effects it has—these are the subject of our collective enterprise.

It is probably well to lay to rest one specter at the outset. We do not hold that the only, or even necessarily major, function of social science research is to aid in policy making. As Riecken has said:

... the social sciences, like the physical or biological sciences, are intellectual subjects, directed primarily toward understanding, rather than action.[1]

There is a profound need to enlarge the zone of understanding of human behavior and society. Those of us interested in the intersection of social science and policy do not question the need for fundamental research. We see no competition with those engaged in developing stronger bodies of verified knowledge and firmer theories to explain patterned regularities of behavior. On the contrary, we welcome these efforts. As social science knowledge becomes sturdier and more predictive, one of the fallouts is that it becomes more trustworthy as a basis for policy advice.

If policy-oriented researchers have no quarrel with discipline-oriented research, the relationship is not necessarily symmetrical. A number of social scientists have written in splendid prose about the dangers and costs of enlisting social science in the cause of government policy making.[2] I believe that the risks they cite are important and real, and they deserve a hearing.

1

Let me try to summarize the arguments:

1. When government sponsors social science research for policy purposes, it diverts social scientists from their true priority of enlarging knowledge.

2. When social scientists accept government funds, they are put in a position of giving advice prematurely on the basis of inadequate knowledge. This situation benefits neither government nor the social sciences; in fact, their brashness brings the disciplines into disrepute.

3. By accepting research problems set forth by government officials, social scientists distort the development of the disciplines. Those areas in which government is interested are advanced, while issues of greater salience for the theoretical core of the discipline are neglected.

4. Social scientists who not only address the research problems that officials set but who address them in the terms and with the value orientations of the incumbent officeholders abdicate their role as scientists and become technicians for the powers-that-be.

5. Using their knowledge and skills in service to any sitting government— whether it be conservative or liberal and reformist or socialist—makes social scientists handmaidens of the state, rather than what they should be: un-attached, untrammeled critics of any and all forms of social arrangement.

These are arguments for maintaining the separation of social science from government and from its even more disreputable bedfellow, politics. But to a considerable degree, they themselves are political arguments. Some derive from conservative assumptions and some from radical assumptions. With all their differences, their common implication is that government and social science are separate realms and should remain so. The less hidebound of the critics would accede that occasional contacts might occur without disaster. Government may from time to time send forth a scoop, like the Viking lander on the Martian surface, to haul in some social science data that look relevant to its business. Social science in its turn may occasionally let down a tin cup to scoop in government financial support for its own undertakings. But there is a sense in these arguments that closer interrelationships, such as doing social science research for policy purposes, would provide benefits and incur costs for the "wrong" groups—that is, for groups that by the critic's lights are undeserving of such consequences.

Despite the cogency of the various cases that can be made against social science for government, there are a number of counterarguments. Most social scientists apparently accept the notion that the two realms can and do overlap. For one thing, in each social science, there is a division of labor. There seems world enough and time for many kinds of pursuits. Those who are attracted by the role of social critic can play that part, while those who want government grants for large-scale empirical work or those who seek government employment to work on applied problems apparently find these opportunities, too. Not everyone has the same interests or the same skills or creativity.

Further, the inwardness of some of the arguments—the contemplation of the internal needs of the disciplines—is not the only perspective that is hallowed by tradition. From the emergence of the social sciences, each of them has had a lusty strand of usefulness and application. Macchiavelli's *The Prince*, Adam Smith's *Wealth of Nations*, and Auguste Comte's *Positive Polity* were deliberately oriented to the solution of practical, wordly problems. It would be a strange kind of social science indeed that did not take the world around it not only as learning ground but as practice ground for its developing insights. While every science goes through periods when primary attention goes to developing tools and methodologies, to building bodies of data, and to constructing models and theories, the strain toward service is never absent. The social sciences are particularly susceptible to calls to the cause of human betterment.

Another point of view suggests that social science is as adroit at exploiting government for pursuit of its own ends as government is at mobilizing social science for its purposes. Social scientists accept government research funding and proceed to divert at least part of their effort to issues of disciplinary priority. A recent study suggests that the government may be a willing partner in this implicit connivance.[3]

But perhaps most significant of all is the recognition that all choices of emphasis in the social sciences are governed by some set of values. Explicitly or implicitly, value considerations guide the selection of topics to be studied, variables to be analyzed, and even the areas of human behavior to be modeled in that most honorable and abstruse of academic pursuits, theory construction. Basic research is no more immune from value choices than research in the fields adjacent to policy making.

And contributing to the deliberations of government is a value that can be viewed as legitimate as any. Given the scope and ramifications of governmental activities, there is much to be said for providing aid, however modest, to improve the effectiveness of government policy. What governments do has massive effects on people's lives, and the record of recent social legislation has shown erratic success. It looks as though governments can use all the help they can get. Contributions from the social sciences may be able to make some difference in how governments handle their ever-expanding range of responsibilities. Further, the contributions need not be narrow and constricted. A wide array of social scientific contributions—data, generalizations, concepts, orientations, critical perspectives—may be able to inform policy making.

The contributors to this volume believe that social science can aid in the making of government decisions. They take for granted that it is neither a foolhardy nor an unimportant thing to do. But they see the issues at the intersect between government and social science in ways that do not always fit the accustomed assumptions. In order to put their discussion in perspective, let me start back with some of the conventional pieties of earlier analyses. This presentation is oversimplified and does disservice to many of the sophisticated essayists who have assayed the relationships between social science and government, but I think it is accurate in contour.

Traditional Wisdom

1. The basic premise of the research-for-policy literature is that using social science research for public policy making is a good thing. Use is good, more use is better, and increasing the use of social research means improving the quality of government decisions. This assumption is such an accepted one that many analyses start with the question: How can we increase the use of social research?

In early essays, partisans of social science engaged in uncritical press agentry on behalf of their craft. There was much hoopla about the rationality that social science would bring to the untidy world of government. It would provide hard data for planning, evidence of need and of resources. It would give cause-and-effect theories for policy making, so that statesmen would know which variables to alter in order to effect the desired outcomes. It would bring to the assessment of alternative policies a knowledge of relative costs and benefits, so that decisionmakers could select the options with the highest payoff. And once policies were in operation, it would provide objective evaluation of their effectiveness so that necessary modifications could be made to improve performance.

The "selling of social research" as a guide to government probably reached its zenith, at least in this simplistic form, in the mid-1960s. Then came a series of setbacks. One was the bad news that came streaming in about the failures in the War on Poverty. True, it was underfinanced and overpromised, but the poverty program had derived much of its intellectual underpinning—at least indirectly—from the social sciences, and its indifferent success caused serious reexamination. Another blow was the fall from glory of the economists. Domestic Keynesianism seemed to have tamed the business cycle and brought about full employment without inflation. Then things went wrong there, too.

Later writings about contributions to policy grew more modest in their claims. Observers wrote of the limitations in research methodology. There was greater sophistication about the probabilistic nature of social research results, about the limitations of the *ceteris paribus* condition in a world where other things were never equal, about problems of generalizability to an uncertain future.

Several writers explicitly recognized that government decision making was a process of advocacy and bargaining, that power and interests were at stake, and that social researchers were becoming partisans in the negotiations. But to many advocates of policy-oriented research, social researchers were still seen as neutral and dispassionate. Their research was entering a political arena, but they themselves were representatives of the truth. Schultze called them partisans of effectiveness and efficiency, a kind of nonpartisan partisan.[4] If the issue of values was not absent, it went unmentioned. People of good will shared a belief in efficiency so that they could work together for the common good. Thus, for all the growing awareness of snares and pitfalls, many observers retained the expectation that social research would be a weight in the scale on the side of rational policy decisions.

As the 1970s wore on, the expectations from social science rose again. There was great interest within government in social indicators, benefit-cost analysis, surveys of need, evaluation research, policy analysis, and social experiments. Government expenditures for social research continued to grow. The National Science Foundation's estimate of federal funding for research in social science and psychology in 1976 was $493 million. Estimates by the Study Project on Social Research and Development at the National Academy of Sciences were even higher, ranging from $650 to over $700 million for fiscal year 1976.[5] As the level of investment suggests, people within government expected that social research, under both grants and contracts, would offer something useful to program and policy. Whatever the setbacks, optimism prevails: Social research should contribute to wiser decision making.

2. A second axiom of the traditional wisdom is that social research is not now well used by government. The theme of neglect is widespread. The House Committee on Government Operations conducted a study on the uses of social research in federal domestic programs in 1967 and published four volumes of testimony. Among the statements: "The extent to which existing knowledge is utilized in shaping . . . welfare programs leaves a good deal to be desired"; ". . . total neglect by the Congress of even social research directly called for by the Congress itself"; "Existing economic, social and psychological data is rarely utilized in shaping national and local health programs."[6]

Three blue-ribbon commissions,[7] as well as many observers before and since, have echoed these reports in elegiac tones. Chapter 11 in this volume, by Michael Q. Patton et al., cites the works of a number of people, including me, to the same effect. To bring the litany up to date, here are two recent citations:

Social science findings in the past have not been totally unrelated to public issues. But the help they offer is slight in comparison with the magnitude of perceived problems such as poverty, welfare, racial antagonism, and urban deterioration. No systematic social theory and research currently illuminate key national issues on a continuing basis.[8]

Of the extensive social research supported by the Department of Defense on the actions of governments and revolutionary movements in foreign nations:

On the whole, for all that it taught those involved, the impact of the research on the most important affairs of state was, with few exceptions, nil.[9]

So research should be used, but it is not. Rather than being part of the solution, social research has itself become a problem.

3. The final taken-for-granted premise is that government officials *could* make better use of social policy research if some relatively modest reforms were made. Changes in procedure, technology, and staffing ought to be able to increase research utilization. The assumption is that appropriate knowledge exists or could fairly readily be brought into existence. The job is twofold: to see that social science knowledge produced is relevant to government and to transfer that knowledge to decisionmakers in ways that enhance their capacity to use it.

A number of schemes have been proposed to improve the fit between government concerns and social science knowledge. A common one is to tinker with research funding mechanisms. Government officials can have more say about what research gets done. By using contracts rather than grants, they can acquire research to their own specifications through processes of competitive bidding. This scheme leaves the investigator little latitude to set his own topic and method, and it prevents his regarding federal funds as a benefice to do the research as he wishes. Another frequent suggestion is to favor for-profit or nonprofit research institutes as researchers for government, rather than social scientists in university departments. Institutes are expected to be more responsive than academicians to the needs of research sponsors. Or new institutions can be set up to conduct government-oriented research, institutions that avoid the disabilities of both universities (with their segmentation into powerful departments) and free-standing institutes (that often cannot attract talented staff). Finally, there are constant calls for more monitoring of research in progress. Federal staff monitors should be out in the field seeing that the research does not stray from its appointed purpose. Reforms of this sort are expected to increase the relevance of research to potential government users.

As for disseminating the products of research, one of the more popular prescriptions is to introduce middlemen, research utilization agents, knowledge brokers, into the process to link the decisionmaker with relevant social science findings. Modeled after agricultural extension agents, research utilization agents are expected to draw from the social science storehouse those findings that will help to solve the decisionmaker's problems. A few attempts have been made to implement this prescription,[10] but almost always for the benefit of practitioners (e.g., teachers) rather than decisionmakers.

Other mild and mannerly reforms have been urged. Since the aim has been to facilitate the transfer of knowledge, these reforms tend to stress communication:

computerized information systems that contain abstracts of research retrievable by key word;
increased personal contacts between researchers and policymakers to develop trust and communication;

training for decisionmakers in social science method and theory;
recruitment of more social scientists into positions of authority;
greater willingness of researchers to interpret and promote their results;
more critical syntheses of existing knowledge to ease the burden both of the
search for appropriate research and the assessment of its validity and appropriateness.

So much for the conventional wisdom. That it contains large elements of truth is unquestioned. Nevertheless, the writers collectively assembled in this volume, whose experience comes from work in four countries, take issue with it at crucial points.

Toward Elaboration of the Issues

1. People say that social science research should be used. But many of the people doing the saying are social scientists who, like Rexford Tugwell on his way to Roosevelt's Washington, expect to "speak truth to power." Such a posture presupposes that (a) there is a clear and single truth, (b) they have it by the tail, (c) it is a whole truth whose revelation is irrelevant to the clash of interests and political stakes, (d) powerful decisionmakers will heed this truth, and (e) decisions embodying such "truth" will be better and wiser than decisions reached on other grounds.

Few social scientists would make such extravagant claims. Yet, many of them talk as though using social research is a simple and straightforward business: Research is truth and they are the passers of the flame. What is behind the wholehearted endorsement of some of these social scientists to "research utilization"?

Above all, I believe that their commitment to social research is grounded in a belief in rationality. They see the world as a complex place, and they seek guideposts and directional principles to find their way through. In their view, social science provides both the theoretical directions and the empirical sound-ings to reach desired goals. To put these resources at the service of policymakers will increase the chances that decisions that are reached will be sound and wise. They believe that social science research can improve understanding of the complex interrelationships of social processes and that in such understanding lies hope for rational policy.

But entangled with this lofty conviction are more self-serving motives. For one thing, government use of social science increases the rewards available. There are more grants and contracts, more positions, more promotions, and more conferences, papers, and journals. The standing of the social sciences is higher on campus and off, and the recognition available to the individual social scientist is greater. The social sciences matter, and the social science career is vindicated.

Further, social scientists can affect the direction that public policy takes.

Their influence is no longer restricted to the small world of the discipline but extends to important happenings. The papers and reports that they write need not find their final resting place in other researchers' footnotes but can make a difference in health care or education or economic policy. They have a sniff of power: the heady sense that their words penetrate conference rooms and oval offices, a glimmer of themselves as *eminence grise*.

Finally, there is the potential for nudging policy in the direction they believe in. Social scientists tend to cluster on the left-liberal end of the political spectrum. The Carnegie study of 60,000 faculty members found that in colleges and universities, which are liberal places to begin with, the most liberal groups on campus are sociologists, social workers, anthropologists, political scientists, and psychologists. On the liberalism-conservatism scale, 41 percent of all faculty scored very liberal or liberal. Compare this with 72 percent of sociologists, 64 percent of anthropologists, 62 percent of psychologists, 61 percent of political scientists, and 57 percent of economists. Faculty members in engineering, business, and agriculture were at the conservative end of the scale.[11] I would guess that there is something involved beyond self-selection of liberals into the social sciences. Questioning the existing order of society is almost inherent in these disciplines; it is part of the calling to seek better structural arrangements for the realization of the human potential. In this day and age, this has almost always meant a leftward tilt.

Since academic social scientists tend to have liberal convictions, their interests in policy influence reflect these convictions. Some of them see the use of objective research evidence as a means to minimize the influence of special interests on public policy—to counteract the lobby, the pressure group, the special pleader, the trade association or large corporation, the politicians who trade favors rather than act in the public interest. Social science, in this view, will advance the common weal by giving voice to the underdog, the deprived, the groups who are underrepresented in councils of power. Through social research, they can help to redress the balance of power tipped too far to the right by the constellation of power and wealth and help move the country toward greater equity and equality.

Thus, while social scientists' concern with the utility of social research rests on a belief in its potential as a rational guide to policy, it is likely to be buttressed by (1) interest in the status and rewards that accrue to social science, (2) desire for influence in the corridors of power, and/or (3) reformist zeal to move public policy in the direction of their own beliefs, which are usually economic liberalism and social egalitarianism. They are not disinterested by-standers. When decisionmakers are confronted with exhortations to use social science research, it is not irrelevant for them to ask: *Cui bono*?

Of course, surfacing the possible self-servingness of the claims to research utility does not vitiate the claims. It may still be true that social research can increase the soundness of public policy. As we will see anon, the contributors to this book tend to think research has value, but they *temper* the claims in the direction of modesty. Several of them, like Rein and Schon, offer a reinterpretation of the types of uses that social research can effectively serve.

2. There are congenital difficulties in the application of social science research to policy. "Improving utilization" is not the easy patchwork job that some have claimed, at least in the higher reaches where policy is made. Several of the authors in this volume take on the executive, legislative, and judicial branches of government. Each of them points out some special problems in his branch. In Chapter 6, Uliassi writes of the flood of information pouring in to the federal bureaucracy, the ambiguity of much of the research that arrives, the contention among experts, and also the competing claims for attention of practical experience and common-sense wisdom. In Chapter 9 on the federal judiciary, Rosen points to problems in meshing social research with legal procedures: rules of evidence, adversary relationships, the unavailability of social research to the courts unless attorneys place it before them, the generality of social science findings as opposed to the specificity of the single case, the concern of the law with order as opposed to the social research emphasis on change, and the overriding interest of the court with *its* business, which is resolving often intractable issues while preserving the fabric of the law, rather than reaching decisions that conform to the "right reason" of social science.

Dreyfus, in Chapter 8 on the Congress of the United States, finds the legislature a place of tumultuous activity where a number of controversial and long-contested issues arise for speedy decision each session—decisions to be made by a limited number of legislators (and their trusted aides) who are both practically and as a matter of democratic principle responsible to their home constituencies. If the findings of social science research are not of preeminent importance in any of these arenas, the sheer competition for attention is not irrelevant. Policymakers are busy people.

Some of the disabilities that look "special" to students of one branch of government actually permeate most areas of government action. Rosen's chapter on the judiciary is full of insights that apply equally to other agencies of government. Notable is the government's emphasis on the resolution of aching controversies with minimal pain (rather than with abstract logic). Administrators, bureaucrats, and legislators as well as judges place a greater premium on negotiating differences and reconciling divergent views than on reaching scientifically elegant solutions. Similarly, not only courts but other governmental units have an enduring respect for order. When the implementation of research threatens to bring about rapid change—topple existing procedures, call for new arrangements and new skills, create a time of confusion and uncertainty, open the gates to more strident demands for further change—then governments often tend to prefer the ills they have than the disorder attendant on even beneficent change.

Other points about the problems of applying research deserve mention. One is the frail character of the knowledge that research produces. One study is rarely enough to place high credence in. Government officials know that social science is beset with fads of attention, with competing theoretical frameworks, and with contradictory empirical evidence. When confronted with the latest words from the social science oracle, they retain a healthy skepticism. On their side, social scientists, too, are aware of the fragility of their knowledge. As a consequence, they often tend to be timorous about drawing policy implications from their work and reluctant to give clear-cut recommendations. Because of the shaky edifice on which they are perched, they lack the zest and confidence of princes' counselors.

Even as research on a subject accumulates and as its methodological and conceptual quality improves, it may provide no firmer basis for choice. This is the theme of Chapter 5, by Cohen and Weiss, who follow the twenty-year development of research on schools and race. They conclude that more and better research was done over the years, but the improvement did not clarify policy choice. Instead, it complicated it. The research did not converge; it diverged and revealed an unanticipatedly complex reality.

Another intrinsic dilemma in attempts to use research is the question of values. As Chapter 4 by Mayntz explains, no social science research is value-free. Explicitly or implicitly, research embodies a set of values; by its focus on certain issues (and its neglect of others), by the concepts it uses, by its theoretical premises, and by the normative basis for its recommendations, research takes a stand. Research can be used instrumentally to resolve problems only where decisionmakers and researchers have accepted the same set of values. Sharpe (Chapter 3), Rose (Chapter 2), and McGowan (Chapter 7) further develop the problem of divergence of values, the undissolvable lump that clogs many dissemination systems.[1][2]

Another obstacle in the application of research arises from the nature of decision-making systems. Social scientists who talk about research use always seem to start at the research end. They ask: How can we induce people in decision-making positions to pay attention to our work? A more fruitful entry into the discussion seems to me at the policy end: How do policies get made? What information do decision-making groups seek to pay attention to?

One of the problems in the policy process is that each actor responds to the incentives and rewards of his own position. A legislator may be engaged by the needs of certain constituents, the President by the desire for reelection, a bureau chief by loyalties to state agencies with which he deals, the Office of Management and Budget by the desire to cut costs, a researcher by the desire to extend a theoretical formulation to another arena. The kinds of information that each actor wants to have are likely to be widely divergent. The aspect of the issue deemed worthy of study varies with the person's view of the problematics— and the opportunities. This suggests that the larger the number of actors who participate in the debate on a policy issue—and on some issues, the numbers are huge—the more diverse are the range of questions that are raised. Diverse standards of relevance will be applied, and one or two sets of data are not likely to be accepted as universally useful, nor as definitive. Research has many rows to plow.

Another limiting attribute of the policy sphere is the occasional amorphousness of the decision-making process. Almost all discussions of the use of research in policy making start from the premise that at some discernible place and time policy gets "made," that there are people who see themselves and are seen by others as decision-"makers," and that singly and collectively they make arrangements to solve a problem. The assumption that there are identifiable actors who make a policy sometimes contradicts reality.

In some circumstances, locating any people who are charged with responsibility for making a decision is difficult. Different organizations have very different decision structures, and in some, the divisions of responsibility are sliced so fine that there seems to be nobody and no group with sufficient authority to move. As Alkin says, "Identification of the project's decision maker(s) is perhaps the most elusive aspect of organizing an evaluation effort."[13]

Nor does there always come a date and a time when choice is made. Options are somehow progressively narrowed by a series of almost imperceptible choices. A variegated group of persons, uncoordinated, takes minor steps. Almost without conscious decision, a decision accretes. As Orlans writes:

... countless proximate decisions are reached in many offices, each with a different brew of fermenting knowledge—and, of course, much else, besides knowledge—until, like Moscow starting to burn, an hour comes and goes in which, we later say, the matter was consummated.[14]

In such amorphous and diffuse decision processes, the use of social research is equally imperceptible. Concepts, generalizations, data, perspectives are absorbed from an array of sources, unreferenced and uncatalogued, and they make their way wraithlike, but sometimes with surprising power, into the emerging decision.

3. A significant reinterpretation that this book provides is the meaning of the terms *using research* or *research utilization.* Much of the sogginess in the whole discussion of policy uses of social research derives from conceptual ambiguities. Upon examination, research utilization is an extraordinarily complicated phenomenon. The term can evoke at least six different meanings.

Instrumental Uses: Problem Solving. When people discuss the use of social research for policy making, the usual meaning involves a direct and instrumental application. Research will provide empirical evidence and/or conclusions that will help to solve a policy problem. The model is a linear one. A problem exists;

information or understanding is lacking either to generate a solution to the problem or to select among alternative solutions; research provides the missing knowledge; a solution is reached.

Implicit in this model is a sense that there is a consensus on goals. It is assumed that both policymakers and researchers tend to agree on what the desired end state should be. The contribution of research is to help in the identification and selection of appropriate means to reach that goal.

The evidence that social research provides for the decision-making process can be of several orders. It can be qualitative and descriptive, for example, rich observational accounts of social conditions or of program processes. It can be quantitative data on either relatively "soft" indicators (e.g., public attitudes) or "hard" factual matters (e.g., number of hospital beds). It can be statistical relationships between variables, generalized conclusions about the associations between factors, or even relatively abstract ("middle-range") theories about cause and effect.

In this formulation of research utilization, there are two basic ways in which social research can enter the policy-making arena. The research can antedate the policy problem and be drawn in on need, or it can be purposefully commissioned to fill the knowledge gap. In the latter event, the assumption is that decisionmakers have a clear idea of their goals and a map of acceptable alternatives, but they lack some specific items of understanding. Thereupon, they engage social researchers to provide the data, the analytic generalizations, and possibly the interpretations of these generalizations to the case in hand by way of recommendations. This process of acquiring social research to order leads to what some observers have called a decision-driven model of research (see Figure 1-1). The expectation is that research generated in this type of sequence, even more than research located through search procedures, will have direct and immediate applicability and will be used for decision making.

Even more, it is often assumed that one specific study will be used for decision making. Whether located or acquired for the purpose, the single study on the topic of concern—with its data, analysis, and conclusions—is expected to affect the choices that decisionmakers make. Particularly the large-scale, government-contracted policy study, tailored to the specifications set by government staff, is expected to make a difference in plans, programs, and policies.

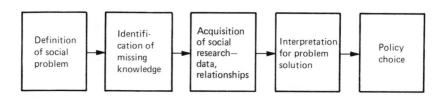

Figure 1-1. Decision-Driven Model of Research Use.

13

This, then, is the typical image of "research utilization." There is variability in notions of how much impact the research should have before it qualifies as "used": whether the recommendations have to be adopted intact, whether they should have some influence on the decision even if not fully implemented, or whether it is sufficient that they be considered even if more compelling considerations prevent their affecting the nature of the decision. Some observers are more lenient than others in the degree of penetration into the decision that constitutes use. But the nature and sequence of use described here is commonly accepted, and it provides the imagery for most discussions of utilization.

But there are other kinds of use, too, and it is well to take a brief tour through some alternative formulations.

Knowledge-Driven Model. Research can be used for policy making not so much because there is an issue pending that requires elucidation as because research has thrown up an opportunity that can be capitalized upon. Examples of this model generally come from the physical sciences: Biochemical research makes available oral contraceptive pills; developments in electronics enable television to multiply the number of broadcast channels. Because of the fruits of basic research, new applications are developed and new policies emerge. The model, probably the hoariest one in the research utilization literatures, looks something like Figure 1-2.[15]

This linear sequence of events assumes that the sheer fact that knowledge exists presses it toward development and use.[16] In social research this is not likely to be the case for several reasons: Social science knowledge is not apt to be so compelling; social science knowledge does not readily lend itself to conversion into technologies, either material or social; development and application are probably less likely to occur unless a social problem has been consensually defined, politicized, and potential solutions debated.

This is by no means to imply that "basic research" in the social sciences is not useful—even for very applied decisions. Certainly, many social policies and programs of government are based, implicitly or explicitly, on basic psychological, sociological, economic, and anthropological research orientations. But when they surface to affect government decisions, it is not likely to be through the sequence of events posited in this model.

Interactive Model. There is another way that social research can enter the decision arena, and that is as part of a complex search for knowledge from a

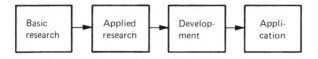

Figure 1-2. Knowledge-Driven Model of Research Use.

variety of sources. Those engaged in developing policy communicate not with one source of information but with many—with administrators, practitioners, politicians, planners, journalists, clients, interest groups, wives, carpool members, and social scientists, too. The process is not one of linear order from research to decision but a disorderly set of interconnections and back-and-forthness that defies neat diagrams.

All kinds of people involved in an issue area pool their talents, beliefs, and understandings in an effort to make sense of a problem. Social scientists are one set of participants among many. Seldom do they have evidence available that bears directly and explicitly on the issue at hand; more rarely still do they have unambiguous evidence. But they can engage in mutual consultations and discussions that progressively move closer to potential policy responses.

Donnison describes this interactive model of research use in the development of two pieces of legislation in Great Britain. He notes that decisions could not wait upon research but had to be made when political circumstances compelled:

Research workers could not present authoritative findings for others to apply; neither could others commission them to find the "correct" solution to policy problems: they were not that kind of problem. Those in the four fields from which experience had to be brought to bear [politics, technology, practice, and research] contributed on equal terms. Each was expert in a few things, ignorant about most things, offered what he could, and generally learnt more than he could teach.[17]

In this model, the use of research is only one part of a complicated process that also uses experience, political insight, pressure, social technologies, and judgment. It has applicability not only to face-to-face settings but also to the multiple ways in which intelligence is gathered through intermediaries and brought to bear. It describes a familiar process by which decisionmakers inform themselves of the range of knowledge and opinion in a policy area.

Research as Political Ammunition. Very often, the constellation of interests around a policy issue predetermines the positions that decisionmakers take. Or debates drag on until opinions are set. At this point, decisionmakers are not receptive to new evidence. For reasons of ideology, intellect, or interest, they have taken a stand that research evidence is not likely to shake.

In such cases, research can still be used. It becomes ammunition for the side that finds its conclusions most congenial and supportive. Partisans brandish the evidence in an attempt to neutralize opponents, convince waverers, and bolster supporters. Even if conclusions have to be ripped out of context (with suppression of evidence "on the other hand"), research becomes grist to the mill.

Social science researchers, particularly if they have been commissioned to do research on the subject, or if they have some stake in the results, are often appalled at the agency's unreceptiveness to their conclusions. They expected a hearing; they receive a deaf ear. After a few experiences of this kind, researchers can become cynical about government's "use" of social research. Many a battle-scarred research veteran ascribes to government agencies only the most self-serving uses of research for justification and agency aggrandizement.

But using research to support a predetermined position is research utilization, too. In fact, it seems to me neither an unimportant nor an improper use. Only distortion deserves reproof; when the researcher knows about misuse of data, he or she has a responsibility to speak out. But just because sides have already been taken is no reason to discount the effects of research. If the issue is still in doubt, what research can do is add strength to the side that the evidence supports. It gives them confidence, removes lingering doubts, and provides an edge in the continuing debate. And since the research finds ready-made partisans who will fight for its implementation, it stands a better chance of making a difference in the outcome.

One of the clear needs in this model of research use is that all parties to the issue have access to the evidence. If, for example, bureaucrats monopolize research that would support the position of clients, then equity is not served. But when research is available to each participant group, research as political ammunition can serve a worthy purpose.

Miscellaneous Uses. Social research can also be used:

to delay action;

to avoid taking responsibility for a decision;

to win kudos for a successful program, to gain recognition and support;

to discredit an opponent or a disliked policy;

to maintain the prestige of a government agency through its support of prestigious researchers;

to keep universities and their social science departments solvent, to support faculty and graduate students;

to serve as a training ground for apprentice social researchers;

to generate further research on topics of social importance.

These are uses. Are we willing to give them house room? Are we willing to say that policy research is confirmed to the extent that it fulfills functions such as these? Or are some of them ipso facto "illegitimate"? When is a use not a use? In the event, it all depends on what you believe in. Value-based criteria have to be invoked.

Finally, we turn to a "use" that seems indistinct and amorphous but that may in the long run have weighty implications.

Research as Conceptualization. Another mode of using research steps back further from the immediate policy issue. Social research can be "used" in reconceptualizing the character of policy issues or even redefining the policy agenda. Thus, social research may sensitize decisionmakers to new issues and turn what were nonproblems into policy problems (a current controversial example is "white flight"). In turn, it may convert existing social problems into nonproblems (e.g., marijuana use).[18] It may drastically revise the way that a society thinks about issues (e.g., acceptable rates of unemployment), the facets of the issue that are viewed as susceptible to alteration, and the alternative measures that it considers.

Global reorientation of this sort is not likely to be the outcome of a single study or even one specific line of inquiry. But over time and with the accumulation of evidence, such use can have far-reaching implications. Thus, it is now fairly commonplace that an organization's behavior is determined as much by its jockeying for influence within the bureaucracy as it is by rational response to outside events. It is accepted that changing the achievement and mobility of poor people is extremely difficult even with well-meaning social service programs. Over time, the gradual accumulation of research results can lead to serious and far-reaching changes in the way people and governments address their problems.

Those, then, are some possible meanings of "using" research. Perhaps the major theme of this book is that the usual definition, the direct application of research findings to solve a specific problem, is not the common pattern. Such uses no doubt occur, but when they do, they are likely to involve research done in-house by an agency's own staff.[19] They are probably also likely to involve day-to-day operations, rather than larger issues of program and policy.

The ways that most social research is "used" are much more diffuse and circuitous. Patton, Grimes, Guthrie, Brennan, French, and Blyth interviewed the principals in twenty health evaluation studies and found that federal decisionmakers used the research to fill in knowledge gaps, reinforce their sense of the situation, reduce uncertainty, and speed up decisions (see Chapter 11). These were not unimportant uses, but they did not involve taking a hunk of new knowledge, turning the lever, and spewing out a decision to match. Addressing the question from another perspective, Caplan's research found that federal policymakers mentioned multiple uses of research (see Chapter 13). But the research they cited tended not to be hard data or single-study conclusions but rather social science generalizations, concepts, and perspectives. This "soft" social science had an influence on the way they conceptualized the issues and dealt with policy.

Knorr, who had expected to find social research used to legitimate decisions already made, was surprised at the number of decisionmakers who said that the research they commissioned had changed their minds—at least a little (see Chapter 12). But she too found that the ways they used it were roundabout: in the early stages of "preparing decisions" rather than in making decisions. The information derived from research underwent further "processing" before it had an effect. Similarly, Rich studied agencies' use of social indicators that had been tailor-made to their specifications (see Chapter 14). He discovered that only in crisis situations, such as the energy crisis, were the data used directly and instrumentally. Under more normal conditions, the uses that were reported tended to be "conceptual"—that is, broadening people's understanding of the issues, providing information for papers, memos, and articles, and leading to further research.

4. So social research is used. It is not the kind of use most people have in mind when they hear the word. Not here the imminent decision, the single datum, the weighing of alternative options, and shazam! Officials apparently use social science as a general guide to reinforce their sense of the world and make sense of that part of it that is still unmapped or confusing. A bit of legitimation here, some ammunition for the political wars there, but a hearty dose of conceptual use to clarify the complexities of life.

Even research that challenges the status quo is found, by Weiss and Bucuvalas, to be welcomed in decision-making circles (see Chapter 15). This is not to say that decisionmakers act on it immediately, but they want to know. If rioters in black ghettoes are not the poorest, least educated, or longest out of work, if drug abusers receiving methadone maintenance do not stop criminal activity, this information calls for new responses. There is a need for fresh thinking and new contexts of cognitive organization. As Etzioni has suggested, many small "bits" of new information can be accepted into one's existing contexts without change of orientation. But at some point, the many new "bits" are out of kilter with the old context. A realistic integration of them can force a major shift in both the organization of one's thinking and the action consequence one supports.[20]

Recent survey data show that government decisionmakers say they are receptive to the ideas, concepts, and theoretical perspectives that social science offers.[21] Social science provides an angle of vision, a focus for looking at the world. It is a source of illumination on the rich details and tangled interrelationships in that world. Whatever else it may or may not do, it serves a global function of enlightenment.[22]

Social science also provides a common language of discourse in our fragmented society. There is a common vocabulary: achievement scores, self-esteem, upward mobility, social role, leadership structure, externalities. The vocabulary tells us which items out of the buzzing, blooming confusion to pay attention to. There is a common syntax that gives rules for combining and ordering these terms. These are the going generalizations. Poverty and oppression lead to disorganization, deviance, and crime; group mobilization and open access to government give each group a voice in the pluralistic negotiations that set policy; decentralization of control to local communities increases the responsiveness of government services. As these illustrations indicate, many of the notions and generalizations that gain currency are important new ways of thinking about policy, but many are unverified, inadequate, partial, oversimplified, or wrong. Much of the social science that affects policy is a pop social science, filtered through popular coverage in newspapers, magazines, and television, attenuated by selective attention, and reduced further by sheer forgetting of details. Much is simply out of date. It was John Maynard Keynes who said:

Practical men, who believe themselves to be quite exempt from any intellectual influence, are usually the slaves of some defunct economist.[23]

He was talking of the power of social science ideas. That social science has pervasive if indirect and often invisible influence seems borne out in the chapters that follow. But a second message implicit in his remark is that the ideas percolating through policy-making channels may be obsolete and themselves defunct.

Academic social scientists enjoy talking of the indirect diffusion of social science into public decision making as a process of enlightenment. But such a diffusion process does not necessarily screen out the obsolete or shoddy; all kinds of social research inputs float around and light in unexpected places. Nor is a circuitous and indirect diffusion of social research an efficient process. Far from it.

Still, to return to our linguistic metaphor, social science provides thinking people, in government and out, with a common grammar. As French once was for diplomats and underworld cant for thieves, it is a way of talking across boundaries. The common terms, data, models, and orientations bring coherence to the discussion of public policy making.

Social science does even more. Social science research, as it penetrates the bureaus, legislative offices, and courtrooms of government, opens up new vistas. Left to themselves, agencies—any agency—becomes routine, stereotypical, unreceptive to new ideas, anchored in tradition, rulebook, and custom. A mustiness sets in, a sameness of response. Even research sponsored within an agency partakes of the agency's accustomed definitions and biases. What outside research can do, and to some extent apparently does do, is bring new assumptions to bear. It looks at problems from a different standpoint, and by redefining the problematic, offers a new perspective for considering solutions.

Organization of the Book

This book originated with the *Policy Studies Journal* issue that I edited in the spring of 1976. That issue had as its theme, "The Research Utilization Quandary," and it contained five of the papers that are included here. Most of them have been expanded for the book.

In addition, in October 1975, I attended the Vienna Roundtable on the

Market for Policy Research conducted by the Committee on Political Sociology, IPSA/ISA, and the Institut für Empirische Sozialforschung (Vienna). Five of the people who spoke at that conference have contributed papers to this volume: Reynate Mayntz from the Federal Republic of Germany, Karin Knorr from Austria, L.J. Sharpe and Richard Rose from Great Britain, and Martin Rein from the United States. I had originally planned a section on "The View from Abroad," but as discussions at the Vienna conference—and the papers themselves—made startlingly clear, the experiences of participants were not diverse but almost interchangeable; the distinctive influences of national culture were swamped by the commonalities of the research-government nexus. Of the four countries represented at the conference, none provided examples of research/ policy relationships that were at all unfamiliar to the others. Accordingly, I abandoned the idea of a separate section on the European experience. Only Sharpe explicitly gives a "transatlantic view."

The book, therefore, is organized according to the following pattern. The first four chapters, by Rose, Sharpe, Mayntz, and Cohen and Weiss, discuss fundamental and intransigent obstacles to transforming social research results into policy decisions. Here are the factors that make instrumental problem-solving applications so problematic: differences in experience and outlook between policymakers and researchers, divergence in values, the unstable and ambiguous nature of social research knowledge.

A second set of four chapters deals with the encounters of the three branches of government with social research. Uliassi and McGowan write about executive agencies, Dreyfus about the legislature, and Rosen the courts.

The next six chapters present quantitative evidence on research-government relationships. Since large-scale studies on research use are a relatively new enterprise, this is the largest body of quantitative evidence so far assembled under one roof. Useem addresses the question of whose purposes government-funded research serves: government's or those of social science. Patton et al., Knorr, Caplan, Rich, and Weiss and Bucuvalas present varied sets of data on the use and usability of social research for government decision making. Much of this evidence suggests that research serves conceptual, "enlightenment" functions rather than instrumental problem-solving purposes. The final chapter, by Rein and Schon, develops the notion of conceptual usefulness by proposing ways to enlist social research in the value-critical task of "problem setting."

Notes

1. Henry W. Riecken, "Social Sciences and Social Problems," *Social Science Information* 8, no. 1 (1969), pp. 102-29. Quotation is from p. 102.

2. Some examples: Robert Nisbet, *Twilight of Authority* (New York: Oxford University Press, 1975), chapter 2 and "Knowledge Dethroned," *New*

York Times Magazine, Sept. 28, 1975, pp. 34-46; Daniel P. Moynihan, *Maximum Feasible Misunderstanding; Community Action in the War on Poverty* (New York: Free Press, 1969); Robert K. Merton, "Role of the Intellectual in Public Bureaucracy," *Social Theory and Social Structure* (New York: Free Press, 1968 ed.), pp. 261-78; Alvin W. Gouldner, *The Coming Crisis of Western Sociology* (New York: Basic Books, 1970), pp. 10, 501-02; Thomas R. Dye, "Policy Analysis and Political Science: Some Problems at the Interface," *Policy Studies Journal* 1, no. 2 (1972), esp. p. 104.

3. Michael Useem, "State Production of Social Knowledge," *American Sociological Review* 41, no. 4 (1976), pp. 613-29 (also, Useem, Chapter 10 of this volume); Pio Uliassi, "Government Sponsored Research on International and Foreign Affairs," in I.L. Horowitz (ed.), *The Use and Abuse of Social Science* (New Brunswick: Transactionbooks, 1971), pp. 309-42, esp. p. 322.

4. Charles L. Schultze, *The Politics and Economics of Public Spending* (Washington, D.C.: Brookings Institution, 1968), pp. 95-97.

5. National Science Foundation, *Federal Funds for Research, Development, and Other Scientific Activities*, Fiscal Years 1974, 1975, and 1976 (Washington, D.C.: U.S. Government Printing Office, 1975), vol. 24, p. 60. The National Academy of Sciences' estimates, to be published shortly, come from personal conversation.

6. U.S. House of Representatives, Committee on Government Operations, Research and Technical Programs Subcommittee, *The Use of Social Research in Federal Domestic Programs* (Washington, D.C.: U.S. Government Printing Office, 1967, four volumes).

7. The Brim Commission was oriented almost exclusively to utilization: National Science Foundation, *Knowledge into Action: Improving the Nation's Use of the Social Sciences*, Report of the Special Commission on the Social Sciences, Washington, D.C., 1968. The Young Committee report appears as National Academy of Sciences, *The Behavioral Sciences and the Federal Government*, Washington, D.C., 1968. The BASS Committee report is National Academy of Sciences-Social Science Research Council, *The Behavioral and Social Sciences: Outlook and Need* (Englewood Cliffs, N.J.: Prentice-Hall, 1969).

8. Leonard Goodwin, *Can Social Science Help Resolve National Problems?* (New York: Free Press, 1975), pp. vii-viii.

9. Seymour Deitchman, *The Best-Laid Schemes: A Tale of Social Research and Bureaucracy* (Cambridge, Mass.: M.I.T. Press, 1976), p. 390.

10. For example, the U.S. National Institute of Education sponsored programs to employ field agents in state departments of education in order to bring research findings to the attention of local school boards, superintendents, principals, and teachers. Margaret McNeely and Ian McNett, "Spreading the Latest Word," *American Education* 11, no. 9 (1975), pp. 24-28.

11. S.M. Lipset and E.C. Ladd, Jr., "The Politics of American Sociologists," *American Journal of Sociology* 78 (1972), p. 71. Confirming evidence on this point can be found in Harold Orlans, *Contracting for Knowledge* (San Francisco: Jossey-Bass, 1973), pp. 1-14.

12. Further discussion appears in Carol H. Weiss, "Evaluation Research in the Political Context," in E. Struening and M. Guttentag, *Handbook of Evaluation Research* (Beverly Hills: Sage Publications, 1975), vol. 1, pp. 13-26.

13. Marvin C. Alkin, Jacqueline Kosecoff, Carol Fitz-Gibbon, and Richard Seligman, *Evaluation and Decision Making: The Title VII Experience* (Los Angeles: Center for the Study of Evaluation, UCLA Graduate School of Education, 1974), p. 94.

14. Harold Orlans, "Comments on James Coleman's 'Principles Governing Policy Research,' " paper presented at American Association for the Advancement of Science, December 1972, excerpted in *Evaluation* 1, no. 3 (1973), p. 20.

15. A very similar model, but with a stage of experimentation, has been prescribed recently by John W. Evans, "Motives for Experimentation," in R.F. Boruch and H.W. Riecken, *Experimental Testing of Public Policy* (Boulder, Colo.: Westview Press, 1975), pp. 15-22. See also R.G. Havelock, *Planning for Innovation through Dissemination and Utilization of Knowledge* (Ann Arbor, Mich.: Institute for Social Research, 1969), chapter 1.

16. There is some evidence that even in areas of need in the natural sciences, basic research does not necessarily push toward application. For example, Project Hindsight indicated faster, and probably greater, use of basic science when it was *directed* toward filling a recognized need in weapons technology. C.W. Sherwin et al., *First Interim Report on Project Hindsight* (Summary), Defense Documentation Center, June 1966. Also C.W. Sherwin and Raymond S. Isenson, "Project Hindsight," *Science* CLVI (June 23, 1967).

17. David Donnison, "Research for Policy," *Minerva* 10, no. 4 (1972), pp. 519-36, citation p. 527.

18. This is how Leonard Reissman says sociologists have learned to "solve" social problems—by redefining them out of existence. L. Reissman, "The Solution Cycle of Social Problems," *The American Sociologist*, February 1972, pp. 7-9.

19. Nathan Caplan, "The Use of Social Science Information by Federal Executives," in Gene Lyons (ed.), *Social Research and Public Policies: The Dartmouth/OECD Conference* (Hanover, N.H.: Dartmouth College, 1975), pp. 46-67. Van de Vall studied 120 research projects in the Netherlands and found that they were more likely to be used by organizational decisionmakers when the research was conducted in-house by staff members. Mark van de Vall, "Utilization and Methodology of Applied Social Research: Four Complementary Models," *Journal of Applied Behavioral Science* 11, no. 1 (1975), pp. 14-38.

20. Amitai Etzioni, *The Active Society; A Theory of Societal and Political Processes* (New York: Free Press, 1968), pp. 159, 166-67.

21. Laurie J. Bauman and Carol H. Weiss, "The Acceptance of Social Research by Decision-Makers: A Comparison of Decision-Makers' and Researchers' Views," paper presented at the American Association for Public Opinion Research meeting, Asheville, North Carolina, May 1976. Nathan Caplan, Chapter 13 of this volume.

22. For discussions of "enlightenment" as opposed to "engineering" functions of social research, see Morris Janowitz, "Professionalization of Sociology," *American Journal of Sociology* 78 (1972), pp. 105-35, and Elisabeth T. Crawford and Albert D. Biderman, "The Functions of Policy-Oriented Social Science," in Crawford and Biderman (eds.), *Social Scientists and International Affairs* (New York: Wiley, 1969), pp. 233-43.

23. J.M. Keynes, *The General Theory of Employment, Interest and Money* (New York: Harcourt Brace, 1936), pp. 383-84.

2

Disciplined Research and Undisciplined Problems

Richard Rose

Far better an approximate answer to the right question, which is often vague, than an exact answer to the wrong questions, which can always be made precise.

—Professor John W. Tukey

Because social scientists study the conditions of man in society and governments seek to influence these conditions, there is a logical relationship between the interests and activities of social scientists and public officials. Yet, there is an uneasy relationship between social scientists and public officials where major efforts have been made to utilize the social sciences in government. Social scientists complain that their work is ignored by public officials or that government departments are trying to exercise too much control. The growth of nonuniversity research institutes, both profit making (e.g., the management consultants, McKinsey & Co.) and non-profit making (e.g., the Brookings Institution), as middlemen between university-based social scientists and government departments is further evidence that something is amiss.

Government officials complain that social scientists fail to interest themselves in the real problems facing their country; they are said to worry instead about abstractions that interest members of an international discipline. When social scientists do come forward with data, ideas, and especially prescriptions about what government ought to do, such actions may not be appreciated by those with the formal authority and power to take decisions. Social scientists may be accused of prescribing naive or politically "impossible" ideas and told to go back to the universities, where their academic (in the pejorative sense) knowledge belongs.

Different Organizations and Divergent Disciplines

The social scientist thinks of himself as a free professional whereas the official in government thinks of himself as a bureaucrat. Like any ideal-type distinction,

This chapter draws upon discussions at an international roundtable on the Market for Policy Research, conducted by the Committee on Political Sociology, IPSA/ISA, and the Institut für Empirische Sozialforschung (IFES, Vienna) at Europa Haus, Vienna, 29 September-3rd October 1975, with financial support from the Ford Foundation and the Austrian government. As co-convenor, I am grateful to the participants for their stimulating comments, but none should be considered responsible for the conclusions drawn herein.

A longer version of this article, with a section considering improvements in the relationship of social scientists and government, appeared in the *International Journal of Social Sciences*, vol. XXVIII: 1, 1976. Published by Unesco.

24

these definitions emphasize one point of difference, notwithstanding many similarities among the two groups and many dissimilarities within each category. The distinction is crucial to understanding how organizational factors influence the different outlooks of the two groups. As the Washington aphorism known as Miles's law puts it, "Where you stand depends upon where you sit."

To describe a social scientist as a free professional, capable of exploring ideas unconcerned by their implications for organizations, is not to claim that social scientists are unconstrained by social influences, but rather, that the constraints are very different from those operating upon politicians and civil servants working in the bureaucratic structures of formally organized government departments. The daily work of a social scientist differs from that of a bureaucrat, because the former is unconstrained by laws stipulating his functions. Nor would a social scientist consider that elected representatives had the technical knowledge to direct his research. While academics are increasingly burdened with committee work as the price of a university job and while the "heavier" forms of social research require research teams, the model of the social scientist nonetheless remains one of an individual scholar gazing contemplatively out the window or looking down at a musty book or the day's latest computer printout.

The social scientist is responsive to an invisible college of professional peers—a group that rarely if ever meets collectively, for its members are scattered throughout universities in many lands and dispersed among universities within his country of residence. The normal mode of social scientific communication is scholarly publication, and the language of discussion is analytic. The social constraints and norms that affect a social scientist's work do not come from government but rather from within his profession.

Whereas society is unitary, the social sciences are subdivided into many specialisms, and development has meant the increasing differentiation of specialisms, both as between disciplines (e.g., economics, sociology, and political science) and within disciplines (e.g., macro- and microeconomics) or the eternally expanding categories of "the sociology of. . . ." A generation ago, many professors in the social sciences did not have a university degree in the subject that they professed, because such a degree had not been offered when they themselves were undergraduates. The rapid expansion of postgraduate training in the social sciences has brought professionalization—that is, the employment of persons with disciplinary training in academic posts concerned with that discipline. Greater depth within a specialism usually means less awareness cutting across specialisms. The focus of social scientists conducting research within disciplinary categories tends to be narrower than that of politicians concerned with the undisciplined ramifications of a problem, or with the interconnectedness of many problems.

University departments initially influence the perception of embryonic social scientists through the systematic instruction and training of postgraduate students. The effect of this training is to give a qualified graduate both professional expertise and a particular definition of what his discipline is about. This definition is sustained by employment in a university or discipline-oriented research institution, where both his initial appointment and promotion prospects are evaluated in terms of his competence in the subject of his discipline. While there is no agreement within a discipline about many matters of major concern, professional associations and the "invisible college" nonetheless provide reasonably reliable criteria specifying how colleagues and superiors can tell whether a given person is doing good work at his discipline. A "good" economist or a "good" sociologist is a person who is good at doing what groups of his fellow professionals think is worth doing, and worth doing well.

Professional social scientists are products of the Enlightenment, and they tend to define their role not in terms of profit, as might an entrepreneur, or higher wages, as might a manual worker, but rather in terms of knowledge in the abstract. The enlightenment of society leads to a more knowledgeable society; this is assumed to be ipso facto a better society.[1] The utilization of such knowledge is not a principle concern of a social scientist, as it is for someone trained in the law and practicing as a lawyer, or trained in medicine and practicing as a physician.

Public officials, whether career civil servants or elected or appointed partisans, are important by virtue of their position in the organization of government. Almost invariably the office that a man holds antedates his own appointment, and the bureau of which it is a part is also well established. The first thing that a public official must do is to become effectively socialized into the norms and values of his office, learning what the organization of which he is a part expects of him. Whereas the social scientist's work is primarily concerned with ideas, the work of a public official is much more concerned with the allocation and management of tangible resources: money, personnel, laws, and administrative decisions that collectively make up the outputs of his organization.

In the course of his daily routine, a public official is constantly concerned about relationships with others in his own and other organizations. Instead of having the freedom to write and publish what he thinks in his own name, the public official must accept that what he does is done in the name of an organization or office and is subject to the approval of those who, by statute or political convention, have the right to veto or revise what he himself would like to say. The characteristic product of a bureaucrat is an anonymous document, a committee report, a ruling issued in the name of his department, or if he is unusually influential, a law. The paper output of government organizations is viewed by social scientists as a "nonintellectual" product. They may even enjoy pointing out to students the contradictions and inadequacies of the analysis contained therein. Sometimes the authors of the document are aware of these attributes. Academic flaws are accepted as necessary conditions for the achievement of the public official's objective, which is to get some kind of agreed document into print. The building of consensus—often by confusing or ignoring intellectually significant analytic points—is more important to him than building an elegant new model that gains in interest because its novelty or controversial nature places it outside the constraints of the mundane world of the bureaucracy.

A public official accepts practical inhibitions upon his freedom of action and limitations upon his ability to analyze problems in return for the advantages of sharing influence in a large organization. He trades off the individual freedom and autonomy of a professional social scientist for participation in an organizational process that makes public policy. A small number of people in any society and a larger proportion in small societies are likely to move back and forth between these two roles, more or less successfully. The longer a man stays in one career, whether that of public official or academic social scientist, the more likely his accumulated experience in one role may constitute a trained incapacity to switch to the somewhat different demands of another role.

A good public official, like a good social scientist, is a person who excels at doing what his peer group and superiors think is worth doing, and worth doing well. However, the criteria for judgment differ radically. In lower-echelon civil service posts, assessment may be in terms of formal procedural skills and qualifications, for example, the ability to administer programs without legal difficulties and avoiding controversy. At the higher policy-making levels of government, a good official is often defined as a person who is good at getting things done. Power and influence, rather than knowledge and ideas, are the tokens of success at the highest levels of government. A public official views knowledge or information as a means to an end, whereas a social scientist views it as an end in itself.

Public officials tend to define their work in terms of the problem immediately confronting them. In this, they are like engineers rather than the philosophers and speculative scientists of the Enlightenment. They wish to apply knowledge within the policy process rather than achieve an understanding that however elegant theoretically is not relevant to the task before them. A public official does not define problems in terms of a body of abstract theories and concepts, but rather by looking at the pile of papers placed on his desk each morning or by answering the telephone and learning of another crisis that must be coped with. Policymakers in Washington want to know who has the action in terms of a current issue, and they wish to get a piece of the action. While no one official expects to control all of the action, he will, like an engineer, want to know whether what he does can produce the effect intended within his relatively narrow, specific, and identifiable range of concerns.

As long as public officials and social scientists stay within the boundaries of their own disciplines, whether academic or bureaucratic, there is little or no communication—or communication problem. Problems of communication arise only when social scientists try to participate in government while remaining academic social scientists, or public officials become involved with social scientists in the hope that this will help government as well as social science disciplines. Common interests do not make for common appreciations of what is important about a given problem area. The divergences between the disciplines of bureaucrats and social scientists create confusion and misunderstanding. Criticisms sometimes involve contradictions; for example, some officials complain that the results of social science research tell them nothing new, and yet they concurrently assert that they dislike novel results that do not fit with the opinions of those inside government.[2]

The enlightenment model of social science gives little attention to the problem of utilizing the findings of research in specific organizational contexts. Social scientists tend to assume their knowledge is tangible, simply because it is difficult to inhibit the movement of anything so intangible as an idea. Good ideas—that is, the learning that constitutes the conventional social science wisdom—are expected to drive out bad ideas, even after allowing for cyclical setbacks arising from the repudiation of conventional wisdom by new intellectual discoveries. The transference of knowledge into government is not a responsibility of social scientists. The appropriate image for transferring ideas comes from meteorology: Social scientists are concerned with seeding the climate of opinion.

Public officials seeking to make use of the social sciences are likely to adopt an engineering approach, in which a problem is specified and appropriate specialists are asked, on a fee-for-service basis, to provide some assistance in disposing of the problem. Social scientists are not themselves expected to make laws or spend public monies, but to advise government officials who can do this. In such circumstances, it is expected that the problem can be specified fairly clearly, and the methods to be employed are well known. In the extreme case, federal departments may sometimes ask for competitive bids for social science research, as if social science work could be evaluated as readily as one might evaluate competitive bids to build a bridge or supply carpets or light bulbs for government buildings.[3] Even though the government may act as if it were a purchasing agent for knowledge, public officials have quickly learned that what they are purchasing cannot be evaluated as easily as specifications for concrete or carpets. Even when the most costly elements of a study can be subject to relatively objective evaluation (e.g., the conduct of a sample survey of the population), the interpretation of the findings is by no means clear-cut, and the policy recommendations arising from opinion surveys involve a considerable inferential leap from quantified date to recommendations for action. Social scientists can influence political discussion by the inferences they draw for government policy, but in doing so they are stepping outside their role as social scientists and moving into an advocacy position.

Whereas the social scientist has a belief that "right reason" provides justification for action, a public official is first and foremost concerned with political feasibility. Hence, even when a social scientist does step into government to provide relevant materials, he will be unable to communicate directly unless he learns the priorities and mode of thought of the bureaucratic discipline of government. The fact that social scientists and public officials both concern themselves with the same problems is less important than the fact that they appreciate these problems in terms of two divergent intellectual disciplines, based upon contrasting organizations that socialize and reward different kinds of achievements.

The Problem of Social Problems

To speak of relating social science to social problems inevitably invokes a model of the application of physical sciences to problems of the physical universe. In the latter instance, theoretical understanding of the physical universe and a technology stipulating techniques for applying theoretical propositions lead to changes in real world phenomena. In this paradigm, science and technology are combined, thereby leading to results that often lead one to say in the mid-twentieth century, "Science can work wonders."

Universities train professional scientists and technologists by giving them instruction in theories, techniques, and applications of a body of knowledge specified by a professional qualifying examination. A chemical engineer or a surgeon is a man who has a certificate attesting to his possession of knowledge, and this qualifies him to solve a set of problems defined within the field of that competence. Within academic quarters, highest prestige is usually given to those professionals who are most proficient at theory rather than applications. The same is true internationally; for example, Nobel prizes are awarded for work in pure science and not for work in the various subdivisions of engineering technology. In the world of public affairs, highest prestige is usually given to those professionals who are most proficient in applying their skills to specific problems affecting their clients. A man with a legal problem does not want the wisdom of a professor of jurisprudence, but the shrewdness of a lawyer who can find a loophole in a confining contract. Similarly, a head of state does not want to employ military theorists whose books are read around the world, but generals who will win battles and wars. The "quick technological fix" may well date from the time millenia ago when lawyers were first employed to find loopholes in municipal or divine laws so that a monarch could do what had hitherto been thought impossible.[4] The traditionally most-honored professions— the law, the army, and the church—were and remain those where the theoretical bases for action are least clear. This fact is irrelevant among clients who judge professionals in terms of their results rather than their assumptions.

The paradigm of science and technology depends for its success upon many assumptions. Especially relevant here is the assumption that the scientific theory in question provides understanding of relationships amenable to manipulation by scientists. This is not, however, always the case. For example, for many centuries astronomers have studied the solar system without being able to alter the solar system. Moreover, the knowledge of astrophysicists runs well ahead of the capability of technologists to build devices sufficiently powerful to test at first hand what they study at a distance. Meteorologists have been incapable of developing a technology to control the weather and are less able to make accurate forecasts of phenomena of interest than are astrophysicists. The differences between the virtually certain application of mechanical technology and the probabilistic application of other technologies present problems for both professionals and their clients. Ironically, where success is most important to people, namely, the practice of medical science, clients appear ready to accept the fact that a doctor's knowledge offers, at best, only a probability of successful treatment.

A second assumption in the paradigm is that there is a consensus about the subject matter of the science and the object of its applied technology. Biologists and computer scientists each can specify what they are studying and that their subject matter differs from each other. Biologists agree professionally that it is desirable to understand vital processes of the human body, and computer scientists agree professionally that it is desirable to invent ways in which computers can do their existing work more efficiently and to develop techniques so that computers can be applied to problems currently outside their scope. Each of these scientific disciplines is clear about what is considered a good thing to do within its field of professional competence.

Logically, assumptions about consensual objectives and an applicable technology mean that a scientific discipline can have consensus or lack consensus about its objectives, and it may provide a good technology for the application of its understanding or lack this. The four possibilities are illustrated in Table 2-1.

1. The normal model of a scientific discipline presupposes a clear consensus about what professionally qualified practitioners should do and an understanding applicable to real-world phenomena. Most of the engineering sciences fit into this category.

2. The "politicizing" of a discipline occurs when a dispute arises within it

Table 2-1
Variable Properties of Scientific Disciplines

	Consensual	Nonconsensual
Applicable understanding	1. E.g., Mechanical engineering	2. E.g., Nuclear physicists
Lacks applicable understanding	3. E.g., Medical research	4. E.g., Psychoanalysis

(or is imported from outside) concerning the objectives to which its undoubted understanding should be applied. In the years following 1945, there were disputes among nuclear physicists about whether and in what circumstances their skills should be applied to the development of military weapons. Today, in nations where industrial development has brought pollution with it, there are disputes about the application of well understood chemical techniques that incidentally pollute the environment.

3. Professionals applying themselves to clearly agreed goals, but without the ability to achieve these ends, often enjoy ready support for their efforts. For example, medical researchers concerned with cancer are agreed upon preventing the occurrence of the disease and its fatal consequences. The fact that no advance has been made comparable with immunization for smallpox or polio-myletis has not deprived cancer researchers of their scientific status or of funds to continue their work.

4. Professional scientists who disagree about the objectives of their work and about the technology appropriate for undertaking it may have their status as scientists challenged. Psychoanalysts often are so challenged, even when there is evidence that their work may sometimes produce cures—that is, satisfied clients. There is no agreement among psychoanalysts about the objectives of their discipline nor is their technology so well defined or applicable as to produce probabilistic type statements about the consequences of their actions.

In a governmental context, the important point that follows from the foregoing distinctions can be expressed in terms of the following hypothesis: *Government will make use of professionals insofar as they demonstrate consensus about their objectives and/or have a technology to apply their theories to real-world phenomena.* The hypothesis is important because it explains two types of phenomena, both of which can be readily observed in societies with a large number and variety of scientists. The first is that governments are very large employers of many types of professionally qualified men, ranging from lawyers through engineers to physical scientists and life scientists. Equally, it explains why governments are unlikely to give employment to many professionals whose objectives are in dispute among themselves and whose understanding is suspect (e.g., psychoanalysts or sociologists).

Governmental encouragement and employment of scientists is not a function of industrialization, but often preceded it. For example, the great irrigation feats of hydraulic engineers in the ancient Middle East were a considerable engineering achievement and one with major political significance. Prior to industrialization in eighteenth-century Europe, governments saw the advantage of encouraging scientific research and applying it to practical problems, whether the provision of canals or of military weaponry. States following the Napoleonic or Prussian tradition (and latterly, the Soviet Union) took the initiative in the application of scientific studies to public policy. The United States, through the Morrill Act of 1862, made explicit statutory and financial provision for the development of a land-grant system of colleges and universities offering instruction in the applied and practical sciences.

Any systematic examination of government employment would demonstrate that governments are not biased against the employment of scientists per se. The uneasy relationship between social scientists and government cannot be explained by any putative "antiscientific" bias of government: It may better be explained by properties of social science. It follows from the preceding hypothesis that insofar as social scientists lack consensus about objectives and/or applicable technologies, then government ought to be expected to make less use of social scientists.

The subject matter of social science is "undisciplined" for many reasons familiar in the literature of the philosophy of social science. When social scientists seek to apply their theories, they usually concern probabilistic relations. Any prescription given for action must contain a ceteris paribus clause; in complex contemporary societies all other conditions rarely remain equal. Social scientists who claim to belong to the same discipline disagree about many fundamental questions concerning theories and objectives of research. In recent years, disagreements have become prominent, and "political" caucuses have formed within professional associations.

The problems and theories of interest to social scientists are heterogeneous. Within this agglomeration it is important to note the extent to which disciplines vary in terms of consensus about objectives and in the development of an applicable technology. (See Table 2-2.)

1. Consensual fields with a high understanding of what to do to achieve results are peripheral subjects in the social sciences and may not even be regarded as such. For example, traffic engineering may be considered a branch of operations research—that is, a "hard" science rather than a social science. Alternatively, consensual topics may be considered not to belong to government public policy, since politics is about conflicts between differently valued choices. For example, a president is unlikely to feel that his job is made easier if a specialist in linear programming can determine the optimum allocation of typists in government offices. Operations research and, in its politically most peripheral aspects, management consultancy typically apply understanding to consensual objectives. Consensus promotes utilization, but it does so at nonpolicy (because nonpolitical) levels.

Table 2-2
Variable Properties of Social Science Disciplines

	Consensual	Nonconsensual
Applicable understanding	1. E.g., Operations research	2. E.g., Economics
Lacks applicable understanding	3. E.g., Classic public administration	4. E.g., Sociology

2. Even though economists are notorious for disagreeing about many matters, public officials are nonetheless ready to consult them. The route that leads public officials, especially elected officials, to high office often does not give them training in the technicalities of economic policy. Yet, high office gives public officials responsibility for major decisions about the economy—decisions that can have a pervasive impact upon public policy. The fact that economists lack a consensus about what government should do is less significant than the fact that within such branches of economics as public finance, public expenditure, investment appraisal, money supply, and so forth, economists do have an understanding that is applicable to the otherwise "undisciplined" problems confronting politicians.

3. Classic public administration involved consensual goals of "good" government. Good administration, like good health, was taken for granted as a consensual objective, and academies and schools of public administration promoted the subject. The proponents of classic public administration doctrines also claimed that they had discovered principles of administration that, if properly understood, could be applied in practice. It was assumed that a sharp distinction could be drawn between politics and administration. Events since the Second World War, both in government and in universities, have disproven these assumptions. Empirical studies of government have emphasized the impossibility of distinguishing clearly between politics and administration, and comparative studies have emphasized how culture-bound and narrow were classical definitions of good government. The attempt to apply principles as prescriptions made it evident that the absence of theoretical justification was not a token of practical efficacy, but rather often accompanied practical inadequacy. As public administration has become more self-conscious about these shortcomings, its new leaders have tended to "go political—that is, emphasize nonconsensual elements of their work.

4. Any reader of sociology journals within nations or comparatively will be well aware that the discipline is nonconsensual. Sociologists may, of course, challenge the claim that they lack understanding of society. What is important here is that the theories of sociologists are rarely capable of development into a technology that a government can apply to reduce the social problems that public officials face. Insofar as sociologists state that their purpose is not to change the world, but rather to understand it, then the lack of a social engineering capability is no fault in their claim to academic status—but it is a fatal weakness to utilization within government.

The work of social scientists is potentially relevant to the work of public officials, especially high-ranking politicians, insofar as it deals with issues about which there is dissensus. The reason is simple: Politics is about the management of conflicting opinions. Activities of government about which there is no dispute are nonpolitical and, therefore, not relevant to the directors of government.[5] The consensual activities of natural scientists and life scientists may be financed by government grants, but they are of little or no concern to high-ranking government officials, until such time as their social implications become evident and controversial. Government officials are concerned with the social, economic and political elements of scientific activities and not with laboratory work per se. For example, medical research is nonpolitical as long as life scientists are seeking to understand biological processes. It becomes political when efforts are made to apply this understanding through decisions of government; for example, through fluoridation of drinking water or government-sponsored birth control programs.

The political importance of dissensus is illustrated by the fact that economists who work on such controversial questions as unemployment and inflation are more likely to have the ear of public officials than do economists whose recommendations concern such agreed-upon goals as the optimum allocation of floorspace in a government building. The fact that the economists have (or claim to have) an understanding applicable to controversial issues gives them effectively more relevance than sociologists, who often address controversial issues and reflect dissensus, but conclude their critiques without making any recommendations that government can act upon. For example, generalizations about the inexorable consequences of industrialization or the importance of changes in cultural values do not interest public officials, because they are not immediately applicable through their existing resources and institutions.

The growth of government activities has increasingly made public officials concern themselves with "undisciplined" problems where their own knowledge and efficacy is lacking. A century ago governments concentrated most of their attention upon the classic defining activities of the modern state: diplomacy, military defense, law, the maintenance of public order, and public finance. In several such fields professional expertise developed relatively early; others (e.g., diplomacy) involved monopoly claims to knowledge based upon information available only to public officials. As European states expanded their activities, governments became involved in the mobilization of physical resources, typically through the application of engineering technologies, to build public works such as canals or railways, to provide long distance communications, and latterly, to encourage both industrial and agriculture output. Social activities, such as they were, tended to involve collective goods aspects of social problems that were amenable to centralized influence by technologies that developed rapidly in the nineteenth century (e.g., *public* health rather than the health of individuals).[6]

Contemporary European governments are under great pressure, both from popular expectations and often from governing parties as well, to provide substantial welfare benefits to society: education, health, security in old age, and such diffuse and abstract properties as "equality." Insofar as an applicable technology is at hand, then the principal concern of a government is meeting the cost of social services. For example, governments know how to pay out pensions to the elderly; their chief problem is finding the money to fund pensions. The technology of elementary education is also well understood and widely diffused; professional educationists are successful technologists insofar as they concentrate upon teaching reading, writing, and arithmetic. Insofar as government asks them to teach adolescents how to be loyal subjects or to develop values novel to the community in which they are born, educationists are likely to be less effective, because they lack applicable understanding; by the same token, government achieves less. In the field of health care, governments know how to produce doctors and nurses and hospitals. It is less clear-cut, however, in Western nations at least, that such inputs of health services automatically and linearly lead to better health and longer life as the result. Governments risk spending more and more money on inputs of health services without securing more and more health for their citizens as an output.

Public officials committed to objectives that social scientists cannot resolve in theory, let alone practice, can adopt any (or all) of several strategies. (First, some can avoid the difficulties of attempting what is uncertain (and conceivably impossible) by concentrating upon procedural elements in the policy process. As long as the bureaucracy is operating satisfactorily, then it is assumed that the program is working. Second, some can concentrate upon measures of governmental output, e.g., money spent, personnel employed, physical plant provided in the form of hospitals, and so forth, rather than upon measures of impact, e.g., illness reduction, increase in learning by children staying extra years at school, and so forth. Third, public officials can turn to social scientists and ask for their help in studying government's problems. Even though a social scientist may belong to a discipline whose leaders show no consensus about objectives and even low understanding of phenomena in question, a Ph.D. in the subject can be expected to bring *some* discipline to the analysis of completely *undisciplined* problems threatening to swamp officials whose expertise lies in controlling government, rather than the complex phenomena of society "out there."

The continuing existence of social problems is not proof of the failure of government, for the political process is designed to generate or publicize problems. Even if public officials resolve a problem to the subsequent satisfaction of all concerned, they cannot rest on their laurels, but rather will be dragged forward to meet another problem that has gained attention, thanks to the skills of parties and pressure groups in articulating demands. In the 1960s, social scientists, like public officials in many lands, tended to be optimistic about the ability of government, of social science and especially of the two working together, to find acceptable means of responding to public problems. Today, optimism is less often found among academics or public officials. Any criticisms that public officials make of the inadequacies of social scientists are double-edged. For public officials to blame social scientists for not providing them with better understanding and technology to deal with undisciplined problems is to admit that the actions that they themselves take are not based upon logic that is explicit or capable of being inferred by observers. The growing importance of the undisciplined problems facing public officials and social scientists is an argument for increasing efforts to use social science to cope with these problems, rather than for dismissing the only technology that government has at hand.[7]

Notes

1. Contrast Daniel Bell, *The Coming of Post-Industrial Society* (New York: Basic Books, 1973), and Samuel P. Huntington, "Post-Industrial Politics: How Benign Will it Be?" *Comparative Politics* VI, no. 2 (1974).

2. See, for example, Nathan Caplan, "The Use of Social Science Information by Federal Executives," in Gene Lyons (ed.), *Social Research and Public Policies: The Dartmouth/OECD Conference* (Hanover, N.H.: Dartmouth College, 1975), pp. 46-67.

3. On competitive bidding for program evaluation, see Albert D. Biderman and Laure M. Sharp, "The Evaluation Research Community: RFP Readers, Bidders and Winners," *Evaluation* II, no. 1 (1974), pp. 36-40. For a wide-ranging discussion of American faith in the "neat engineering solution"—and of Europeans' faith that American techniques provide such a solution—see Reyner Banham, "Europe and American Design," in Richard Rose (ed.), *Lessons from American* (London: Macmillan, 1974), pp. 67-91.

4. Sometimes, the fix failed to take. See, for example, Sophocles' *Oedipus Tyrannus.*

5. Since dissensus requires that political figures be aligned on both sides of an issue, social scientists will have their statements ignored if there is a negative consensus among public officials that their views are impractical, nonsensical, or incomprehensible.

6. For the relevant historical evidence, see Richard Rose, "On the Priorities of Government: A Developmental Analysis of Public Policies," *European Journal of Political Research* IV (1976).

7. Cf. the slogan in the American wild west saloon: "Don't shoot the piano player; he's doing the best he can."

3

The Social Scientist and Policymaking: Some Cautionary Thoughts and Transatlantic Reflections

L. J. Sharpe

Bored by the tedium of institutional analysis but disenchanted by barefoot empiricism, many social scientists have found no alternative succor in the aridities of "value-free" grand theory. It is not, therefore, surprising that under the mixed promptings of a quickening official interest in the application of social science to public policy making, a more radical student clientele, and the pervasive influence of a second-hand "systems theory," they have increasingly turned their attention to postlegislative politics, to the study of "substantive" public issues, to "outputs," and to policies. From such predispositions it has been for some social scientists a relatively short step to taking a direct interest in public policy making. Such concern has in turn given birth to a small body of literature, and it is the primary concern of this chapter to provide a critical comment on it.[1]

Much of what is said in this literature, it must be admitted at the outset, is informative and largely unexceptionable—that is to say, it raises what seem to me to be the key issues and explores most of the more important problems. In some cases, and the work of Cherns[2] is a good example, there is also a realistic appreciation of the policy-making process and therefore of the severe limits governing the extent to which social science research can directly contribute to public policy making. But it must also be said that some of this literature, although less naive than apparently Dr. Kissinger was before he went to Washington,[3] tends nevertheless in its different ways either to be too optimistic about potential contribution of social scientists to policy making, or to ignore many of the barriers lying in the path of expanding its contribution. Even Cherns, when he turns to the possible modes of harnessing the social scientist to the policy-making process, offers a fairly elaborate framework that seems to imply that such linkages could be extensive. So the overall effect of his analysis tends to leave the impression of overoptimism.

Part of the reason for this overoptimism is a tendency to formal abstraction with few concrete examples of where social science has made, or seems likely to make, a direct contribution. Clearly, the danger of an excessively abstract approach is not merely the obvious one that it tends to avoid reality, but also that it can so easily slide into discussing the ideal or desired conditions rather than the probable. This is especially so when the discussion is being conducted by social scientists who, it may be presumed, feel duty bound to take a

This chapter is a revised version of an article that first appeared in *Policy & Politics*, Vol. 4, no. 2, 1975. Published by Sage Publications.

38

somewhat lofty expansionist view of social sciences' (or at least their own disciplines') potential contribution to government. Since one of the minor curiosities of the literature is the relative absence of anyone who can be identified as a politician or administrator, such tendencies are perhaps to be expected. When the argument is also placed in a broader and hazier discussion of the need for faster economic growth, the problems of social conflict, and the increasing complexity of modern society, as it is in many cases, the claims for social science as a saviour become distinctly bolder. If, to this heady mixture, is added a pinch of moral uplift on the social responsibilities of social scientists and the need for them to justify their keep, reality recedes even further into the background, and any social scientist who questions the need, or possibility, of more social science in government is liable to appear churlish if not actually traitorous.

Important as these tendencies are for encouraging overoptimism about the possible contribution of the social sciences, it is likely that another characteristic of the literature is even more important, and this is the extent to which it is either American or is strongly influenced by American experience. Of the twenty-six citations in Cherns' 1968 article, only four are British, although the article is apparently discussing the British situation. Why does this American influence matter? Before answering this question, two important exceptions to the case of overoptimism must be noted. The first concerns the discussion of the role of economics in public policy making. For a number of reasons economics has a greater potential contribution to make to public policy making than the other social sciences. The most obvious of these is that it deals with the central policy issues: the allocation of resources. It also deals in measurable effects, which among other things enables it to establish what Shonfield has called a "causal nexus"[4] between existing policies and a wide range of economic indicators of the consequences of these policies on different aspects of the economy.[5]

The second aspect of the literature on the potential contribution of social science to government that must be absolved from the charge of overoptimism relates to trained social scientists working as permanent civil servants or to permanent research units within government itself. Although there are still relatively few of the former, they have grown rapidly in numbers, and examples of the latter include the Home Office Research Unit, the Research and Development Group of the Department of the Environment, the Civil Service Pay Research Unit, and the Behavioral Science Research Division of the Civil Service Department. That this type of in-house social science aid to policy making has an important part to play in modern government cannot be gainsaid, although it will be, as I will suggest, always a limited one. The main charge of overoptimism that this chapter is concerned with relates principally to the discussion of university-based social science research and to the temporary secondment of individual academic social scientists to government.

To return to the question posed a moment ago, why does it matter if the literature on the need for social scientists in government is largely American inspired? At a fairly high level of generality, it probably doesn't matter much because there are obvious points of broad similarity between the two countries and, judging by the 1966 OECD report on this subject, with other Western democracies as well.[6] But if we want a reasonable modicum of accuracy, it has to be recognized that American society is decidedly more sympathetic and receptive to the social sciences than is British society.

It is difficult to pin down this kind of broad difference between the two countries with any precision, but no British social scientist who has ever visited the United States can have failed to be aware that he was in a *milieu* that took his calling seriously. The nearest analogy is perhaps that of an English chef visiting Paris. One reason is that the social sciences as a whole have higher status as academic disciplines in the United States than they do in Britain, and they have been firmly established as such for a longer period than they have in Britain.[7] Further, American culture is more predisposed than most to believe in the beneficial effects of rational inquiry as an aid to decision making of any kind. It is, after all, the home of scientific management, and there seems to be a much wider acceptance of the utility of harnessing the latest technique to do service in the decision-making process—to reducing the process to a technology—that is somehow alien to British political practice. What is perhaps more relevant, this tendency is linked to the wider American democratic tradition. Price has made the point that the effect of the scientific spirit of the Founding Fathers was to destroy "the traditional theory of hereditary sovereignty and to substitute the idea that people had the right, by rational and empirical processes, to build their governmental institutions to suit themselves."[8]

Lasswell's discussion of the social sciences, or as he prefers to call them "policy sciences," emphasizes their role in public policy making:

It is probable that the policy-science orientation in the United States will be directed toward providing the knowledge needed to improve the practice of democracy.[9]

Such an exalted place for social science has no parallel in the British political tradition. On the contrary, it is profoundly suspicious of the university world altogether and social science in particular. It gives much greater weight to knowledge as accumulated experience—*he who does knows*—and in its extreme form sees practical experience as the only legitimate source of knowledge. As G.H. Hardy has it:

Statesmen despise publicists, painters despise art critics, and physiologists, physicists, or mathematicians have usually similar feelings; there is no scorn more profound, or on the whole more justifiable, than that of men who make for men who explain. Exposition, criticism, appreciation is work for second-rate minds.[10]

This elevation of practice over commentary, exposition, and theory is also reflected amongst other things in the extent to which so many of the professions in this country, not least those which play a large part in government, still conduct their education and training outside the ambit of the universities. The epitome of the government's response to a policy problem in the United States is to select the professor with the highest reputation in the field, give him a generous research budget, and put him on a contract. The epitome in Britain is to set up a committee of inquiry made up largely of distinguished practitioners in the chosen policy field with a token academic who may or may not be invited by his colleagues to organize research.

There has undoubtedly been a strengthening of the social science input to the activities of committees of inquiry and royal commissions in recent years. Some royal commissions have actually designated a social scientist as research director who has undertaken or commissioned extensive research.[11] Similarly, on other commissions and committees, the social scientist member has undertaken such a role unofficially.[12] However, it remains to be seen how far these developments reflect a permanent change in attitudes, and even if they do, there will be some way to go before we approach practice in the United States where university social science departments are by British standards much better adapted to, and often heavily dependent on, government for their maintenance.[13] The long debate about whether or not the social sciences are, or ought to be, the "policy sciences,"[14] C. Wright Mills' attack on "abstracted empiricism,"[15] and Merton's concern lest academic social scientists be reduced to the role of "bureaucratic technicians"[16] all have their origins in the fact that a large slice of American academic social science is sustained by research sponsored by government or other extramural agencies. Moreover, the long-standing tradition of American social science, "which emphasizes empirical focus, reliable technique, and precise data,"[17] has made it much more amenable to such ties.

The exploration of causes must admittedly always be a bit speculative, but what cannot be denied are the palpable indications of the much greater importance attached to academic social science as an aid to policy making by government in the United States as compared with Britain. This may be graphically illustrated by the much greater amount of money spent on it by the federal government. In 1970, it allocated £145 million for social science research when the comparable figure for the United Kingdom was £5 million,[18] and in 1971 the U.S. figure increased to nearly £200 million.[19]

Another dramatic reflection of the very different attitudes of the governments of the two countries to the role of social scientists in government is the extraordinary extent, by British standards, to which university social scientists have been brought directly into the U.S. federal government over the past decade and a half. Kissinger, who as Secretary of State has one of the most important posts in the executive branch, is only the most celebrated example of a long line of very distinguished academic social scientists who have been brought in to fill some of the most important offices of the federal government since 1960. Others include Rostow, Roche, Bundy, Gullion, Schelling, Yarmolinsky, Schlessinger, Galbraith, and Moynihan. A handful of academics have been appointed to relatively minor ministerial posts in Britain in recent years—Bowden, Balogh, Kalder, and Crowther-Hunt, for example—and one—Sir Claus Moser—was appointed to a senior civil service post as director of the Central Statistical Office. During the period 1964-66 the first Wilson government also brought in a number of academic social scientists—the now-famous "Whitehall Irregulars"—but they were mostly economists, and the example has not been followed on the same scale by any government since. Taken together, these changes hardly compare with the American attitude towards academic social scientists in government, which has been summarized by Moynihan thus:

... there is no place on earth where the professor reigns, or has done up until very recently, as in the United States. For the past thirty years in our society the intellectuals—the professors—have influenced almost without precedent in history. The economists primarily (I am leaving aside the whole phenomena of the physical sciences), but increasingly also the softer social scientists, the sociologists, the political scientists and the psychologists.[20]

Another major difference between the political-cum-administrative traditions of the two countries that suggests caution in assuming that the American experience is very relevant to British conditions occurs on the "user" side of the policy-making partnership: the politicians and the civil servants. Let us look at the politicians first. The greater receptivity of American government to social science may not only reflect higher public esteem, but also the much greater extent to which politicians employ "aides" and research assistants of all kinds. The American politician does not expect to do his own speech writing, letter writing, fact gathering, background reading, and, some would add, thinking. He employs a team of aides. Furthermore, many congressmen rely heavily upon university contacts in their home districts and states for policy consultation. Robert Peabody estimates that upwards of two hundred congressmen regularly hold informal brains trusts at their home state universities.[21] Thus, the whole ethos and style of American politics is strongly impregnated with the tradition of drawing upon the outsider as a vital element in policy making.

In Britain, by contrast, most MPs, even those with cabinet aspirations, seldom employ anything more than a secretary and possibly a personal assistant. The latter, until the advent of the Rowntree Trust Scheme that finances research assistants for opposition front benchers,[22] usually performed their tasks out of personal admiration rather than monetary reward. British politicians once they decide to make politics a vocation develop—have to develop—a very strong sense of self-sufficiency that seldom leaves them until they attain office, when they can then look to the civil service for all the policy-making aid they want. And they are likely to have a great deal more respect for these civil servants than they ever had for academics. Also the absence in the United States of a highly organized permanent party organization producing a detailed manifesto—a steady flow of policy statements and discussion documents—means that the individual congressman and senator is forced back on his own resources and hence to outside help. One of the effects of the British system is that there must be a cadre of high intellectual quality in the leadership group of the major parties to an extent that is unknown in the United States. In the case of the Labour party, the cadre tends in fact to include a high proportion of ex-social science and history academics, or academic *manqués*. In 1964, which was something of an *annus mirabalus* of this phenomenon, the cabinet of the first Wilson government contained no less than six ex-social science dons including, of course, the prime minister himself.

Let us now turn to the other half of the policy-making partnership: the higher civil servants. Here again there are some important differences between the two countries. In the first place, the British civil service is permanent, enjoys security of tenure, has high academic standards of competitive entry, promotion by merit in a strongly hierarchical career structure, has an exceptionally strict code of political neutrality, and recruits virtually the whole of its higher echelons from its own ranks. At the level where new policy is made, it is also dominated by generalists rather than technical specialists who share a strong sense of corporate identity.

Although the American federal civil service now shares to some degree all these characteristics, except the dominance of generalists and a sense of corporate identity at the top, it has none of them to quite the same extent as the British civil service.[23] Yet, it is likely that it is the effect of these characteristics that make it very much less receptive to the assistance of social scientists, or indeed of any outsider, for they all combine to give the British civil service at its upper reaches a relatively high status, a sense of omniscience, and intellectual security to an extent that is not possible at the equivalent level in the American federal civil service.

This difference is reinforced by the fact that unlike their American counterparts, the British are not subject to the effects of the separation of powers doctrine that requires them to explain their proposals to congressional committees in public; nor do their proposals have to face the critical scrutiny of the professional staffs (often again recruited from the universities) of the congressional committees. As Lyons has put it:

The need for knowledge and analysis in making government decisions on complex issues is increased by the process of checks and balances inherent in the operations of the American political system. Not only is the government accountable to the general public, but the separation of powers within the government requires that the President and Congress account to each other.[24]

Perhaps the most decisive reason why the American administrative system is more receptive to academics is that, lacking the equivalent of an administrative class within the federal civil service who act as the confidantes and advisers to the executive politicians, each regime in Washington imports its own close advisers—the "in-and-outers"—and they usually include a strong leavening of academics.[25]

There may be a further consideration that makes American government more dependent on the assistance of academic social scientists. The United States is unique among Western democracies in lacking a permanently organized social democratic party that is able to compete on approximately level terms with the other major parties and whose broad egalitarian aims have the effect of promoting the interests of the poorest section of the population.

This characteristic of the American political system means that the federal government has to conduct periodic bursts of activity in order to maintain some sort of parity of welfare with comparable countries in relation to the poor. Instead of being a product of a continuous doctrinal battle within the political system about the speed and direction of the secular trend to greater equality within civil society (which is very roughly what seems to happen in other Western democracies), social amelioration has often to come from on high—from the executive branch—in large doses dressed up as emergency measures to combat a temporary national crisis.[26]

Such was a lot of the New Deal legislation, the social legislation of the Second World War period, and the War on Poverty initiated by Presidents Kennedy and Johnson. But such sudden demands on government cannot be achieved by the existing agencies of the federal government, and since the problem is seen as largely nonideological, the national predisposition to see social science as a saviour comes into its own. During the heyday of the War on Poverty for the decade ending in 1968, federal funds available to the social sciences increased no less than sevenfold.[27] Riecken has summarized the general attitude at these periods when discussing the conclusions of a number of reports on the need for more social science in government made in 1968, thus:

Overall the tone of these reports is consistent—a heavy emphasis on the desirability, need and prospect of bringing social sciences into closer conjunction with the practical affairs of society. This is perhaps a response to the current awareness, widespread and uneasily acute, that all is far from well in American society, and the expectation that rational methods, grounded in scientific work, can help to steer the country through its troubles.[28]

Not only are federal agencies unable to cope, there are also insufficient civil servants imbued with the necessary sense of hope and drama or equipped with the necessary knowledge of the conditions and arcane habits of the recipients of the proposed new enactments that will "make America over." Ambitious social science professors with a liberal bent may be seen as ideal candidates in many respects for filling the breach in such exciting times. Thus, the notion of making good the deficiencies of government by expanding research is also matched by the notion of improving the quality of administrators by importing social scientists into government. So, when Rexford Tugwell after Franklin Roosevelt's first election announced that the academics who like himself were *en route* to Washington could "speak truth to power," he was articulating what now amounts to a traditional link between social science and American government that has few parallels in other countries. Among American political scientists who specialize in American political institutions a sojourn in Washington seems to be regarded as an essential feature of their careers.

So much for overoptimism about the potential contribution of social scientists that seems to be derived from American experience. Another important cause of overoptimism is the widespread assumption that governments are always in need of, or actively seek, information. But it seems doubtful whether this is the case. It is more likely that government has too much information, not too little—too much, that is, by its own estimation. Government is concerned with decisions that have to be made within fairly short time limits, and this means that one of its main tasks is to close off as many options as possible by establishing criteria of rejection. Rigorously applied, this can mean, if the policymaker is lucky, that the decision "selects itself" with the minimum of friction and time wasting and the maximum of plausibility. These are not the conditions under which information will be actively sought, for any new information will almost certainly delay matters. But it may well generate further options as well, without providing any new criteria of rejection. Keynes, who had rather more experience of government than perhaps any other British social scientist before or since, pointed out this essential feature of government long ago; yet it is seldom recognized in the literature: "There is nothing a government hates more than to be well-informed; for it makes the process of arriving at decisions much more complicated and difficult."[29]

Another misunderstanding about the extent to which social science can aid decision making is the assumption that social scientists have the information that decisionmakers need. The first, relatively minor, fault with this argument is that a great deal of academic social science is not about phenomena but about concepts. This was Beveridge's point when he claimed that economics was really a branch of medieval logic and that economists ". . . are persons who earn their livings by taking in one another's concepts for mangling."[30]

Of much greater importance is the fact that even where social science research is about the real world, it is not in the form that is useful for policy making. This is not so much a problem of pure versus applied research, but simply that academic research is general, whereas policy is usually highly specific and in addition requires a knowledge of the institutions and processes in which it is to be applied. Cherns has stated that problem as well as anyone. Social science research, he claims, ". . . can only have specific use if it is concerned both as taking a narrow view of the problem it is tackling and has a strategy for its use designed into its methodology. Research of this kind turns out to have low generalizability which does not necessarily mean, but often does, that it is also trivial."[31] Since we may presume only a minority of social scientists want to engage intentionally in trivialities, we are brought face to face with the fact that it has proved very difficult to uncover many instances where social research has had a clear and direct effect on policy even when it has been specifically commissioned by government. Cherns recounts his own embarrassment when forced by a beady-eyed request to provide evidence of such effects in relation to research sponsored by the Human Sciences Committee of the old Department of Scientific and Industrial Research, and he reminds us that the Heyworth Committee on social studies faced a similarly fruitless task, as did five separate investigations in the United States in relation to research sponsored by the federal government.

This last point is worth noting in passing since it suggests that although American government may commission more social science research, it may be no more inclined actually to use it than British government. Doubtless, American policymakers, no less than British, commission some research not to elucidate a policy problem but to parry short-political pressures by buying time. If we are to believe many of the claims made on behalf of social science as an aid to public policy making, this must be at least in part the explanation for the puzzling disparity between the scale and quality of American social science research and its access to government on the one hand and the effectiveness of American government on the other.[32]

It is true that there are a number of factors that may obscure the link between research and policy. Cherns points out, for example, how difficult it is to gauge the link because the time span may be too protracted, because we lack adequate measures of change, and finally, because we often don't know the "before" conditions accurately enough.[33] He might have added that the effect of social science research on a policy choice may also be obscured because it was purely negative in effect—that is to say, option C was chosen because option A (initially the most favored) was ruled out by the findings of the research although the implications of that research (option B) were politically unacceptable. Nevertheless, when due allowance is made for these factors, examples of a direct link between social science research and actual policies are remarkably scarce.

I would now like to turn to what is an extremely important aspect of the contribution of social science to public policy making, particularly in relation to the secondment of academic social scientists directly into the policy-making process. This is the general predispositions of the two parties—academic and policymaker—to each other. The first problem is the difference in time scales of university research and government decision making. The policymaker usually wants decisions as soon as possible: Time is one of his scarcest resources, partly because of intense short-term public pressures on policymakers, partly because governments have a fixed time span, and partly because the legislative process is an insatiable consumer of time, and it is a process that cannot be bypassed. So if time runs out, the most elaborately prepared, most urgent, most worthy proposals remain mere intentions. Even when a longer time scale for policy formulation is deliberately chosen, such as a royal commission, committee of inquiry, or an intradepartmental working party, the tempo is still likely to be too fast for the academic. This is because governments have to be careful who and what research they commission. They will usually require "peer review" as well as internal vetting. Cumbersome financial approval procedures will also have to run their inexorable course, and mundane problems associated with the seasonal character of research personnel recruitment lengthen the process still further. The academic engaged in research for government will also be inclined to resist being rushed, precisely because he is now being asked to produce something that may possibly determine events rather than impress his academic peers—and determine events, moreover, in an institutional and policy setting that he may discover is largely unfamiliar to him. The academics' time scale is relatively posterity; the policymakers' can seldom be longer than next week to next year.[34] Robin Huws Jones made this point most tellingly in discussing government attitudes to sociological research when he confessed to ". . . a disloyal spasm of sympathy with the complaint that the sociologists' cry is 'Give us the job and we'll spend the next seven years sharpening the tools.' "[35] Such considerations have led one American observer who has had a great deal of experience in commissioning outside research for government to conclude: "The time required for the initiation, conduct and reporting of grant-supported research very nearly guarantees that the results will not be available in time to be useful in policy formulation and implementation."[36]

The second problem derived from the different predispositions of policymaker and social scientist is associated with the handicap that the social scientist has to shoulder, when compared with, say, the technologist or engineer, because he deals with facets of human behavior, or the operation of institutions, that form part of the working experience of policymakers. This working experience is moulded into a series of plausible explanations that in reality may or may not be accurate, but that are jealously guarded by the policymaker with all the pride and obstinacy that any professional guards the current orthodoxies of his specialism. And he is unlikely to discard them easily unless he can be presented with an alternative explanation that is backed by proof—that is, has been validated by controlled experiments. This proof, in the nature of things, the social scientist cannot provide. The nearest that social science has so far got in Britain to a controlled experiment in relation to public policy is action research, notably in the Education Priority Area programs and the Community Development projects. But it is doubtful whether these experiments will offer the policymaker with something that approximates to, and he recognizes as, validation.[37] No social scientist who has to advise a group of civil servants and politicians is likely to forget that mixture of suspicion tinged with incredulity that they often seem to feel—almost instinctively—towards social science research findings, in relation to a policy or political process about which they claim familiarity, that refute their own interpretation.

There are some indications that these attitudes may be changing, partly because the status of the social sciences has risen slightly, but mostly because the intractability of some policy problems has made policymakers more willing to consult outsiders. In Britain, the creation in 1970 of the Central Policy Review Staff, which advises the cabinet as a whole,[38] and the setting up in 1974 of an advisory team of social scientists under the leadership of Bernard Donoughue in the Prime Minister's Private Office are both reflections of this change although both are small and in some respects are in-house rather than outsider teams.

The creation of the Civil Service College in 1968, which itself maintains a largely social science-based research program and is responsible for extensive in-service training courses, also reflects and possibly stimulates a more receptive attitude towards the social sciences in the central departments. The expansion of departmental research budgets (in 1975 the research budget for the Department of the Environment was, for example, running at £15 million), some of which is spent on university-based social science research, may be another indicator.

There has also been some reorganization of the research and policy sections of the other major departments following the Rothschild Report,[39] which also seems to have stimulated interest in social science research. Perhaps the most extensive of these changes has occurred in the Department of Health and Social Security. A further likely agent of change is the SSRC itself, which at one time set up a Social Science and Government Committee. It was this committee that prepared the way for the establishment of "Social Trends" as a permanent feature of government publication and that again is likely to stimulate more interest in the social science dimension of policy making.

We must be careful not to inflate these trends into a major change in the relationship between social science and government. Even if the role of the social sciences increases, there remain other obstacles to improving the impact of social science that relate not so much to the receptivity of the "user" as to the social scientist himself.

In the first place the social scientist is not immune from stereotyped attitudes towards the policymakers. Social scientists who are interested in political institutions and public policy tend to regard with suspicion, almost instinctively, those at the top level of government. This is hardly the place to explore the precise origins of these attitudes,[40] but it is of some significance that a common feature of much of the academic theory of democratic organizations is derived from the assumption that, whatever the outward forms may be, power is inevitably concentrated at the top. More specifically, that the conventional account of how democratic institutions work is mythical. Whether it is Schumpeter's theory of how the modern democratic state works, Weber's theory of bureaucracy, Michel's iron law of oligarchy, the various elite-mass theories stemming from Mosca, or the elitist account of community power, they all have this characteristic more or less in common. Reared on such intellectual diet and imbued with no more than the average enthusiasm for democracy, it is perhaps hardly surprising that our social scientist when first transplanted into government tends to see his new colleagues in a slightly jaundiced light. This is not the most propitious beginning for successful collaboration.

The academic also tends to feel aggrieved at the way policymakers handle research findings. Whereas he likes to think of himself as a seeker of the truth pure and unadorned, the policymakers seem to him to be manipulating it by choosing those aspects of research findings they find congenial and ignoring or suppressing the rest. Secondly, the academic social scientist requires an unusual combination of patience, understanding, enthusiasm, and above all, belief in his discipline if he is to continue as an effective participant in the policy-making process. This combination of qualities is not easily come by among professionals, and it must be said in all frankness it is rare among academic social scientists. This is because the social scientist is himself only too aware of the precarious edifice of knowledge on which he is perched. As Lippman has suggested, he shares the policymakers' estimate of himself and he "...has little inner certainty about his own work...only half believes in it...his data is uncertain, his means of verification lacking."[41] His whole professional posture and training is against closing off avenues of analysis and is in favor of opening them up and revealing their hidden dimensions, and where he thinks his views may be acted upon, of careful qualification, of never being pinned down, and of not coming to a final conclusion if he can help it. He may also have feelings of guilt and embarrassment if he gets embroiled in issues that have strong party political overtones.[42] In the sweaty-palmed atmosphere across the polished mahogany tables of Whitehall, he is vulnerable, and the policymaker senses his vulnerability from the degree of necessary indeterminancy in his findings:

This very indeterminancy then leads to tension between the expert and the policymaker, since the results of research are rarely decisive. The policymaker must still perform a difficult act of judgement based on his own views and experience.[43]

This is not to say that the academic social scientist cannot take a direct hand in policy making, only that it is very difficult for him to do so and remain an academic. He may settle for a different role—that of a specialized civil servant or a rather detached, well-informed politician—but the role of academic will be very difficult to sustain for any length of time.[44] For any academic with an interest in the policy-making process per se and no more than a normal ration of personal vanity, such a role can be highly rewarding. Especially so if it means, as it usually does, that he has access to information that he would find hard to acquire so easily as an ordinary university teacher. He may also succumb to considerable and flattering pressure not to beat a hasty retreat back to the university since the need for government policy statements to ". . . have some rags of legitimation cast about them by quantitative research"[45] is on the increase in a society where more and more of the informed public is exposed to social science at the universities. If he is at all sensitive to his professional standing in the academic world, he will of course have to weigh these rewards against the possible loss of professional standing if the sojourn is too protracted. The vigilance of at least some of his academic peers in relation to his new career is unlikely to flag and if he does get the ear of the policymakers, they may tend to see it, as Shonfield has suggested, ". . . in terms of a sleight of hand by which one of their number has managed arbitrarily to capture the use of power of a politician—in the sort of way that Lysenko used Stalin."[46]

The academic in government will certainly find his role difficult to sustain if his research breaks new ground and his findings refute received opinion. For that is precisely the point where the professional policymakers have to desert him. No research for public policy making can outrun to any great extent the intellectual capacities and comprehension of the policymakers (the lesser problem that we will return to in a moment), nor can it run too far ahead of the parameters of received opinion. The risks for the policymaker, both politician and civil servant, are far too great.[47]

There remains one final aspect that merits a brief mention and that is the delicate one of ideology or values. All social science research that is likely to be of any use to policymakers will imply some values. This may be so even in relation to the techniques it employs. The apparently innocent sample survey, for example, when used as a consumer test of public policy may be viewed by politicians as a disguised referendum that seeks to outflank them as the people's representatives.[48] Since the British political system is presaged on a conflict of values through the party system, there will always be potential grounds for conflict between a social scientist and policymakers. However, much of the discussion of the problem seems to avoid the real consequences of this fact, either by exaggerating the conflict in terms of claiming that all social science is inherently a challenge to the status quo, or that it is inevitably the acolyte of the status quo, or, alternatively, by simply ignoring the problem of values altogether. It is clear, however, that the latter view is unacceptable, and the first two, although considerably more frank, both tend to mistake one branch of the social sciences for the whole. A more realistic approach to the value problem must surely accept that social science research may be a challenge, or it may be a reinforcement to the status quo; it all depends on what the subject is. And the consequences of both are that the conflict can only be minimized if the social scientist himself chooses which political master, which party, and which policy he wishes to be involved with. To put the matter more directly, most social scientists have a clear idea which party they support and a Conservative party supporter is unlikely to work very long within or for a Labour government (and vice versa) without coming under severe psychological strains that are likely to undermine his performance qua social scientist in any case.

Where does this largely pessimistic discussion leave us? Not I think with the totally negative conclusion of Miller who believes that such is the interpenetration of social science and politics in policy making that there is ". . . a direct incompatibility between careful evaluative research and the political process."[49] Cherns is probably closer to reality when he concludes that experience to date suggests the role of the social scientist who wants to directly influence public policy is largely confined to providing the policymaker with aids in his selection of means, and where there has been a wide discrepancy between aim and achievement.[50] Provided we exclude the very considerable contribution that social scientists can make indirectly to public policy making by changing the climate of ideas about how a policy problem is viewed, the fairly modest role that Cherns assigns to the social scientist in policy making is probably about right.

Notes

1. In relation to social science and policy making in Britain, see, for example: *Social Research and a National Policy for Science,* Tavistock Pamphlet No. 7 (London: Tavistock Institute, 1964); *Report of the Committee on Social Studies* (Heyworth) Cmnd 2660 H.M.S.O., 1965, chapter VII; *Report of the Committee on the Civil Service* (Fulton) Vol. 1, Cmnd 3638 H.M.S.O., 1968, chapter 5; T.S. Simey, *Social Science and Social Purpose* (London: Constable, 1968); F.F. Ridley, "Policymaking Science," *Political Studies* 18 (1970); A.H. Halsey, "Social Science and Government," *Times Literary Supplement*, March 5, 1970; M. Stacey, "Sociology and the Civil Service," *SSRC Newsletter*, No. 13, November 1971; D. Donnison, "Research for Policy," *Minerva* X, no. 4 (October 1972); J.B. Cullingworth, "The Politics of Research," in J.B. Cullingworth (ed.), *Problems of Urban Society*, Vol. II (London: Allen and Unwin, 1973); M. Abrams, "Social Surveys, Social Theory and Social Policy," *SSRC Newsletter*, No. 24, July 1974. For a wider, European view see, for example: *The Social Sciences and the Policies of Governments* (Paris: OECD, 1966); Y. Dror, *Public Policymaking Re-examined* (Scranton: Chandler, 1968), especially chapter 17; and the contributions by de Jouvenel, Trist, Suchodolski, Friis, and Dror, in Cherns et al., *Social Sciences and Government* (London: Tavistock, 1972).

2. This is spread over four overlapping articles: A.B. Cherns, "Social

Sciences and Policy," in Cherns et al., *Social Sciences and Government*; "Social Sciences and Policy," in P. Halmos (ed.), *The Sociology of Sociology*, Sociological Review Monograph No. 16 (Keele: University of Keele, 1970); "Social Science Research and its Diffusion," *Human Relations* 22, no. 3 (1969); and "Uses of the Social Sciences," *Human Relations* 27, no. 4 (1968).

3. Dr. Kissinger is reported to have said at the time, "When I first started advising at high levels of the Government in the early days of the Kennedy Administration, I had the illusion that all I had to do was walk into the President's office, convince him that I was right and he would naturally do what I had recommended," *Guardian*, March 20, 1972.

4. A. Shonfield, "Research and Public Policy," in Cherns et al., *Social Sciences and Government* (London: Tavistock, 1972).

5. P.A. Samuelson also makes this point in his "What Economists Know," in D. Lerner (ed.), *The Human Meaning of the Social Sciences* (New York: Meridian Books, 1959), as does Y. Dror, somewhat more obscurely, in *Design for Policy Sciences* (New York: Elsevier, 1971), p. 8. But in the British context at least, it is not a view that has received universal acceptance even among economists. See, for example, T.W. Hutchinson, *Economics and Public Policy in Britain 1946-1966* (London: Allen and Unwin, 1968).

6. *The Social Sciences and the Policies of Governments.*

7. Simey, *Social Science and Social Purpose*, chapter 3.

8. D.K. Price, *Government and Science* (New York: New York University Press, 1954), p. 4. Edward Shils also emphasizes the importance of the "lay culture" of the United States in enhancing the status of social sciences. See his *Torment of Secrecy* (London: Heinemann, 1956), pp. 40-41.

9. H.D. Lasswell, "The Policy Orientation," in D. Lerner and H.D. Lasswell (eds.), *The Policy Sciences* (Stanford, Calif.: Stanford University Press, 1957), p. 15.

10. G.H. Hardy, *A Mathematician's Apology*, as quoted in I.M.D. Little, *A Critique of Welfare Economics* (Oxford: Clarendon, 1957, 2nd ed.), p. 1.

11. For example, the Donovan Commission on trade unions and the Redcliffe-Maud Commission on local government.

12. For example, the Seebohm Committee on the personal social services, the Fulton Commission on the Civil Service, and the Kilbrandon Commission on the Constitution.

13. C. Cunningham, "Research Funding in the United States," *SSRC Newsletter*, No. 13, November 1971.

14. See Simey, *Social Science and Social Purpose*, chapters 4 and 5, for a discussion of this debate.

15. C. Wright Mills, *The Sociological Imagination* (New York, Oxford University Press, 1959), chapters 3 and 10.

16. Merton, "Social Scientists and Research Policy," in D. Lerner and H.D. Lasswell (eds.), *The Policy Sciences* (Stanford, Calif.: Stanford University Press, 1957), p. 293.

17. Merton, "Social Scientists and Research Policy," p. 306.

18. Cunningham, "Research Funding in the United States," p. 19.

19. D.P. Moynihan, "The Role of Social Scientists in Action Research," *SSRC Newsletter*, No. 10, November 1970, p. 2.

20. Moynihan, "The Role of Social Scientists in Action Research," p. 2.

21. Personal communication to the author from Professor Peabody.

22. The Rowntree scheme did precipitate an increase in ministerial advisers when in 1974 many of the incoming Labour government retained their Rowntree advisers (the so-called "Chocolate Soldiers" or "Rowntree Smarties") on taking office. But in mid-1976 the total number of advisers including the Prime Minister's Private Office was only about thirty-five, of whom probably about eight were academics.

23. For a succinct account of the main features of the federal civil service as compared with the British, see *The Civil Services of North America*, Civil Service Department, H.M.S.O., 1969.

24. Gene M. Lyons, *The Uneasy Partnership* (New York: Russell Sage, 1969), p. 14.

25. Richard Neustadt, "White House and Whitehall" in Richard Rose (ed.), *Policymaking in Britain* (London: Macmillan, 1969), p. 296.

26. R.E. Lane, "The Decline of Politics and Ideology in a Knowledgeable Society," *American Sociological Review* 31 (1966), p. 659.

27. H.W. Riecken, "Federal Government and Social Science Policy in the United States," in Cherns et al., *Social Sciences and Government* (London: Tavistock, 1972), p. 176.

28. Ibid., p. 189.

29. J.M. Keynes, as quoted in R.M. Titmuss, *Poverty and Population* (London: Macmillan, 1938), pp. 5 and 6.

30. Sir William Beveridge, "The Place of the Social Sciences in Human Knowledge," *Politica* II, no. 9 (September 1937), p. 466.

31. Cherns, "Social Science and Policy," p. 55.

32. See David Eversley's pertinent comments on this disparity in relation to planning and the role of social science for policy making generally in his *The Planner in Society* (London: Faber, 1973), chapter 10.

33. Cherns, "Introduction," *Social Sciences and Government*, p. xxvii.

34. "The average length of time the Committee of Economic Advisors is given to explain a specific topic before it goes to the President for a decision is reported to be one week," Amitai Etzioni, "Policy Research," *The American*

Sociologist (supplementary issue "Sociological Research in Public Policy") 6 (June 1961), p. 9.

35. *The Almoner* 12, no. 2, p. 61, quoted in A. Sinfield "Which Way for Social Work?" in P. Townsend et al., *The Fifth Social Service* (London: Fabian Society, 1970), p. 28.

36. James D. Cowhig, "Federal Grant-Supported Social Research and 'Relevance': Some Reservations," *The American Sociologist* (supplementary issue, "Sociological Research and Public Policy") 6 (June 1961), p. 67. Cowhig was in 1971 a staff associate of the Research Application Directorate of the National Science Foundation and had been a program evaluator for HUD.

37. See Halsey, "Social Science in Government," and his *Educational Priority—F.F.A. Policies and Problems*, vol. 1, H.M.S.O., 1973.

38. See C. Pollett, "The Central Policy Review Staff, 1970-1974," *Public Administration* 52 (Winter 1974), for the most comprehensive description and appraisal of the CPRS over the first four years of its life.

39. *A Framework for Government Research and Development*, Cmnd. 4814, H.M.S.O., 1971.

40. For a discussion of the predispositions of social scientists towards policymakers, see L.J. Sharpe "Government as Clients for Social Science Research," *Zeitschrift für Soziologie* 5, no. 1 (1976), pp. 70-79.

41. W. Lippmann, *Public Opinion* (New York: The Free Press, 1965), pp. 233-35, quoted in Lyons, *The Uneasy Partnership*, p. 7.

42. See Y. Dror, *Design for Policy Science*, p. 9, for an interesting though somewhat terse discussion of the "weaknesses" of social scientists for public policy making.

43. Lyons, *The Uneasy Partnership*, p. 10. See also M. Allbrow, "The Role of the Sociologist as a Professional: The Case of Planning," in Halmos, *The Sociology of Sociology*, p. 11, for an interesting discussion of the role of the sociologist in planning policy.

44. Robert K. Merton, *Social Theory and Social Structures* (Glencoe, Ill.: Free Press, 1957), p. 2.

45. Hope, *Social Research Policy and Social Policy—I Indications of the State of Society*, p. 22.

46. Shonfield, "Research and Public Policy," p. 70.

47. Moynihan, "The Role of the Social Scientist in Action Research," p. 4.

48. For a revealing example of some of the perils of conducting sample surveys for policy making, see Allbrow, "The Role of the Sociologist as a Professional."

49. W.B. Miller, as quoted in D.P. Moynihan, "The Urban Negro Is the 'Urban Problem,' " in F.R. Harris (ed.), *Social Science and National Policy* (New York: Aldim, 1970), p. 19.

50. Cherns, "Social Sciences and Policy," pp. 54 and 60.

4

Sociology, Value Freedom, and the Problems of Political Counseling

Renate Mayntz

The acrimony and hostility that have characterized the recent controversy between adherents of a so-called critical (or neo-Marxist) sociology and adherents of the analytical (or neopositivistic) theory of science about the possibility of a value-free social science[1] become understandable if it is recognized that much more than an epistemological question is at issue here: The controversy revolves fundamentally about the social scientist's role in society and especially in relation to politics. Starting from this observation, this chapter is concerned with the practical implications of methodological positions. It tries to show how a faulty perception of the nature of social science knowledge obscures to the social scientist himself the role he plays as he engages in political counseling.

In the polarization of views that has been characteristic of the debate just referred to, the opponents on both sides have tended to forget that the value freedom of neopositivistic social science is apparent rather than real. No substantive social science is ever free, in its concepts and propositions, from normative elements. Methodologically speaking, its statements may be empirical propositions and not value judgments; but these propositions are not value free in the sense of being completely neutral with respect to the values we hold, as may be intuitively true of some mathematical formulae or an equation describing a chemical reaction. Max Weber, whose name has become firmly associated with the postulate of value freedom, means by this postulate only the impossibility of deriving *value judgments* from a scientific theory. He explicitly denies that our concepts are value free and points out instead that basic cultural values operate as selective criteria in the formation of sociological concepts and in the formulation of sociological questions and propositions.[2] The normative element in our concepts may of course be more or less pronounced. While the evaluative element in such tell-tale Marxist terms as exploitation, alienation, and emancipation is obvious (and intended!), it becomes less conspicuous in the abstract terminology of structural functionalism. But who would seriously claim that such terms as *normative integration, instrumental motivation, innovation,* or *goal displacement* are strictly value neutral? The value connotation can also change with the theoretical context; thus role conflict has a negative valence as determinant of deviant behavior, but a positive one as motor of innovation.

The normative implications of our concepts and propositions derive from

This chapter was originally presented as a paper at the Plenary Session 2 of the 8th World Congress of Sociology in Toronto in August 1974; it has been abridged somewhat for publication here.

the fact that the questions we ask about reality reflect specific cognitive interests, which in all empirical sciences are ultimately of a practical nature and hence partial to specific values.[3] This fact is obvious in the case of medicine or engineering. But in the social sciences, too, the role that values play in defining research questions has been generally recognized. The normative element attaches particularly to the focal dependent variables—that is, the phenomena to be explained by a theory. A theory usually starts with the definition of a problem that, unless it is of an intrinsically logical nature (i.e., derived from already-existing theory), implies a statement that something is not as it should be, or that a valued state of affairs is threatened. Thus, not only organization theory with its interest in efficiency and system maintenance, but also Parson's theory dealing with the abstract problem of social integration or socialization theory with its implied interest in successful socialization, all contain clearly perceptible normative elements. The same is true of studies of social mobility and of education, which reflect an interest in the values of social justice and equality of opportunity.

Although the role of values in defining problems for scientific analysis is generally accepted in the abstract, it is often ignored and sometimes explicitly denied that this makes our theory—concepts, questions, and propositions—proclaim specific values. Of course, the normative element in much of sociological theory remains implicit and rests in the selectivity that operates in our choice of concepts and formulation of questions. Two reasons in particular may be responsible for the continued implicitness of the normative element in "neopositivistic" sociology: one objective and one subjective. The objective reason is the pluralistic and inconsistent character of its normative content, which contrasts sharply with neo-Marxist theory. The subjective reason lies in the desire to establish a reputation of scientific objectivity. The prominence of objectivity as a professional value among the older generation of sociologists may in turn be related to the fact that until recently, the status and the potential influence of the discipline upon practical matters seemed predicated exactly on the objective nature of its results.

As we move from concepts and research questions to theory building, values enter the scientific process at yet another level. This level has to do with the fact that even the convinced neopositivist stops applying the methodological principle of systematic doubt rather early on the way. Of course, no sociologist denies that much of sociological theory is of a hypothetical nature and still waits for empirical testing. And yet, in everyday practice we tend to forget this fact and to accept speculative theorizing for a valid explanation of social reality. This danger is especially pronounced where we attempt to get at the forces underlying the accepted everyday facade of social life. In trying to explain what is normally not even questioned, it is hardly possible to avoid producing, with the explanation, a new definition of reality, which easily becomes a new convention if it is not questioned in turn.[4] Again, the more complex the interdependencies we study and the more macroscopic the questions, the more difficult is conclusive evidence to come by. However, it is hard to remain in a subjective state of uncertainty. The individual sociologist usually does not even notice the precise instant where he starts to accept a hypothesis not yet sufficiently tested as valid truth.

Where evidence is inconclusive or data permit alternative interpretations, our choice of an interpretation is directed by the beliefs and values we hold. Nor is this peculiar to social scientists. Burtt has shown that even in natural science, metaphysical convictions determine the choice between different possible interpretations of empirical facts.[5] But the effect that the content of our belief systems has on the interpretation of social science findings has not been systematically examined,[6] though individual pieces of theory may in retrospect be recognized as normatively biased and even ideological in content. This happened for instance in the case of the "organic" or "professional" model of organization that emerged from the empirically based criticism of the presumably superior efficiency of bureaucratic organization and was offered as a more valid description of reality.[7] In general, however, the influence of values on the interpretation of research findings is probably even more difficult to perceive and avoid than their influence on formulating concepts and questions. At the same time, the influence of values at the level of interpretation may impair the validity of sociological propositions much more seriously than the use of value-imbued concepts that, if properly operationalized, remain irrelevant for concrete research operations.

Our willingness to rest contentedly with plausible interpretation rather than follow the maxim of systematic doubt is not just a sign of mental sloth. It is probably connected with the fact that the objective validity (or scientific truth) of scientific statements is not merely a value in itself, but has a largely instrumental function in securing its acceptance—that is, social consensus. It is a sociological commonplace that knowledge is a social phenomenon. For practical purposes, knowledge is what the scientist can persuade his audience to accept as such.[8] But the basis of such acceptance can vary and may under certain conditions depend more on normative congeniality than on demonstrable validity. It may well be that the apparently greater carelessness with which the new left sociology engages in speculative theorizing is not only due to the fact that it often deals with more complex phenomena at a more macroscopic level, where empirical testing is difficult, but can primarily be accounted for by the fact that its reference group, "progressive" social movements and students, is more easily persuaded by normative appeals than is true of the reference group of established neopositivist sociologists. Correlatively, the function of continued emphasis on the principle of value freedom could be to convince a group of sociological consumers interested in application, and hence in knowledge that really works, that our advice is sound.

It has been argued so far that even the convinced neopositivist cannot help but produce what in *functional* terms is at least partly an ideology: a world view that contains untested elements of belief, evaluations, and hence implied prescriptions for action. If this is true, the stereotyped view of the "value-free" scientist as provider of merely instrumental knowledge to policymakers should be as false as the belief that there is really value-free social science knowledge. This is in fact the thesis of this chapter.

In its extreme form, the stereotype of the politically instrumentalized "value-free" scientist has been developed by the adherents of the new left: "engaged" sociology. They maintain that while their own approach leads them to participate as scientists in defining the goals for collective action, the methodological position of value freedom inevitably implies a decisionist orientation. Applied to the relationship between science and politics, this results—so the argument goes—in a specific form of division of labor, where the policymaker sets goals in a decisionist (or irrational) manner, while the scientist plays the part of a value-neutral provider of instrumental knowledge. Thus, instrumentalized by policymakers, value-free science can rationalize politics only at a merely technological level: It can make it more effective, but not better in a normative sense.

Characteristically, adherents of the postulate of value freedom share major elements of the "means provider" stereotype, even if they reject the accusation of their being uncritical with respect to political decisions. Following Weber's own analysis of the possibilities of criticizing political goals scientifically, they point out for instance that the separation between (political) goal setting and (scientific) selection of means holds only analytically, while in practice the known or available means influence the definition of goals. Similarly, they will point to the rationalizing effect of showing up the unintended side effects or costs of pursuing a given policy. The value-free scientist can also show whether a certain policy is consistent with given values. But these contributions to goal setting remain of an indirect nature. To point out available means or probable side effects of a specific policy requires only knowledge of situations and of causal relations. The dimension of the normative is touched directly only where the scientist reflects about the *cui bono,* the utilization of the technical solutions he provides.

A correlate of the view that the "value-free" sociologist cannot participate directly in political goal setting is the view that expert knowledge cannot per se legitimate the authority to define the goals of collective action. Organization sociologists have frequently pointed to the progressive erosion of bureaucratic authority and the increasing importance of expertise for the legitimation of authority. But if expert knowledge is in fact value free and does not permit the derivation of evaluations and hence of prescriptions with reference to the choice of ends, expertise can legitimate decision making only on the basis of an already existing value consensus. Quite logically, therefore, all technocratic models of the relationship between science and politics imply the absence of a controversy over values, if not explicit value consensus.[9]

Since the image of the sociologist as value-neutral provider of instrumental knowledge is based on a mistaken conception of the nature of sociological theory, it is not surprising that the sociologist who gets actively involved in political counseling—that is, sitting on government advisory bodies or doing contract research related to specific policy issues—finds that the accepted view of his role is wrong on several counts. That this situation has not been widely recognized is only partly due to the limited experience of our profession with political counseling. The main reason lies in the strong ideological support that the false image receives.

The stereotyped conception of the value-free scientist's relation to the world of policy making is emphatically shared by political and administrative decisionmakers. In a study conducted in Western Germany, Hannes Friedrich found that senior civil servants, who in their official capacity have to deal with scientific advisors, attribute predominantly service functions to scientific advice.[10] In particular, they mentioned such functions as providing factual information and analyzing problems situations and trends of development. Rarely do they grant to scientific advice a part in the crucial tasks of making proposals for action or of defining policy goals. This view clearly reflects the interest of the questioned officials in retaining, unchallenged by the intrusion of scientific advisors, the right to develop policy proposals themselves. A similarly competitive situation would develop between politicians and scientists if the latter were to claim the authority of defining policy goals for themselves. Thus, for administrative and political policymakers the "value-free" conception of the scientist's role with respect to goal setting serves the function of a protective ideology. Pretending to *explain* why scientists are rarely asked to contribute to political goal setting, it *justifies* the normative attribution of a restricted instrumental function to scientific advice, which (at least in the German Federal Republic) is reflected in the official task definition of advisory bodies and individual advisors and in the fact that they report predominantly not to parliament or to political leaders, but to bureaucrats of the second or third rank down.

Nor is this stereotyped conception inimical to the interests of the scientist himself. If the value-free sociologist may not engage in goal setting, he can still rationalize politics in a sense that means more than just making it more effective with reference to each isolated end; the chance of doing this rests in the possibilities for a scientific criticism of political goals pointed out before. This attribution of a rationalizing function not only serves to keep the scientist out of the fray where advocates of conflicting goals battle with each other, it is also attractive for another reason. The idea that the scientist makes political decisions more rationally reflects the old dichotomy between politics as the realm of irrational passions and science as the bulwark of reason. The evaluative connotation in this dichotomy is clear and flattering to the scientist. Thus, the self-image of the "value-free" scientist is anything but modest. It reflects a strong moral conceit that harks back to the classical view that "truth" implies the morally "good"—a conviction of which not even critical rationalism and neopositivism seem to have cured us.

But even if functional for those concerned, the false notion of the "value-free" scientist advisor can shatter under the impact of direct, personal experience. The first thing that the social scientist called upon to give advice to policymakers will find is that he has no difficulty at all in prescribing courses of action, even if the goal to be pursued has not yet been defined. In other words, he finds that he can formulate policy goals himself—not as a citizen, but by virtue of his professional knowledge. The most common way in which this happens is by signalizing problems that call for a determinate political action. In the German Federal Republic, social scientists were the first to point out the need for comprehensive educational reform and also indicated the direction it should take. They could do this easily since their choice of education as a problem area for scientific investigation implied, whether they made it explicit or not, a certain normative conception of the functions that the educational system should perform, for example, to provide mobility channels for the talented, to provide equal educational opportunities to children from different social backgrounds, or to provide the needed qualifications to the economy. When their research findings indicated that, for instance, girls of Catholic parents living in rural areas were the most severely disadvantaged group, this finding was published and publicized not simply as a value-neutral finding, but as proof of a problem that called for political action. Similar examples could easily be drawn from other areas of social science research.

I for instance found it relatively easy to develop, on one occasion of policy-related research, a distinctly normative conception of the functions of the bureaucracy with respect to policy making. This conception made it possible to derive structural prerequisites that, when compared with the conditions actually obtaining in the federal bureaucracy, permitted making specific recommendations for organizational reform.[11] The value premise underlying this applied theory was the conviction that the directive capacity of the government should be strengthened, which is a postulate that in turn can be justified with reference to the needs of system survival under specific conditions.

The prescriptions of the social scientist are thus not simply deduced from his empirical data, but are based on value postulates that, if not spelled out explicitly, are at least implied in the formulation of our concepts and questions. The prescriptions are "imperative" for all who share this value. The value postulate that lies at the basis of a given system of knowledge cannot of course be justified within this theory. But this inability does not seriously restrict the normative potential of empirical science *in practice*, because in practice the discussion is rarely about ultimate values. Normally, we are busy in the middle ranges of the means-end tree, and as long as there exists a tacit goal consensus between policymaker and scientist, there is no need even to spell out the value premises underlying scientific prescriptions.

The problems start where this condition is not fulfilled. In fact, while the social scientist engaged in political counseling will find it easy to do what he is supposedly incapable of—that is, define goals for political action—he will meet other problems for which the stereotyped image of his role has not prepared him. According to the stereotype, politics requests from science information on the best alternative to reach a given policy goal, which implies that such knowledge will be utilized if it is available. Only deficiencies in the available scientific information should accordingly restrict the utilization of social science knowledge. That such deficiencies exist we all know. Not only are certain areas of knowledge too sparsely developed. To become more useful to policymakers, sociological research and theory building would also have to shift its emphasis toward prediction rather than ex post explanation, toward thinking in developmental terms rather than in static cross-cuts, and toward the analysis of complex system dynamics rather than simple interdependencies. Besides, the social scientist should learn to include in his advice instructions on how to get from the status quo to the recommended goal state—that is, he should be more concerned with the question of which variables can in fact be manipulated to effect a recommended innovation.[12]

Granted that social science knowledge is seriously deficient for purposes of practical application, this is not the only and not even the main reason that restricts its utilization. The expressed demand for scientific information often remains definitely below what is available and could be had for several reasons. The time pressure under which policymakers normally operate reduces the level of expressed information need. The expectation that the utilization of more information would overstrain the available information processing capacity, or increase rather than reduce uncertainty, similarly lowers the level of information demand. Finally, the demand for a specific piece of information presupposes that its relevance to the problem is recognized, which becomes more difficult as the problem gets more complex and is more unique in character.[13]

While these factors lower the level of expressed demand for all types of instrumental knowledge, the utilization of social science knowledge is restricted in addition by the resistance that its implied normative content can evoke. Where policymakers do not share the value orientation implicit in a specific theory, they will not think of asking its advocate for advice. Thus, implicit consensus about the criteria of success may contribute to the rather intense cooperation between science and politics in the field of economic policy, while lack of such consensus could explain the failure to establish effective advisory relationships in some fields of social policy. Neo-Marxist sociologists who espouse their values consciously recognize this source of resistance easily. But the sociologist who is not even conscious of the normative implications of his theories may be seriously flummoxed by it.

But not only do policymakers fail to use all the scientific advice they could have, they also use what they get for purposes quite different from those the scientific expert had in mind. The scientist often assumes that his advice is sought by policymakers to help in reaching a substantive policy goal. But the values of the policymaker are only partly those of substantive policy; largely they are political—that is, the increase and preservation of power. And as policy goals are sometimes defined in an instrumental rather than a normative perspective—that is, subject to political expediency—so scientific advice is not only sought as an instrument to achieve some substantive policy goal. In the previously cited study, two-thirds of the questioned officials referred explicitly to the political functions of getting scientific advice. Most frequently mentioned were the functions of justifying decisions (or nondecisions) that they had made already or would make anyway and of supplying "objective" reasons for the rejection of demands they do not wish to fulfill and thereby counteracting, for example, the pressure of organized interests. The respondents also admitted that scientific advisors are selected because what they are known to advocate fits the present purpose.[14]

The tendency toward political instrumentalization of scientific advice is one of several reasons that make the effectiveness of the scientist's advice an overriding problem for him. Where it is not instrumentalized, his knowledge, though asked for loudly and paid for heavily, often comes to rest in some drawer and is simply not acted upon. This situation is frustrating to the scientist who is in fact normatively committed to his proposals and wishes to see them realized, and it is even more frustrating because by misperceiving both the quality of his knowledge and the social context of its utilization, he fails to see *why* his advice is not acted upon.

As for the quality of his knowledge, the scientist tends to overestimate its certainty and hence its compelling nature. In fact, however, even in natural and engineering sciences, let alone social science, results are often so equivocal and knowledge so imperfect that the policymaker himself is forced to choose between equally credible but contrasting views and proposals. This of course holds particularly for the prediction of future events, whether technological innovations, "spontaneous" social developments, the impact of a determinate policy, or the effects of a new form of organization. As for the situational context, the merely intermittent contact between the scientist and his employer often results in a growing disjunction between the work of the former and the intentions of the latter. By failing to recognize that while he is working to answer a given question, the situation that gave rise to it has already changed, the scientist may in the end provide a solution to a problem that is no longer perceived as such. Or he himself may redefine the problem he was asked to solve in the course of his inquiry, so that in the end he again answers the wrong question. Lack of familiarity with the operation of the political-administrative system may also induce the scientist to impute to the recipient of his advice not only the desire but also the authority to implement what is pointed out to him as the correct solution—which is often quite unwarranted and can only lead to the disappointment of the scientist's hope for effectiveness of his proposals.

These problems in the utilization of scientific advice that the stereotyped image of the relation between science and policy making neglects direct attention to the communication aspect of this relationship. It is generally recognized that there exists a communication problem between scientists and the policymakers they advise. Thus, most of the criticisms made by the German officials in the previously mentioned study of the limited usefulness of scientific advice can be reduced to the existence of a communication problem, whether the officials point to the abstractness of the scientists' arguments or accuse them of being unable to accept the definition of a problem as the bureaucracy sees it, so that they miss the point in their proposals.

The communication problem can be aggravated by specific institutional forms of cooperation, but it is basically not an organizational one. Science, politics, and administration constitute different cultural systems; each is characterized by its own perspective and pursues different interests and follows their separate procedural norms. It is recognized that communication between these systems requires some sort of translation, but the true nature of the communication problem escapes attention where science is held to be "value free." The problem is not simply one of cognitive content or of "language"—that is, of the too descriptive phraseology and perception of the policymakers on the one hand and the unfamiliar and abstract scientific terminology on the other. The problem is rather one of selective attention and of different value orientations. The scientist cannot be satisfied to try to make his political or administrative discussion partner "understand" what he is saying in a cognitive way, but he is compelled to convince him also of the values implied in his proposal.

This process of persuasion may be difficult for two different reasons. The first is obvious: namely, lack of consensus at the level of the value premises implied by a concrete policy proposal, though even here the nature of the disagreement is not easily recognized if both sides maintain that they are not talking about goals, but means (or "facts"). The second difficulty for the essentially normative persuasion in which the scientist must engage to defend his recommendations can derive from the political orientation of their recipient. Politicians are not only normatively oriented towards substantive policy goals, they are also constrained to orient their action at the needs of political survival. To this purpose, they must attempt to collect visible success for themselves, their party, and the government and avoid losing support. Actions that serve these goals are rational for politicians. But the criteria of political rationality may militate against measures that would be rational as means of reaching a given substantive policy goal. These measures may therefore be objected to for this reason, not only by politicians but also by high bureaucrats who, for the sake of their own success, identify with the decision criteria of their political superiors.

The articulation between different systems of rationality criteria is a difficult task, and it is not only the scientist counseling politicians who is confronted with it. Within the central bureaucracy, the same type of articulation is needed between the political leadership (the department chiefs and their politically recruited aides) and the professional specialists in the basic operating units who are charged with the details of program development. Here it is the divisional leadership upon whom the mediating function devolves. To fulfill this function successfully, the divisional leader must possess substantive expertise and full information about the details of program development in the operating units, and information about the strategic goals and political constraints operative at the level of the political leadership. He must, in other words, be a man of two worlds who not only understands the language of politics as well as the language of the specialist, but who is able to make the specialist and the politician understand each other's point of view.[15]

Sometimes the bureaucracy also performs a mediating function between science and politics. But more often than not the scientist is left to his own devices in solving his communication problem. He could probably do so better if he had a correct view of what he does and of the context in which he does it. The communication problem as such would persist, however, because it is only aggravated and not generated by the stereotyped image of value-free social scientists supplying instrumental knowledge to action-oriented policymakers.

Notes

1. This controversy is well illustrated at least for West Germany in the volume Th.W. Adorno et al., *Der Positivismusstreit in der deutschen Soziologie* (Darmstadt und Neuwied: Luchterhand, 1969).

2. Much more clearly even than in the essay "Der Sinn der 'Wertfreiheit' der soziologischen und ökonomischen Wissenschaften" this comes out in the essay "Die 'Objektivität' sozialwissenschaftlicher und sozialpolitischer Erkenntnis"; see Max Weber, *Methodologische Schriften* (Frankfurt/Main: S. Fischer, 1968), edited by J. Winckelmann.

3. See Jürgen Habermas, *Erkenntnis und Interesse* (Frankfurt/Main: Suhrkamp Verlag, 1968).

4. According to Erwin K. Scheuch, this is what happened in the development of the new left sociology. Sociology, though critical in principle of all social conventions, largely developed within advanced capitalistic societies, so that the specific content of its criticism perforce assumed an anticapitalistic tone. This particular content, but not the methodological principle of systematic criticism behind it, has recently become popular among the young and the intelligentsia—as a new progressive dogma. See "Pyrrhus-Siege der Soziologie," *Die Zeit*, No. 41, October 9, 1970.

5. Edwin A. Burtt, *The Metaphysical Foundations of Modern Physical Science* (Garden City, N.Y.: Doubleday, 1954, 2nd rev. ed. [1932]).

6. This has been argued specifically by Martin Rein, "Social Policy Analysis as the Interpretation of Beliefs," *Journal of the American Institute of Planners* XXXVII, no. 5 (September 1971), p. 299.

7. See Renate Mayntz, "The Study of Organizations—A Trend Report," *Current Sociology* XIII, no. 3 (1964, published 1966), pp. 113-15.

8. This is not only a "sociologistic" interpretation of science, but also recognized by reflective natural scientists; see, for instance, John M. Ziman, *Public Knowledge—The Social Dimension of Science* (London: Cambridge University Press, 1968), especially pp. 9-11.

9. This is elaborated extensively by Wolfgang Schluchter, *Aspekte büro-kratischer Herrschaft* (München: List Verlag, 1972), especially chapters 1 and 5.

10. Hannes Friedrich, *Staatliche Verwaltung und Wissenschaft, Die wissen-schaftliche Beratung der Politik aus der Sicht der Ministerialbürokratie* (Frank-furt/Main: Europaische Verlagsanstalt, 1970), pp. 139-61.

11. See Renate Mayntz and Fritz W. Scharpf, "Kriterien, Voraussetzungen und Einschränkungen aktiver Politik," and "Vorschläge zur Reform der Minis-terialorganisation," both contained in the volume edited by the two authors, *Planungsorganisation—Die Diskussion um die Reform von Regierung und Ver-waltung des Bundes* (München: Piper, 1973).

12. See, for instance, the argument by W. Williams, *Social Policy Research and Analysis* (New York: American Elsevier, 1971), pp. 7 ff., according to which information provided by social science generally takes on the form of "macro-negative" evidence showing the dimensions of major problems in broad terms rather than specifying what would work in a program.

13. These reasons were pointed out in the context of an empirical study of expressed information demand, which also showed that in an experimental gaming situation only 11 percent of the information held available and needed for an optimal problem solution was requested by the participants. See Eberhard Witte, *Das Informationsverhalten in Entscheidungsprozessen*, J.C.B. Mohr, Tübingen 1972.

14. Friedrich, *Staatliche Verwaltung*, pp. 161-89.

15. This articulation process is described in more detail in the study by Renate Mayntz and Fritz W. Scharpf, *Policy-Making in the German Federal Bureaucracy* (Amsterdam: Elsevier, 1975), see especially chapter V, pp. 78-86, and chapter VI.

5

Social Science and Social Policy: Schools and Race

David K. Cohen
and
Janet A. Weiss

Introduction

The last twenty years were palmy ones for research on education and race. National racial policy advanced after *Brown*, and as efforts to eliminate segregation and discrimination multiplied, research on the problems prospered. What was a trickle of studies in the few years before 1954 became something of an academic torrent; as efforts to eliminate segregation moved closer to center stage, research on the problem multiplied. In part this was the result of government efforts to promote studies of current policy, and in part it was due to the fact the researchers' priorities are influenced by what they read in the papers.

In any event, the contacts between race research and policy increased. Researchers regularly found themselves testifying in courtrooms, evaluating government programs, or consulting with educational agencies. Sometimes they even found themselves in the newspapers and more often in the various magazines that publish popular science. Through all this period, research on education and race improved in all the usual ways researchers recognize. Methodology is now more sophisticated than it was twenty years ago. Basic concepts have been overhauled and refined, and new distinctions have been hatched. Various central scientific hypotheses have been weighed; some, perhaps, have even been tested. Evidence has accumulated at a startling pace, and some of it has been analyzed. Certainly, a much broader variety of analytic skills have been devised and used. And finally efforts to connect research and policy have multiplied, motivated by government, by private foundations, and by many researchers' desires for relevance.

But while research has improved and its contacts with policy have multiplied, it has only produced new arguments and complications. As a result, research has not become more helpful for particular policy decisions. Research has proliferated, but so have arguments among researchers. Methods of study have improved, but the results are less accessible: How many of the people who could read the Social Science Brief filed in *Brown*, for example, could also read the Coleman Report's sections on integration and school effects? Research projects have multiplied, but so have competing ways of defining problems and

The research for this chapter was supported partly by grants from the Carnegie Corporation of New York to the Center for Educational Policy Research, Harvard University, and by the American Jewish Committee to the Huron Institute.

interpreting results. In our view, this situation is not the fault of bad research, nor do we think it could be remedied by better research. The prosperity of research quite naturally contributes to a sense of growing complexity and to confusions over policy advice.

That, indeed, is the theme of this chapter: For the most part, the improvement of research on social policy does not lead to greater clarity about what to think or what to do; instead, it usually tends to produce a greater sense of complexity. This result is endemic to the research process. For what researchers understand by improvement in their craft leads not to greater consensus about research problems, methods, and interpretation of results, but to more variety in the ways problems are seen, more divergence in the way studies are carried out, and more controversy in the ways results are interpreted. It leads also to a more complicated view of problems and solutions, for the progress of research tends to reveal the inadequacy of accepted ideas about solving problems.

The ensuing complexity and confusion are naturally a terrific frustration both to researchers who think they should matter and to officials who think they need help. They expect direct policy guidance from social research and assume that knowledge in the social sciences ought to be convergent. As knowledge improves, more scientific agreement about the issues in question is expected, but knowledge in the social sciences generally is not convergent. Rather than picture the research process as scouts converging on a target, it might make more sense to picture the process as outriders offering different visions of what passes them by. Multiplying the outriders tends to multiply the visions—up to a point, of course—and sharpening their sight tends to refine their differences.

Thus, if the result of scientific improvement in some aspects of physical science is convergence—at least for a time, within important conceptual limits[1] — the result of improvement in the social sciences is a richer, more diverse picture of things. Naturally enough, if one expects the first and gets the second, one is bound to be disappointed, even angry. But it may make sense to locate the trouble in the expectation of convergence rather than in the science.

Our point in this chapter is to explore this view of social policy research and to suggest the criteria of research quality that we think it implies. We will do so by showing how the research process works in the case of schools and race. We have three main points in mind. The first is that as research on social policy matures, it tends to help redefine social problems. Research is often critical and questioning, and it reveals inadequacies in accepted views of a social problem. As practical experience in problem solving turns up unexpected and puzzling results, research excellently reports, amplifies, and embellishes them.

A second point is that the improvement of research method tends to increase divergence in the treatment of evidence and to multiply mystification in the interpretation of findings. Methodological sophistication is a cardinal academic virtue, but it does not increase consensus on research issues. Rather, it clarifies differences, reveals previously unsuspected problems in data and analysis, and progressively removes research from the everyday world in which most judges, legislators, and bureaucrats walk and think.

A final point is that as research on a social problem matures, the angles of vision multiply. Social problems typically are framed initially in terms of a particular discipline, profession, or research tradition, but as research on a problem prospers, other traditions and disciplines are drawn in. Each involves a different angle on social reality or different assumptions about how social investigations should be carried out. The result is a richer and more diverse vision of the problem and its possible remedies.

Shifting Social Problems

In the beginning, the problem was lawful school segregation. The years immediately surrounding the *Brown* decision saw little ambiguity on this point, even though there was enormous controversy over the issues. According to the research centering on that decision, the legally mandated system of racially dual schools was a problem because it damaged the persons and impaired the opportunities of black Americans. The discussion of remedy was cast in similar terms—that is, eliminating the socially stigmatized black institutions and mixing blacks into the population of white schools.[2]

There was not a great deal of evidence underlying these points: The research was often thin, and the ratio of speculation to empirical findings was sometimes remarkably high. But for all this, there was not much diversity of opinion. The main division lay between those researchers who thought segregation was the problem and those who thought it was the solution. Most arguments in early desegregation research lay between the exponents of racial inferiority[3] and everyone else.

Today most researchers continue to oppose the doctrine of inherited inferiority among blacks. But they can't agree on much else. The desegregation of Southern schools brought the country closer to compliance with the Constitution, but it didn't produce the other results that earlier law and social science had suggested. In particular, desegregation didn't have the expected effects on school performance. The news on this point accumulated slowly throughout the early 1960s in a modest number of reports on desegregated districts. In some cases desegregation seemed to be associated with gains in achievement (and in some cases it didn't), but in no cases were the gains substantial.[4]

In the summer of 1966, the *Equality of Education Opportunity Survey*[5] (the so-called Coleman Report) was dropped—rather like a long-acting, repeating bomb—into this moderately confused scene. The survey reported that racial segregation had no independent impact on Negro school achievement although schools' social-class composition did seem to affect achievement. How this finding might be related to earlier research or legal ideas about racial segregation was not clear. And finally, the *EEO Survey* found no consistent relationship between school desegregation and racial attitudes. The net effect was to call into question several accepted ideas about race and schools.

The next major study didn't help. The U.S. Civil Rights Commission undertook a presidentially commissioned analysis of northern school segregation,[6] and the results were a little curious. The Commission accepted Coleman's findings about the noneffects of schools' racial composition, but found, in further analysis of the *EEOS* data, that racially integrated classrooms had a positive effect on achievement—in high school. The report also explored the relation between desegregation and racial attitudes in more detail, but it found no consistent "improvement" in racial attitudes associated with desegregation. Desegregated schools seemed as likely to produce tension and conflict as understanding and interracial harmony.

There ensued many smaller studies of particular districts as desegregation accelerated, but these accumulated the same small and inconsistent differences.[7] The questions thus multiplied. If desegregation didn't consistently or appreciably improve things for black students, what about earlier assertions that segregation damaged the hearts, minds, and future opportunities of black youth? These queries might have lain mercifully quiet in academic groves and bureaucratic files had it not been for the fact that research only reflected experience. Desegregated schools turned out to be more uncomfortable than anyone had expected, and often they were downright dangerous. This finding stimulated second thoughts all round and thus invited blacks to reflect on the comforts and advantages of separate institutions.[8]

If research helped to redefine the problem of segregation, the process was reinforced by social and political trends. Population shifts produced an increasing number of central cities with heavy black majorities in the public schools. Some social scientists interpreted this as evidence that racial balance was impossible within central-city schools. They maintained that desegregation would therefore have to occur on a metropolitan scale. They tried to support this conclusion with evidence that the academic effects of integration disappeared in majority-black settings and with research on the success of small-scale, city-suburban busing programs.[9]

But the notion was not warmly received. Black politicians in the central cities, especially those with an interest in the mayors' offices, quickly developed an allergy to metropolitan school desegregation. And some social scientists took exception to the idea that desegregation required the dilution of black student bodies in mostly white settings. By the 1970s that approach struck many as a sort of *raffine* racism.[10]

These reservations were reinforced by the movement for black community control. Somehow the conjunction of black demands for self-government with white proposals for metropolitan dispersal of black students seemed odd, if not downright embarrassing. Increasingly, social scientists held that the central problem in matters of education and race was no longer segregation; rather they argued that the racism that had engendered segregation also made desegregation as much a problem as segregation.

This brief account hardly captures all of the ways in which ideas about the problems of schools and race have changed. But the central point is that early and relatively clear definitions of the problem tended to blur under the pressure of experience. Once upon a time the problem was legally mandated dual schools, but by 1970—not to mention the later years of Boston and Detroit—that issue seemed almost quaint.

This phenomenon occurred in several ways. For one thing, segregation turned out to be more complex than had been expected. In 1954 no one really thought school desegregation suits would reach school flagpoles, teachers' rooms, and student clubs. For another, at the beginning of efforts to solve social problems, there is almost always a preferred solution—a social device that is appealing precisely because it offers a simplified view of how things can be improved. "Disestablishing the racially dual school system" was precisely such a device, but it turned out to hide a swamp of complexities.

And last but not least, the segregation problem became less clear because social reality changed in several ways. First, population shifts in central cities gradually frustrated efforts to desegregate schools. As a result, what had been a complex problem involving single jurisdictions became a supercomplicated problem crossing jurisdictional lines within metropolitan areas. Second, events beginning with *Brown* tended to legitimize black grievances, to encourage their expression, and to focus attention on them. As a result of school desegregation, blacks developed a much more refined sense of racial injustice in schools, a much decreased willingness to stand the pain, and a sharply reduced appetite for white people's solutions. All of this worked a change in social reality: What would have been an entirely acceptable integrated high school in 1954 would have seemed an outrageous insult in 1974.

So, trying to solve this social problem changed the way the problem was seen; it complicated and diversified views of the problem; it made once-appealing solutions seem limited; and it suggested alternative solutions. The result was not just that the problem came to seem more complex, but also that in some ways it came to seem different. The current view that desegregation is a major social problem is at cross-purposes with many ideas surrounding the *Brown* decision.

Research played several roles in all this complexity. For one thing, research on social policy is part of the intelligence apparatus by which society learns what seems to be happening. Research and evaluation taught Americans about the ambiguous impact of integration on achievement, about its contradictory effect on attitudes, and about the problems of the desegregation process. What is reported to society profoundly influences what society learns.

Second, social problem research played a critical role by picking apart earlier ideas and assumptions. The *EEO Survey*, for example, used powerful statistical techniques to blow apart many established ideas about schools and race. The intent was not critical, but the effect was to raise basic questions about the effects of desegregation. And third, research and social commentary by researchers often turns out to be a way of expressing new social tendencies and intellectual currents. Much of the "research" associated with the movement for community control partook of this quality and thus legitimized new ideas by introducing them in scientific garb.

Thus, research sometimes reports a complicating reality, and sometimes it complicates our picture of reality through criticism and the introduction of new ideas. In both ways, it helps to make our understanding of social problems more complex, and because formal inquiry is somewhat less absent-minded than the daily media, it provides a historical record of these changes for researchers and their consumers. This only heightens the sense of complexity and change. Research usually is not the primary moving force in all this, but because of the growing importance of formal studies in social reportage, it is rarely unimportant. In one way or another, it is a significant force in redefining and complicating our views of social problems.

Research Methods and Frameworks

One might think from the account so far that social problems, not research, are to blame: The problems sneak up on the unwary investigator slowly, seductively let down their veils, and reveal their alluring complexity. The hopeful analyst is captivated but befuddled. That research contributes its share to befuddlement, though, is evident in considering the improved methodology.

Two improvements were central. For one thing, computer technology and the avalanche of money for large-scale studies made it possible for researchers to collect evidence on many factors in any social situation. Methodologists and data analysts adapted and developed statistical techniques that permit analysis of many such factors at one time, and so social scientists can now attack social phenomena with much more finesse than was possible three decades ago. These advances encouraged the collection of much more diverse and representative data. Investigators not only can report findings that are statistically more credible for national policy, but they can consider all sorts of interesting subgroups. All of this has helped research to become more self-conscious. There is heightened awareness of problems of analysis, methodology, and design. They are now a central interest in the social sciences and a focus in most debates over policy research.

A second improvement was the diversification of desegregation research since the early 1950s. At the outset most investigations were psychological, but gradually economists, sociologists, and anthropologists were drawn in—as were researchers from education and law. The relative importance of psychology has diminished, and research has flowered under the influence of several different disciplinary and professional orientations.

These advances are good for research, but one reward for the better studies has been a clearer idea of just how muddy the waters really are. Research on the effects of segregation and desegregation reveals this nicely. Early work on racial awareness and self-esteem[11]—the research summarized in the Social Science Brief—supported the idea that segregation caused psychological damage to black children. This broadly psychological emphasis was given specific focus by research that maintained that desegregation would never improve the achievement of black students because of their inherited intellectual inferiority.[12] In the political atmosphere of massive resistance, some social scientists felt that answering these racist studies was essential. They tried to show that desegregation did raise black students' achievement and IQ test scores.[13] This tendency was given added force by the post-Sputnik pressure for better achievement and by the growing fashion of programs to improve the academic performance of "culturally deprived" students.

The result was to ensconce achievement test scores as the variable of chief interest in research on race and schools. At the outset, these studies were few in number and straightforward in design: The relation between schools' racial composition and test scores would be presented in simple one- or two-way tables. In some cases it seemed as though black students were better off in desegregated schools, while in some cases it didn't. But the results were easy to read, and they dealt in a currency everyone thought they understood.

The *EEO Survey*, published in July of 1966, changed all that, for it brought a formidable array of methodological refinements to bear on the question. The *EEO Survey* was based on a nationally representative sample of schools and was designed to permit complex multiple regression analysis of the relative impact of racial composition, school resources, student background, and school social-class composition on achievement and attitudes. In these analyses, schools' racial composition was found to have no significant independent association with student achievement. In addition, there seemed to be little relation between school resources and school achievement. The two issues tended to merge after the report's publication, and Coleman's report was attacked almost as soon as it hit the streets. Henry Levin and Sam Bowles took Coleman to task for a series of high methodological crimes.[14] The *EEO Survey*, they argued, had used the wrong regression statistics; it was flawed by problems of nonresponse; it used analytic techniques that understated the impact of school resources; it was therefore useless for policy guidance.

The episode certainly undermined the report's credibility, but it also nicely illustrates disciplinary differences in the use of analytic techniques. Coleman is a sociologist, and he used the regression statistic dearest to that discipline (the standardized beta coefficient, which reflects the relative importance of several forces in a complex system of relationships). Bowles and Levin are economists, and they held out for the regression statistic most familiar to economists, which reflects the unique impact of one variable in an input-output system (the unstandardized beta coefficient). Adding disciplines to the scientific fray sharpened issues and created new arguments.[15]

In the aftermath, the Civil Rights Commission produced its reanalysis of the *EEO Survey* data. These results further complicated things because of the *EEO Survey*'s nationally representative character. The findings about classroom integration in *Racial Isolation* were based on data from high schools in the northeastern urban United States. There did seem to be an effect of integration in this region, but the Commission also published an appendix volume wherein lay parallel analyses of classroom integration from other regions. Sometimes these results showed no positive impact of integrated classrooms, and sometimes they showed a negative impact. Often they were inconclusive. Having nationally representative data did not produce more definitive conclusions.

Later in the decade, reanalyses of the *EEO Survey* data became a growth industry supported by government grants, public-spirited foundations, and scholarly animosity. One group at Harvard, under the scientific leadership of Daniel P. Moynihan, produced a raft of refinements and further qualifications.[16] David Armor, for example, found that school integration helped black students, but only if they were in more than token-integrated, but less than majority, black schools. Whites, it seemed, were good for blacks if taken in medium doses, rather than in very small or very large ones. Economic contributors in Moynihan's volume continued to moan over the *EEO Survey* and attack its results, while Jencks and other sociologists upheld the statistical virtue of Coleman's original findings with new and better analytic techniques. Another reanalysis group at the U.S. Office of Education attacked Coleman's and Jencks' findings on school effects while simultaneously repelling the advances of Levin, Bowles, Kain, and Hanushek on the *EEO Survey*'s methodology.[17] As one would expect from an agency that spends most of its time giving away money to public schools, the Office of Education group found that school resources did make a difference.

The reanalyses continued for years and produced more questions, more qualifications, and more occasions to exercise new analytic muscles. Some researchers thought Coleman had overstated the impact of social-class integration.[18] Others, reanalyzing the Civil Rights Commission's work, found that the effects of classroom integration seemed to hold at the ninth grade but not at the twelfth grade.[19] Jencks and company, in *Inequality*, thought there might be a small effect of school racial mixing in elementary schools, but they emphasized the modesty of the effect and the uncertainty of the evidence.[20] Shortly thereafter, the Civil Rights Commission reentered the picture—this time by denouncing the inadequacy of previous research on the subject and proclaiming its unreliability for policy guidance. The Commission commissioned a more comprehensive, complex, longitudinal study to resolve the issues.[21] The reanalyses, then, produced a swarm of contrary ideas, a host of refined analytic techniques, and a growing despair over the prospects for clear conclusions on the issues.

The controversies continue. They have moved on from what now seem old-hat, simple multiple regression techniques to more complex analytic methods such as path analysis and multistage regression. They also have moved to new and more complex analytic issues—the effects of schooling on adult success, rather than just achievement—and they have moved on to new bodies of data, the *EEOS* having been rubbed raw in various scientific embraces. The effect of schools' racial composition occasionally appears in these supersophisticated combats in mathematical sociology and econometrics, but the issue seems to have been dwarfed by larger questions about whether schooling itself makes a difference and obscured by the proliferation of complex analytic techniques. The only conclusion on which most researchers now seem to agree is that the data collected in the 1960s are inadequate and more studies are needed. Science marches on.

Our story of the improvement in desegregation research doesn't end here. As research on test scores accumulated, so did questions about that approach to assessing school integration. One reason was that some researchers became uneasy about reporting the persistent black-white gap in achievement scores—a gap that seemed unresponsive to any intervention. Another reason was that by the middle and late 1960s, sociology and economics had entered research on education and race in force, and they contemplated other outcomes of desegregation. Finally, the more test scores were used, the more psychologists questioned their meaning.

Some researchers questioned the technical basis of the tests; and others questioned their cultural foundations. On both counts, the tests' credibility suffered. The more research that was done, the less clear it seemed that test scores were a sensible way to assess the impact of integration. This discovery encouraged studies on other outcomes of desegregation. Researchers recalled that desegregation was supposed to have something to do with hearts as well as minds—with interracial attitudes and behavior as well as test scores. They cautioned that excessive reliance on tests would produce a distorted picture. The sophistication of studies on the social-psychological impact of desegregation increased appreciably as a result, but these improvements did nothing to offer clear policy advice.

Early research on racial attitudes had seemed to show that racial attitudes would benefit from interracial contact in equal status situations.[22] These studies viewed racial attitudes as a self-evidently important outcome of biracial settings, partly because social psychologists assumed that there were those links between attitudes and behavior. But in a period when bigoted attitudes were openly expressed, liberal social scientists understandably regarded the reduction of such expression as a good in itself.

As research on desegregation's effect on interracial attitudes flowered in the middle and late 1960s, dissatisfaction with the older attitude measures increased. They were few in number; they needed technical improvement; and as desegregation spread, the available sorts of interracial situations grew and demanded new measures appropriate to the circumstances. By the late 1960s, the result was a rich growth: forced-choice questionnaire items, social-distance scales, measures of racial stereotyping, doll-choice measures, sociometric preferences, simple Likert scales, and semantic differentials.[23]

The improvement here is plain: Attitudes are not simple, and it makes perfect sense to pursue them in a variety of ways. But one problem was the lack of comparability. Studies seldom repeated measures, let alone replicated study conditions. The issues were a little different, the populations were varied, and the measures were different. The variation did not seem to be a serious problem until researchers began to notice the tendency of attitude measures to be weakly related. Even within studies, there were almost always low correlations between scales measuring interracial attitudes.[24] If different ways of measuring the same conceptual variable did not lead to the same conclusions, then the proliferation of measures raised questions of generalizability. Most studies stood as socially scientific islands; each was more or less gleaming, but most were somewhat incomparable to the others.

A second problem arose partly from evidence about the weak relationships among measures. This problem increased uncertainty about the validity of any single measure and made using more measures seem even more sensible. But the focus of most work of this sort was demonstrating and explaining the effects of interracial schools on racial attitudes, and the weak connections among measures meant that explaining the causal connection for one measure of racial attitudes need not necessarily hold for another. Interracial schools that seemed to produce a good racial climate based on a self-administered questionnaire seemed to produce a bigoted climate based on observers' reports.[25] These findings confused interpretations of both reality and the research. Researchers learned that the way they measured attitudes seemed to influence the sort of attitudes they "found." Such self-consciousness is a good thing, but it doesn't produce much clarity about the policy implications of research findings, nor does it build confidence in the solidarity of research results.

A third problem was the relation between attitudes and behavior. Social psychologists who had focused research on attitudes had, of course, assumed that a change in attitudes would lead to a change in behavior. But by the mid 1960s, social psychology had changed its tune. One reviewer concluded:

Most socially significant questions involve overt behavior rather than peoples' feelings, and the assumption that feelings are directly translated into action has not been demonstrated.[26]

In the case of integration, research showed that the attitude-behavior link was fragile. In one study of biracial groups, white students from integrated schools were more likely to dominate blacks than whites from all white schools.[27] In another study, white college students who expressed more prejudice actually took more suggestions from blacks in group tasks than did white students who expressed less prejudice.[28] It is easy to conjure up after-the-fact explanations for such findings, but that is a little off the point. The advance of research on racial attitudes has revealed no strong or consistent connection between attitudes and behavior. This result is an interesting and important research development, but it rather weakened the ground under an entire line of policy-relevant studies based exclusively on attitude research.

Partly as a consequence of these findings, measures or reports of behavior came to be included routinely in research on desegregated schools. This research created a whole new set of outcomes to explain and greatly complicated the job of understanding the effect of school factors on student outcomes. And substituting behavioral for attitudinal variables—as many researchers did—made later studies increasingly incompatible with earlier ones.

In an effort to sort out the hodge-podge of findings, social scientists turned their attention to the social circumstances that might mediate the effects of interracial situations on attitudes and behavior. They turned up a formidable list. In some studies they weighed the impact of teachers' and principals' racial attitudes. In others, they probed whether students' social and economic class backgrounds affected student reaction to desegregation. Other studies explored other influences: segregation of classrooms, length of students' experience in interracial schools, the extent of minority students' participation in extracurricular activities, the age or grade level of students, community attitudes, and the degree of internal tracking and grouping.[29]

For each one of these influences, at least one study claimed that the factor in question did mediate the relationship between interracial settings and racial attitudes or behavior. But factors that seemed important in some studies seemed unimportant in others. Ordinarily, it was not possible to know just why this was so. As a result, the findings seemed unstable, and little was learned about the relative salience of the situational influences on racial climate. One study did try to quantify and compare the relative importance of many of these factors, but Crain and his colleagues found that most situational influences had no impact on the racial attitudes measured.[30] Some had very weak effects, and in some cases the effects varied between different measures. Complicated multivariate analyses of situational factors that mediate the impact of racial composition of schools on student attitudes and behavior did little to clear up the contradictions of earlier studies or to offer much guidance for policy.

Thus, social-psychological research was a useful balance to the heavy reliance on test scores, but it didn't exactly clarify matters. By adding another disciplinary perspective on desegregation, it complicated the picture. This phenomenon became widespread in the late 1960s and early 1970s, as sociologists and economists entered the field, but it was most striking in the work of some anthropologically oriented social scientists. They rejected all forms of quantitative and survey research and undertook direct observational studies of desegregated schools. These ethnographies offered a different disciplinary approach to the study of schools and race, and they presented rather a different picture of desegregation. They found social segregation within schools, insensitivity and racial stereotyping on the part of teachers, defensiveness and denial by teachers and administrators, and a mixed and often unhappy experience for black children. The most recent effort reported on a desegregation program carried out in a way that most communities would probably regard as either quite acceptable or ideal.[31] But the integration experience seemed a demeaning and unhappy one for most of the black children involved, though none of the school staff appear to have known about their feelings. This finding was rather a different portrait than emerged from the various quantitative evaluations of desegregation, and it resulted in rather more astringent conclusions. The author, an integrationist, held that desegregation simply ought not to occur under such conditions.

In summary, then, the improvement of research has had paradoxical results. On one hand, we have a less simple-minded and more plausible account of social reality. Artifacts are reduced, distortions due to faulty method are often eliminated, overblown interpretations are corrected, and more careful analyses are presented. The technical sophistication of recent research on desegregation is such as to inspire more confidence than twenty years ago that the results of any given study are valid. But these changes have led to more studies that disagree, to more qualified conclusions, more arguments, and more arcane reports and unintelligible results. If any given study is more valid, the inferences to policy from the lot seem much more uncertain.

One reason for this uncertainty, as we have pointed out, is that methodological refinement in social research often is not convergent but rather tends to sharpen differences. The research has grown, and grown more sophisticated, but the findings have not been cumulative. A good part of the reason is that no strong theory suggested what influences should be observed or what outcome variables are most important. Given this situation, social science tends to proliferate under the influence of empirical ideas, weak theories, intuitions from practical experience, suggestions from other fields, or the analytic possibilities suggested by new methodologies. The fruit of such scientific developments is sometimes rich and always varied, but not necessarily very coherent. Another reason is that the progress of research on a social problem tends to draw in diverse research traditions, and the consequence is more differences in approach and interpretation. Still another reason is that research on social problems tends to move backward, from relatively simple ideas about problems and their solutions to ever more basic questions about both. The net result is a more varied picture of reality, but such results don't lend themselves to straightforward policy guidance.

Conclusion

One thing is clear from this story. The more research on a social problem prospers, the harder it is for policymakers and courts to get the sort of guidance they often say they want: clear recommendations about what to do, or at least clear alternatives. Predictably, the result is frustration. In both the race and school finance cases, for example, one can see the judges becoming more exasperated with the complexities and contradictions of research.[32]

But while we expect continued frustration in this connection, we don't think that social science is irrelevant to social policy, nor do we think it should be. At its best, social research provides a reasonable sense of the various ways a problem can be understood and a reasonable account of how solutions might be approached. Such general advice about controversial and problematic issues is a useful contribution to social knowledge, even if it is not crisply relevant to particular decisions.

But this view doesn't explain exactly how we should think about research and its relation to policy. One alternative is to think of policy formation as a process of competition for values and social goods and to think of research as ammunition for the various parties at interest. The growing diversity of approaches and findings may frustrate any given user of research, but the net satisfaction of all users will increase as more of them find studies that suit their special purposes. It goes almost without saying that this view will seem satisfying in proportion to the fairness of the competition.

But if this view is plausible, it isn't complete. Our account also suggests that the improvement of research has not simply been a matter of sharper argumentation. In addition, we know more. Research has helped provide a better picture of the desegregation process; it has taught us something about how desegregation does and doesn't work, and why; and it has helped broaden our picture of whom desegregation affects. Typically, however, these improvements do not offer a handy solution. Indeed, among the things we can learn from the accumulated studies of the last few decades are cautions about easy solutions, simple formulations, and social science findings. On this view, then, research on a social problem might be portrayed as a contribution to social wisdom. As more is learned through experience and investigation, simpler and appealing ideas give way to more qualified advice.

Finally, the studies cited in this chapter suggest that research is part and parcel of social enthusiasms. When whipping up the brains of America's youth was in fashion in the late 1950s and early 1960s, research on race and schools stepped to the tune of test scores. When desegregation was "out" and community control was "in," fate-control studies were all the rage. And when school desegregation came North early in the seventies, many liberal and moderate northern politicians who had supported this reform in the South suddenly developed cramps. Research on race and schools has suffered a similar affliction, which is evident in the recent work of Armor and Coleman, among others.[33]

On this view, research and policy might be pictured as the subjects of sea changes in social thought. Research contributes something to these changing climates of opinion, but it also responds to them. Research and policy affect each other, but both seem to bob along on larger waves.

These three pictures of the relation between research and policy imply rather different criteria for evaluating the contribution of research. If we think of social science as political ammunition, we would evaluate the quality of desegregation research at least partly in terms of fairness in its distribution. If, alternatively, we think of research as an incremental growth in social wisdom, then we would evaluate it in terms of its contribution to such general guidance. And if we imagine policy and research to be both swept away on waves of social enthusiasms, we might retreat, puzzled at the difficulty of devising any evaluative criterion.

Regardless of which picture is most appealing, our account suggests that on the evaluative criterion advanced by most advocates of policy research—does the research contribute more precise guidance for particular decisions?—most research would fail miserably. We think the problem here lies not so much with the quality of research as with a misconception of the research process. To expect more precise guidance for particular decisions is in most cases a dream hopelessly at variance with the divergent and pluralistic character of social policy research. Rather than helping, the dream generally seems to distract research workers from a clear view of their work and its role.

Instead, we think it is useful to picture the research process as a dialogue about social reality—that is, as a historical conversation about social problems and how they might be solved. A dialogue is good to the extent that the various relevant views are present and to the extent that points of difference are clarified. A dialogue is good to the extent that the whole represents a satisfying, if necessarily diverse, account of the ways in which an issue can be framed, explored, and resolved. We have tried to show how, as research prospers, the conversation is enriched.

This is not to suggest that the progress of research on race and schools has been entirely satisfying, for some parties have been better represented at the social science smorgasbord than others, nor is it to suggest that truth will complaisantly out, for dialogues are subject to fashion changes. While they can produce what we think of as wisdom, it is often only a passing fancy that later loses its appeal. But our chief point is simply that it is helpful to see social research this way. To those who ply the trade, it offers a more sensible view of their work. Among those who would like guidance, it presents a basis for more reasonable expectations. It also helps explain why improved knowledge doesn't always lead to more effective action.

Notes

1. For a discussion of these points, see Thomas Kuhn, *The Structure of Scientific Revolutions* (Chicago: University of Chicago Press, 1962).

2. Social Science Brief (Appendix to Appellant's Briefs: The Effects of Segregation and the Consequences of Desegregation: A Social Science Statement), reprinted in Kenneth B. Clark, *Prejudice and Your Child* (Boston: Beacon Press, 1963, 2nd ed.), pp. 166-84.

3. Henry E. Garrett, "A Note of the Intelligence Scores of Negroes and Whites in 1918," *Journal of Abnormal and Social Psychology* 40 (1945); Henry E. Garrett, "The Equalitarian Dogma," *Mankind Quarterly* 1 (1961); Audrey Shuey, *The Testing of Negro Intelligence* (Lynchburg, Va.: Bell, 1958).

4. See the extensive reviews in Nancy M. St. John, *School Desegregation* (New York: Wiley, 1975), and in Meyer Weinberg, "The Relationship between School Desegregation and Academic Achievement: A Review of the Research," *Law and Contemporary Problems* 39, no. 2 (Spring 1975), pp. 240-70.

5. James S. Coleman et al., *Equality of Educational Opportunity* (Washington, D.C.: U.S. Government Printing Office, 1966).

6. U.S. Commission on Civil Rights, *Racial Isolation in the Public Schools* (Washington, D.C.: U.S. Government Printing Office, 1967), vols. 1 and 2.

7. St. John, *School Desegregation*, p. 80.

8. See, for example, Charles V. Hamilton, "Race and Education: A Search for Legitimacy," *Harvard Educational Review* 38, no. 4 (Fall 1968).

9. The USCCR report, *Racial Isolation*, was the first in this line of thought.

10. Derrick A. Bell, Jr., "Waiting on the Promise of Brown," *Law and Contemporary Problems*, no. 1 (Winter 1975), pp. 341-73.

11. Kenneth and Mamie Clark, "Racial Identification and Preference in Negro Children," in T. Newcomb and E. Hartley (eds.), *Readings in Social Psychology* (New York: Holt, 1974, 1st ed.).

12. Garrett, "The Equalitarian Dogma," and Shuey, *The Testing*.

13. For example, Thomas Pettigrew writes about the desegregation of the Washington, D.C., schools: "Though Negro students, swelled by migrants now comprised three-fourths of the student body, achievement test scores had risen significantly for each grade level sampled and each subject area tested approached or equalled national norms. Furthermore, both Negro and White students shared in these increments." See T.F. Pettigrew, *A Profile of the Negro American* (Princeton, N.J.: Van Nostrand, 1964), p. 128.

14. Samuel Bowles and Henry M. Levin, "The Determinants of Scholastic Achievements—An Appraisal of Some Recent Evidence," *Journal of Human Resources* 3 (Winter 1968), pp. 3-24.

15. For fuller treatments of this phenomenon, see David K. Cohen and Michael S. Garet, "Reforming Educational Policy with Applied Social Research," *Harvard Educational Review* 45, no. 1 (February 1975).

16. Christopher Jencks et al., *Inequality* (New York: Harper & Row, 1972); Marshall S. Smith, "Equality of Educational Opportunity: The Basic Finds Reconsidered," in Frederick Mosteller and Daniel P. Moynihan (eds.), *On*

Equality of Educational Opportunity (New York: Random House, 1972); D.J. Armor, "The Evidence on Busing," *The Public Interest* (Summer 1972); Pettigrew, *A Profile*; and Coleman et al., *Equality*.

17. George Mayeske et al., *A Study of Our Nation's Schools* (Washington, D.C.: DHEW, 1972).

18. Smith, "Equality of Educational Opportunity."

19. D.K. Cohen, T.F. Pettigrew, and R.T. Riley, "Race and the Outcomes of Schooling," in Mosteller and Moynihan (eds.), *On Equality of Educational Opportunity*.

20. See, for example, the citations in St. John, *School Desegregation*.

21. *Design for a National Longitudinal Study of School Desegregation* (Santa Monica, Calif.: Rand Corp., 1974).

22. Gordon W. Allport, *The Nature of Prejudice* (Garden City, N.Y.: Doubleday Anchor Books, 1954), and Samual A. Stouffer et al., *The American Soldier* (Princeton, N.J.: Princeton University Press, 1949).

23. See St. John, *School Desegregation*, chapter 4.

24. James M. Jones, *Prejudice and Racism* (Reading, Mass.: Addison-Wesley, 1972); also St. John, *School Desegregation*.

25. See, for example, R. Hope (1967) cited in St. John, *School Desegregation*, and Judith Porter, *Black Child, White Child* (Cambridge, Mass.: Harvard University Press, 1971).

26. Allan Wicker, "Attitudes versus Actions: The Relationship of Verbal and Overt Behavioral Responses to Attitude Objects," *Journal of Social Issues* 25 (1969), p. 75.

27. J. Seidner (1971) described in Elizabeth G. Cohen, "The Effects of Desegregation on Race Relations," *Law and Contemporary Problems* 39 (Spring 1975), pp. 271-99.

28. I. Katz and L. Benjamin, "Effects of White Authoritarianism in Biracial Work Groups," *Journal of Abnormal and Social Psychology* 61 (1960), pp. 448-56.

29. Examples of this kind of research include Appendix C1, USCCR, *Racial Isolation*; J.E. Teele and C. Mayo, "School Racial Integration: Tumult and Shame," *Journal of Social Issues* 25 (1969), pp. 137-56; E. Useem, "White Students and Token Desegregation," *Integrated Education* (1972), pp. 44-56; and C. Willie and J. Baker, *Race Mixing in the Public Schools*, 1973.

30. Armor, "The Evidence on Busing," pp. 90-126; T.F. Pettigrew, E.L. Useem, C. Normand, and M.S. Smith, "Busing: A Review of the Evidence," *The Public Interest* (Winter 1973), pp. 88-118; D.J. Armor, "The Double Double Standard: A Reply," *The Public Interest* (Winter 1973), pp. 119-31.

31. Raymond Rist, *The Invisible Children: School Integration in American Society* (Cambridge, Mass.: Harvard University Press, forthcoming 1976).

32. See *Hart* v. *Community School Board*, 383 F. Supp. 699, 744 (E.D.N.Y. 1974), and *Hobson* v. *Hansen*, 327 F. Supp. 844, 859 (D.D.C. 1971).

33. Armor, "The Evidence on Busing," and J.S. Coleman et al., *Trends In School Segregation* (Washington, D.C.: The Urban Institute, 1975).

6

Research and Foreign Policy: A View from Foggy Bottom

Pio D. Uliassi

As everyone who follows such matters knows, opinions vary on the significance of the social sciences for foreign policy making. True believers are most commonly found on the private side of the government-academic divide, and skeptics in the ranks of Washington's bureaucracies—especially, it is often alleged, in Foggy Bottom. But there are exceptions. A team of behavioral scientists, for example, recently concluded (with evident reluctance) that "no substantive knowledge from the behavioral sciences appears of immediate and unambiguous relevance to ACDA problems."[1] On the other hand, many people in the State Department at times display an unsuspected interest in research, without (it almost goes without saying) betraying an unseemly enthusiasm for it.

In discussing the State Department's use of research, it is convenient to begin with a reminder that foreign affairs officials are flooded with information, some of which has plausible claims to the standing of social science, from three main sources. First, there are reports and studies done within the bureaucracy itself by foreign service officers abroad, or by the hundreds of intelligence analysts scattered about Washington, or by people designated as policy planners. Second, there is commissioned research done under contract to one of the many executive agencies that play a role in foreign affairs. Finally, there is a vast amount of uncommissioned research, most of it done on American campuses, that reaches Washington in one form or another (often diluted from its pure scientific state): Bureaucrats, after all, occasionally converse with academics, attend conferences, read newspapers, periodicals, and books, and a few intrepid ones even scan the pages of professional journals.

One can draw a number of implications from looking at the information universe of policymakers in this way. One is that agency budgets for commissioned research alone probably cannot be taken, as they sometimes are, as valid indicators of relative interest in the social sciences, much less of their actual use for policy purposes. A far more important implication is that research flowing from each of these conspicuously different sources probably is distinctive in some respects, even when making allowances for considerable substantive overlapping. But this generalization is only a rough one, and the devil, as usual, lies in the details: How specifically does intramural research differ from commissioned studies? How do both differ from the larger body of social science produced by people with no links to, often with no particular interest in, and

The views expressed in this chapter are those of the author and do not necessarily reflect the official positions and attitudes of the Department of State.

sometimes with scorn for, federal policy agencies? And how does research of such different kinds fare in competition for the attention of people in positions of influence and authority?

Any serious assessment of the role of research in foreign policy would have to address these as well as other problems—something impossible to do in a short chapter. Here I will limit myself to some observations on the State Department's experience with "external" research—that is, studies carried out by people who are not regular employees of the government—and more narrowly to external research commissioned directly by the State Department. I should add that the Department's view of social research is latitudinarian and encompasses not only the behavioral sciences but (to the dismay of some critics) the more traditional social studies and the humanities as well—indeed any disciplined effort to understand any aspect of international and foreign affairs.

External Research

In recent years, the State Department's annual budget for external research has approached $1,000,000, which is a modest sum when compared to the budgets of some other agencies but hardly inconsequential.[2] To take a typical recent instance, in fiscal 1974 the Office of External Research (which manages the Department's program) sponsored forty-three studies, ranging from modest essays to more ambitious empirical investigations; it organized thirty-one seminars and conferences involving some one hundred fifty scholars; and it arranged for the services of thirty-five consultants. Before turning to the question of whether and how research may affect policy, it is worth looking at these activities a bit more closely.

The program covers an unusually broad range of subjects or problems, even though the projects actually carried out are only a fraction of the suggestions made by various departmental units. Among the topics found in last year's dozen or so more costly projects, for instance, were law enforcement in the oceans; international cooperation in research and development; the "absorptive capacity" of oil-producing countries; political terrorism; private U.S. foreign affairs organizations; international disaster relief; aspects of United States-Soviet relations; and the West European left. The more modest, and far more numerous projects, including most seminars and conferences, were equally diverse. This range has both advantages and disadvantages. There is a good deal to be said for the educational functions of such a program. However, it obviously makes no provision for "basic" research or for sustained investigation of a few especially critical problems. (This year the State Department is directing most of its funds to studies in four areas—China, the Soviet Union, Latin America, and Interdependence—but these are still quite broad rubrics.) The fact is that no one knows how "best" to allocate resources in a severely constrained budget: whether to invest them intensively or to disperse them more widely, and thinly, to cover the innumerable concerns of the Department as the least specialized of the foreign affairs agencies.

One other feature of State's external research is worth noting because it illustrates again the educational emphasis that has developed over the years. The program is designed to involve a large number of departmental officers with social scientists outside the bureaucracy. Consultants as a rule work closely with the Department's own analysts. Seminars and conferences draw people from all parts of the Department. Most of the larger research projects are formulated, monitored, reviewed, and discussed at various stages by working groups consisting of analysts, operational officers, and policy planners. Such close participation is costly and sometimes cumbersome, but it is supposed to serve several purposes: to make external research more relevant to the perceived needs of the Department; to discourage the parochialism that might result from having any project too exclusively inspired and monitored by a single client; and to encourage the kind of intellectual exchange that many people believe is more telling, in its effects, than the mere distribution of formal reports that often are quickly consigned to the files and as quickly forgotten.

These at least are the hopes. What in fact can be said about the actual uses of external research in the State Department? Of course we know what people read and hear through the program, but it should come as no surprise to learn that it is virtually impossible to trace a direct connection between whatever is transmitted through these activities and the substance of policy. It would be rash to conclude, from this observation, that the kinds of projects sponsored by the Department are, despite all, still irrelevant to its real concerns; or that State Department officers are, as some ungenerous critics believe, uncommonly recalcitrant about accepting the knowledge and wisdom of their social scientific betters. The actual situation is far different and more promising.

Uses of Research

In a conventional model of applied research, "findings" may have policy or operational "implications" that have to be "communicated" to practitioners, who in turn have to "accept" and "implement" them. But this is a mechanical scheme that bears little resemblance to what can actually go on in complex situations. Discussions of the social sciences and foreign policy indeed frequently suffer from the failure to recognize how intrinsically difficult it is to document the effects of research even when it does have some impact on decisions. There are, I think, at least three reasons for this difficulty.

One is the fact that commissioned research constitutes only a small part of the total fund of knowledge that is available to policymakers and is not always easily distinguishable from material stemming from other sources. (Of course, the same thing should be said about intramural and uncommissioned research.) In addition, "scientific" knowledge, from whatever source, supplements and complements (and sometimes contradicts) common sense knowledge or the insights and wisdom presumably acquired through practical experience by people who consider themselves professionals in foreign affairs. Under such circumstances, even those who are intimately familiar with the inner life of an institution are hard put to identify the origins of the information, perceptions, judgments, and opinions that affect policy, except occasionally in a general way.[3]

A more fundamental reason for the elusive connection between research and policy is that research seldom provides unambiguous answers to the kinds of questions that most concern policymakers. Social scientists can, and usually do, argue about what conditions or events bearing upon policy may mean, what courses of action might be taken to achieve given ends and with what consequences, and what the relationship of objectives may be to broader interests and values. As one moves through the many stages from description to prescription in policy research, uncertainty and contention among experts usually increase. Awareness of agreements and disagreements related to policy matters is of course invaluable to policymakers, or should be. The patent failure of the social sciences to achieve scientifically validated certainty, nevertheless, gives policymakers considerable latitude in choosing among alternative views of almost any element in their policy deliberations and choices.

This observation leads to a related matter. Foreign policy, as it is fashionable to say these days, cannot be understood fully as the behavior of a hypothetical "rational actor"; organizational routines and bureaucratic and other forms of politics have a lot to do with what happens. Knowledge of course enters into the process, unless behavior is to be completely out of touch with reality, but knowledge is politically mediated. Thus, research, even if it is not consciously or unconsciously ignored or distorted, legitimately can be interpreted and used in different ways by competing individuals, groups or organizations in pursuit of the interests they believe should be served by policy.

These observations should in no sense support the notion that social research has no bearing on policy. They only suggest, it seems to me, that it is unrealistic to adopt what amounts to an "engineering" model of the uses of research in foreign policy, except rarely in some technical fields. "Enlightenment," however, vague and old-fashioned it may sound, probably evokes a more accurate image of the actual contributions of research.

Method and Substance

Enlightenment, however, may take different forms. In reviewing the experiences of the State Department, I find two tendencies among advocates of applied research. Some emphasize the methodological and others the substantive contributions of social science to foreign policy.

An illustration of the first tendency comes from a panel of experts, assembled by the State Department to assess the role of research in foreign affairs, who concluded that the social scientist's "most useful contribution can be in the area of method and process even [sic] more than in his contribution of 'new knowledge'."[4] A small number of the State Department's more experimental projects in recent years have been partly inspired by such a conception of social science as technique. These include conferences and studies dealing with data banks, the applications of quantitative methods to intramural research, "net assessment" procedures for policy analysis, and problems of resource allocation. It is hardly surprising that those who have been closely connected with such projects as researchers or clients sometimes differ profoundly in their conception of the social stances; but most of them evidently share a belief that policy can be significantly improved by "modernizing" and "rationalizing" the operations of what they perceive to be a somewhat archaic and untidy establishment.

Most State Department officers, however, look to the social sciences (on the increasing number of occasions when they look to them at all) for direct help on substantive matters. Almost all the studies and conferences sponsored by the Office of External Research deal with policy-related conditions, trends, problems, and issues; most conclude with some general implications for policy at least; and some explicitly examine options that presumably fall within the bounds of courses of actions that "realistically" are available in a particular decisional setting. Few people in the Department would claim unequivocally that such research is "applied" in readily perceivable ways; but most of them would agree, I believe, that commissioned studies—and especially the face-to-face encounters associated with research—somehow help them to be better informed, more open to alternative ways of looking at the world, and more judicious than they would be if they remained more tightly enclosed within the intellectual confines of their own bureaucratic environment.

Notes

1. The Ohio State University Research Foundation, *Utilization of the Behavioral Sciences by the U.S. Arms Control and Disarmament Agency*, Final Report ACDA/E-221, (prepared for the U.S. Arms Control and Disarmament Agency), January 1975, vol. I, Summary, page 2.

2. Annual surveys of government spending on foreign affairs research may be found in *FAR Horizons*, a quarterly newsletter published by the Office of External Research of the Department of State. In fiscal year 1974, for example, total government "obligations" were $29,071,000. The budget of the Department's Office of External Research does not include the grant and contract

expenditures of the State Department's Bureau of Educational and Cultural Affairs. The latter for the most part serve purposes quite different from policy-related analysis for internal departmental use.

3. For an example covering China policy, see the lengthy review article by Tan Tsou, "Statesmanship and Scholarship," *World Politics* XXVI, no. 3 (April 1974), pp. 420-51.

4. Report of Panel A, *A Report Prepared for the Conference on Social Research and Foreign Affairs*, Airlie House, Warrenton, Va., October 16-18, 1970 (Xeroxed).

7

Management by Evaluation

Eleanor Farrar McGowan

Federal efforts to direct social change have not been marked by outstanding success. Since the early 1960s, the government has launched a variety of programs designed to reform society by reforming education or health or urban affairs. But some fifteen years later, it is hard to find programs that have lived up to early hopes.

Various theories have been advanced about why things go wrong: unmanageable program size, unclear goals and objectives, fuzzy legislation, little central guidance.[1] One persistent idea, in addition, has been the belief that increased rationality in planning or evaluation will set things right. This chapter discusses one effort to rationalize the management of planned social change through rigorous evaluation. The story suggests that rigor didn't help very much. In my view, the chief reason is that the unclarity of social innovations cannot be usefully dealt with by the typical approaches to program evaluation. Such rational approaches, in fact, tend to confuse things precisely because they are not suited to the imprecision of most social innovation. Rational strategies like impact evaluation often create more problems than they solve.[2]

This chapter will explore that idea by using the case of one recent federal education program—Experimental Educational Project (EEP).[3] It is hard to imagine an innovation less suited to scientific R&D. Its goals were vague, in good part because the innovation sought to redefine ideas about what was wrong with schools. It held—contrary to most modern ideas about education—that the chief problem is too much schooling rather than too little.[4] EEP was based on the assumption that schools were boring, that much of what they taught was irrelevant, and that they created social problems by accumulating restless, semisocialized adolescents in institutions that taught them little and prepared them for adult roles and for work even less.

The program proposed to get young people out of the classrooms and into work—to end the structural isolation of youth by putting them in contact with adults in work situations. It was hoped that if young people experienced different kinds of work, they could make more informed career choices when the time came and would develop the personal skills necessary to evolve a career.

But if the ideas were fashionable and the innovation appealing, it presented a familiar dilemma for its managers and developers. It was based on a series of broad and novel intuitions, not solid theory or research. Thus, there was no real basis for choosing one way of implementing the innovation over another. Precisely because it was an appealing melange of broad ideas, there was no self-evidently superior way to manage its development.

91

Early History

EEP was developed in four innovative high schools started by four independent developers under the sponsorship of the U.S. Education Agency (USEA). In its first year the development process was rather undirected—a typical case of R&D on-the-hoof—and the four developers did pretty much what they wanted.[5] But the following year, EEP was transferred to another arm of USEA, and there things changed. The new group was charged with making education research and development more rational and scientific. And its managers believed that greater rationality could improve innovations and increase learning from them—by preventing the looseness that surrounded development efforts like EEP's.[6]

When EEP's new managers reviewed their inheritance, they thought ". . . it was a mess, had no goals. The idea was good, but [the developers] didn't know what they were doing."[7] In their view, the developers were proceeding in precisely the wrong way. They proposed to remedy this state of affairs by using a series of program evaluations to direct the implementation process. The first step was to hire a team of three university consultants who were told to visit the developers and devise an overall evaluation procedure for the project. The managers hired outside help partly because their staff was small. But another reason may have been political: the hope that involving experts would protect against criticism and display their own managerial competence. Certainly USEA's director encouraged it. One staff person, reflecting on the role of the consultants some months later, said, "[The managers] . . . hired them mostly to protect their asses. They didn't want to make a mistake."[8]

The consultants' reports recommended that the project undertake two evaluations the following year. Their purposes were explicit: to clarify and specify the program's goals, to reveal how to achieve them, to help monitor the developers' work, and to insulate the project from criticism. According to the consultants, evaluation ". . . should help to identify . . . program goals and subgoals in ways which make it clear what the mission of the program is and how that mission related to student characteristics." The report termed it "especially desirable" that the developers pay particular attention to the identification of goals that could be measured.[9]

The consultants expected USEA to use evaluation evidence to understand how the program affected students, to make decisions about where and how to spend money, and to make decisions about monitoring, replicating, and disseminating the innovation. In addition, evaluation would justify the program to the public and especially to the Congress. Evaluation was thus a broad management device, designed for many purposes and aimed at many audiences. But the question of whether evaluation was suitable for these purposes apparently never came up. In particular, the developers were never asked. In the view (of one EEP Washington staffer), "[The managers'] . . . idea was to keep evaluation visible for USEA, and to a lesser degree, the developers."[10] She thought the evaluation was designed for more than just its stated purposes: It was intended to manifest a commitment to rigorous evaluation for all to see. Thus, in this case, evaluation probably also served an expressive role.

The First Evaluation

The consultants' report was then issued as evaluation guidelines. When the four project directors saw it, they were shaken. They were told to use a "rigorous experimental design" in preparing their evaluation plans; they were urged to use random control groups; they were told to develop "rigorous experimental models that would obviate the need for research five years from now"; and they were told that there was to be "no trial and error stuff."[11] The developers felt the guidelines asked for inappropriate information. It seemed to them that the Washington staff didn't really understand EEP; in fact, one project director tried to point out discrepancies, but was essentially told, "Tough—that is how it is."[12]

In effect, then, the evaluation guidelines seemed to carry several messages. One was that the managers wanted information that seemed rational and scientific; another was that they were not open to questions about whether such information would be appropriate or useful; a third was that the top program managers seemed to know and care more about evaluation than about the innovation itself. Thus, the evaluation created quite a stir in the program. It surfaced conflicting views of what the innovation was all about and how to manage it.[13]

This first episode ended paradoxically. The EEP staff evaluator and the developers' evaluation staffs tried to develop a rigorous experimental design, but could not. They then threw out the guidelines and collaboratively developed an evaluation aimed at helping the developers with their program models. It was surprising to all that the top EEP managers seemed not to notice or care.[14] While reasons for this aren't entirely clear, one probably was that their attention was shifting to another evaluation. This time the plan was for an even more rigorous effort: an outside, third-party study of EEP's impact on students.

External Impact Evaluation

The EEP managers were prepared to let a half-million-dollar contract for this external impact evaluation to a major national nonprofit evaluation firm. The developers thought it was foolish in principle, but also became worried about the cost.[15] USEA's political fortunes had slipped, and its reduced appropriation eliminated half a million dollars that had been designated for spreading EEP to additional school sites.[16]

The developers thus argued for an external third-party audit of the developers' own internal impact studies—as an objective and much cheaper evaluation of EEP's impact. They proposed that the $500,000 external evaluation be replaced with an external audit costing $20,000 and that the balance of the half million be spent on diffusion.[17] They argued that USEA needed to quickly disseminate programs like EEP, which seemed likely to be well-received by the public and well-regarded by Congressmen.

But the EEP managers were upset by this suggestion and rejected it.[18] A year afterwards, one member of the Washington staff said that their decision was based solely on what the managers thought the evaluation would symbolize. She argued that the managers never seriously considered cost, political utility, or the possibility that disseminating EEP might help the USEA.[19] Several people corroborated this argument by saying that the managers were less concerned with devising an appropriate assessment of EEP than with the management style the study symbolized. These staffers felt that the symbolism served important managerial, political, and professional purposes in USEA. The top USEA staff encouraged it,[20] and it was a message to the developers to shape up and be more systematic.[21]

The external evaluation turned out much like the earlier guidelines. The contractor intended to measure project goals and student outcomes with which the developers didn't agree, and they intended to use control groups—which the developers felt were inappropriate. The developers argued that the evaluation would reveal few reliable changes in students because it measured the wrong things the wrong way and that it would therefore show that EEP didn't work. But the EEP managers would hear none of it. They regarded the objections as defensive and self-serving.[22]

The argument went on and so finally did the evaluation—with some changes. But in general it reinforced the effect of the earlier evaluations. It did not resolve the uncertainties that surrounded EEP; it did not clarify its goals, nor did it help implementation. In fact, the entire evaluation episode seemed to encourage new problems within the EEP system: It created considerable invalid information by encouraging the developers to report only what the Washington managers wanted to hear; it drew the developers attention away from the development work they considered central; and it seemed to reduce trust all around.

The evaluations, then, were part of a rational strategy, but each was designed by third parties who didn't know much about the innovation. Thus the studies were not substantively useful and in fact subtracted from the project in several ways. Efforts to create more rationality and better information produced less of both, and efforts to manage EEP with evaluation were overwhelmed by the uncertainty of the innovation. The result was more uncertainty.

But in other ways, the evaluations proved useful. They fit EEP into the culture of USEA, which probably helped the program in internal budget struggles. They enabled the program managers to practice their specialties—evaluation. And they were useful theatrically and symbolically. In addition, they stimulated the labs to produce evidence that—though the EEP managers later said was inappropriate and irrelevant—helped EEP to pass a USEA panel that reviewed all programs desiring dissemination funds and to get the funds.[23] Thus, though the evaluation guidelines seemed irrational in some ways and caused terrific problems, they were explicable and useful in others.

Conclusion

In the end, then, EEP's implementation did not differ much from that of larger federal social programs. EEP is an attractive collection of ideas, but they are all uncertain and unsettled. EEP's managers at the USEA were aware of the uncertainties and sought to manage them by the application of large doses of managerial rationality. But these efforts solved none of the problems they were supposed to and created a few others. This is not to say, however, that the management had easy alternatives. USEA's director made it clear he expected just the sort of evaluations the EEP managers commissioned, and they perceived that other federal bureaus with oversight responsibility for their programs would expect such studies as well. Rationality seemed essential for bureaucratic and political reasons, quite apart from anyone's beliefs about its efficacy.

But the story of EEP reveals a paradox that strikes me as central in considering the implementation of social innovations. On one hand, these programs are spawned in broad and vague terms, partly because such ideas are appealing to federal reformers and partly because the political process encourages the loose and contradictory thinking they embody.

But while such ideas seem more appealing for these reasons, they are thereby less workable and more problematic for federal executive agencies. The Washington managers responsible for their implementation typically feel caught: On one hand is their own weak grasp on the ideas, the looseness of the development process, and their limited control over the field agencies actually doing the work; on the other is their accountability to Congress and other executive oversight bureaus, and frequently a desire for social reform. This dilemma, combined with the American passion for rationality regularly produces the sort of mismatch between innovative ideas, federal influence, and rational management strategies so elegantly displayed with EEP. Thus, while one may believe there is a better way to manage the development and implementation of such innovations, it is hard to imagine that such alternatives will soon materialize in practice.

Notes

1. See, for example, Jeffrey L. Pressman and Aaron B. Wildavsky, *Implementation* (Berkeley, Calif.: University of California Press, 1973); Jerome

T. Murphy, *Grease the Squeaky Wheel* (Lexington, Mass.: D.C. Heath and Company, 1974); Milbrey W. McLaughlin, *Evaluation and Reform: the Case of ESEA Title I* (Cambridge, Mass.: Ballinger, 1975).

2. D. Schon, *Beyond the Stable State* (New York: Random House, 1972), chapter 10.

3. The names and acronyms of both the project and the agency have been changed to protect confidentiality.

4. The following description of EEP is taken from Eleanor F. McGowan and David K. Cohen, "Planning for Field Tests and Design of EEP," unpublished paper commissioned by U.S. Education Agency, November 1974.

5. Interview 51, April 1975. To protect the confidence of USEA staff and developers, who candidly shared their thoughts and information during many site visits and interviews, the field notes and interviews have been numbered sequentially by date and will be cited in this chapter by number and date. The interviews, transcripts, and field notes are contained in the author's personal files and will be made available to persons having scholarly interest in these data.

6. The debates and arguments on these points have been nicely summarized in R. Levien, *The National Institute of Education* (Washington, D.C.: Rand, 1971).

7. Interview 42, April 1975.

8. Interview 48, February 1975.

9. Robert Boruch, William Goodwin, and Edward Palmer, "Recommendations on Internal Formative Evaluation," USEA Experimental Education Project, March 1973.

10. Interview 48, February 1975.

11. Interview 51, April 1975.

12. Interview 49, March 1975.

13. Interview 4, June 1974.

14. Interview 48, February 1975.

15. Interview 4, June 1974.

16. Interview 56, July 1975.

17. Interview 48, February 1975.

18. Interview 54, April 1975.

19. Interview 48, February 1975.

20. The agency's director had told the EEP managers that he wanted "everything evaluated to the nth degree before it goes out" (Interview 49, March 1975).

21. This project director told a story of their proposal, prepared in the spring of 1973, which raised a series of basic research questions about EEP. The staff identified many of the issues they were still uncertain about and wanted

time to do research on. They proposed to work on those. A USEA site team came out to review the proposal and visit the site. The project director said, "... they were horrified and embarrassed by the proposal—and rejected it. It was a very, very bad scene—lots of argument and misunderstanding." He said it was a very strange event, because (1) one reason the proposal had been written that way was because the staff did have those questions, and (2) the staff had perceived the EEP managers to be serious about research and development—that was the message they'd gotten on various occasions. So they figured, "Well, if USEA is serious about these research questions, we can ask them, and they'll give us money to do it." Then the site team came out and said, no, you can't have money for that. You should go ahead with the development work and keep this thing moving toward replication. He said it was very strange. "We'd been operating for a year, and we realized we didn't know a damn thing about the basis for our model. We wanted to find something out. We thought we were working for R&D people—we had to go ahead full speed and get the thing developed. It was the old game and we're still playing it." He was asked by the interviewer if that still held, and he said, "Absolutely. We've been playing the old game since then" (Interview 4, June 1974).

22. Interview 51, April 1975.

23. Interview 52, April 1975.

8 The Limitations of Policy Research in Congressional Decision Making

Daniel A. Dreyfus

The Problem of Congressional Information

In 1801, Thomas Jefferson, in his first inaugural address, told the members of Congress that he looked to them "with encouragement for that guidance and support which may enable us to steer with safety the vessel in which we are all embarked admidst the conflicting elements of a troubled world." In 1972, Ralph Nader's Congress Project observed:

Congress is, or ought to be, the watchdog of the public purse. Even if it no longer initiates legislation, even if it abdicated much of the budget making process, even if the President can play a shell game with the funds the Congress has appropriated, Congress should vigorously and constantly yap at the executive's heels to make sure that funds are not squandered, that incompetent administrators don't fritter taxpayer dollars away on worthless or marginal projects, that the executive is obeying the laws and enforcing the laws.[1]

One might conclude from these quotes that in the space of the bicentennial experience Congress has been demoted from its position as the nation's navigator to the role of an inadequate watchdog. The critical reader, however, will recall that Jefferson did not seek "guidance or support" for the Louisiana Purchase, and the instigators of Watergate would probably choose a phrase other than "yapping" to characterize congressional response. In fact, the only lesson contained in the two quotes is that excessive rhetoric that misrepresents rather than illuminates the role of the Congress is a time-honored American tradition.

In the past few years, Congress has been subjected to a great deal of critical attention both from within its membership and from outside. "Reforms" in the congressional system that have been instituted recently appear to stem from inconsistent assumptions of the nature of the institution. The erosion of the seniority system presumes that a purely collegiate "one-man-one-vote" organization will somehow still be able to forge complex compromises about critical political issues. The new congressional budget process, alternatively, assumes that Congress is just another bureaucratic management organization.

Considering the fine lack of agreement among scholars and other observers concerning most aspects of congressional behavior, it is remarkable that nearly all commentators on the shortcomings of the legislative branch believe that Congress needs more policy research.[2]

In a philosophical sense, of course, the Congress itself is primarily a policy analysis mechanism. The functions of the legislature are to sense the needs of society for policy initiatives, to define and articulate the options, and to determine and assert the will of the collective social decisionmaker. These functions in the broad sense include everything that policy research can encompass.

Criticisms of congressional policy making rest largely upon the fact that it is usually done in ad hoc ways. Problems are seldom actively sought out by Congress. They are nominated by the executive, the media, and interest groups. The options considered by the Congress and the arguments concerning those options are often provided by the same sources. The most vital contribution of the Congress itself is its selection among policy options that legitimizes the final choice. Congressional decision making is often based upon nebulous criteria and instinctive, almost mystical determinations of the public will. Furthermore, the whole process is frequently obscured by rhetoric designed to rationalize rather than to explain the decision.

In essence, the Congress is often criticized because it does not engage in sufficient, independent, scientific, and orderly policy analysis accompanied by all of the accoutrements of data collection, technical advice, and comprehensive exposition of the decision process. The thesis of this chapter is that the circumstances of the congressional role make a more rigorous application of policy research nearly impossible and practically unwarranted.

The Nature of Congressional Decisions

It is commonplace that decisionmakers do not approach small decisions with the same sophistication of analysis as big decisions. Nevertheless, much discussion of institutional decision making or "policy making" neglects to differentiate between big and little decisions. Observers of situations that involve decisions differing widely in significance can often arrive at conclusions about the policy process that are contradictory or entirely irrelevant.

Scholars such as Dror and Redford have described at least two levels of decision making.[3] The literature on management information systems has suggested further subdivisions.[4] For this discussion, congressional decisions can be crudely divided into two levels. The first—dealing with little decisions—will be called "legislative oversight and policy adjustments." The second—involving big decisions—will be called "major policy making." The relationship of policy research to the congressional decision making is quite different in the two levels of decision processes.

Legislative Oversight and Policy Adjustment

The thousands of small decisions that Congress makes each session are concerned with incremental adjustments in bodies of existing policy. They involve minor additions to and subtractions from existing executive authorities or small redirections in existing programs and activities. The annual process of budgetary authorizations and appropriations, as Wildavsky has noted,[5] also are mainly incremental changes in established policies. The myriad congressional budgetary decisions made each year, with few exceptions, belong in the category of legislative oversight and policy adjustment.

The Congress deals with the mass of such decisions by delegating them to the specialized attention of committees. Of course, committees also importantly participate in major policy decisions; but with regard to oversight and minor policy adjustments, the committees, or even subcommittees, for all practical purposes, decide for the Congress.

Sometimes congressional policy will be established by informal comments made during committee hearings, by staff contacts with agency officials, or by letters signed by the committee leaders. Where legislation is involved, bills pass on the consent calendars or with minimal floor debate and prearranged amendments. Often, furthermore, a legislative measure that includes one or more significant and controversial provisions may also provide a vehicle for numerous other provisions that are examined only by the committees of jurisdiction.

Where these limited and specialized decisions are concerned, Congress serves primarily to legitimize the policy proposals of others, principally the executive. In doing so, it examines the proposed incremental changes for conformity to previous congressional policy and attitudes, expressed or implied. Congress also provides an additional potential point of access to the political process for interests that may lack leverage or have no voice at all in executive decisions. In the first instance, Congress presumably remembers its previous attitudes or can rediscover them quickly. In the second, it is incumbent upon outside interests, the media, or special pleaders (such as Ralph Nader) to make other viewpoints or demands known.

In 352 days of working time, the 93rd Congress enacted 772 of the 26,222 measures introduced. These included 39 appropriations acts involving thousands of program items. Nonlegislative issues, one of which was the response to the Watergate issue, also consumed great amounts of time.

Probably only a hundred legislative measures and issues could be classified as major policy making. With regard to the rest, neither the members nor their principal staff advisors had the time or energy to consider fully the facts that were conveniently available. Senator James Buckley has frankly and aptly characterized the problem of absorbing information:

In session and out, a Senator is constantly on the run, trying to keep abreast of the most immediately pressing matters through meetings, briefings, and staff memorandums, his attention drawn in a thousand different directions.

As for trying to do all the "necessary reading"—the bills, reports, studies, background material; all that required to develop in-depth personal understanding and knowledge—there is only one thing to say about it and that is that it can never be done. The amount of reading necessary to keep a Senator minimally informed on matters of maximum importance is always double that which he can possibly accomplish in the time allotted. My reading takes place in my office, at home, in airports, on airplanes, in taxicabs, in waiting rooms, and just about anywhere I can find sufficient light and (as always) time—and there is never enough.[6]

Clearly, further research and analysis on minor decisions is seldom desired, and if it were available, it could not be absorbed.

Major Policy Making

Only a few major policy decisions are considered by the Congress each year. Such decisions involve fundamental revisions of existing policies, programs, or activities; important reorganizations of federal agencies; and very large increases or reductions or outright terminations of ongoing activities.

Congressional deliberations on major policy decisions have high public visibility. A large percentage of members and the leaders of Congress participate directly in negotiations and debate, and the dominance of the responsible committees is diminished. Usually, the president becomes the spokesman for the executive position.

Because major policy decisions contemplate divergences from past practice and involve experiments with unprecedented policy concepts, they are excursions into the unknown. The specialized bureaucratic experience and technical expertise of executive agencies and client groups are not entirely persuasive. Predictions of the outcome of various policy options become very uncertain and, as a result, a broader set of viewpoints can gain credibility.

These situations, the grand debates on controversial national issues, are the kinds of congressional decisions that many people believe warrant an independent congressional capability for technical research and policy analysis.

In those issues, it may be argued, Congress is the real decisionmaker. Then, it is not endorsing or modifying a policy formulated elsewhere, but choosing among potential policies that differ from one another in matters of crucial concern to society. Then, there is the greatest justification for Congress to invest the time and other resources to look beyond the justifications of the executive branch and outside advocates, to reassess the facts, to pose the issues for itself, and to seek out and evaluate the broadest range of options.

Closer examination of the nature of controversial issues, however, reveals a different notion of the congressional role. In order for an issue to be truly controversial at the national level, there must already be widespread adherence to at least two viewpoints or policy options. Unless two legitimate, credible, and reasonably well-defined options exist, the issue can not result in significant debate.

By the time that important, controversial issues receive intense consideration by the Congress, they will already have been the subject of examination by a broad spectrum of interested analysts. Commentators within and outside of government will have verified and criticized the principal arguments for all of the options and viewpoints. Even the political positions will have been defined, at least in general terms.

Where issues substantially turn upon technical matters, as they did in the supersonic transport debate and do in the current nuclear breeder reactor controversy, there must be some lack of technical certainty in order for the issue to remain controversial. There will, therefore, have to be credible and qualified expert judgment available to support each side of the debate, and additional expert testimony is more apt to serve primarily to reinforce political debate rather than to enlighten the discussion.

The role of Congress is to evaluate the political strengths of the various viewpoints, to assign political measures to the intangible and otherwise unquantifiable factors that make the decision controversial, and to arrive at either a political victory or a compromise that will result in a feasible and legitimate policy.

The challenge to the Congress in such issues is not to discover new factual knowledge or previously overlooked alternatives. Indeed, the likelihood of anything really new emerging at that stage of issue development would be remote even with the most exhaustive search, and the nature of congressional decision making severely limits the search that is possible.

Limitations on Legislative Decision Making

Major policy decisions treated by the Congress are rarely the result of congressional formulation. Almost by definition, the important issues facing the Congress are formed by national and world affairs. They arise out of the circumstances of society. Critical and controversial political decisions, furthermore, can only be made when social pressures for decision are intense. Only then have they sufficient priority to command attention. Only then are signals from the polity adequate for evaluation of the political consequences, and only then would a prudent politician be compelled to make a hazardous choice.

Once a decision's time has come, the Congress usually does not enjoy the latitude to defer its action. The severe criticism currently being leveled at Congress for its inability to formulate a comprehensive response to the incredibly complex and unprecedented energy crisis is an example of the pressures generated by pressing public policy issues.

Nor are major public issues easily anticipated in advance. Public concern for environmental matters in the late 1960s, for example, ripened from routine administrative policy making into the demand for unprecedented federal involvement within a few months.

Many formal and informal mechanisms, ranging from the as yet untested Office of Technology Assessment to the well settled Brookings Institute, have been devised to provide early warnings of emerging public problems. Prediction of the future, however, is a notably inexact pursuit. Someone has probably predicted every major issue of modern times, but legions of issues that were also predicted have never materialized. Most major congressional issues become full blown without much advance notice and are discovered rather than predicted.

There is seldom any opportunity to do policy analysis in anticipation of future issues, therefore, and little time to do it once congressional action has begun in earnest.

In addition to the need for quick response to often unanticipated issues, however, another characteristic of the congressional decision process imposes a more restrictive constraint upon the utility of independent policy research. For the Congress to fulfill its primary purpose, the members must remain individually responsible to their electorates for their decisions, and the elective process insures this responsibility. The ultimate judgments about the political consequences of each vote can be made only by each member himself or by some generalist staff person who is sufficiently intimate with him to be, and to be accepted as, an extension of his own political personality.

There are only 535 members of the Congress; only 100 Senators. Each member will delegate important political judgments to only a few, in some instances only one or two, trusted staff members. As a result, the ultimate consideration, distillation, and value judgments about all of the research and policy analysis presented to the Congress concerning all of the major issues of government must be made by a few hundred individuals in the Senate and perhaps less than a thousand in the House.

A gnawing desire to somehow introduce more analysis, more knowledge, and more comprehension of increasingly bewildering issues into congressional decision making is felt within the institution as well as by sympathetic observers. Professional staffs in both the Senate and House have proliferated in recent years, established legislative agencies such as the General Accounting Office (GAO) and the Congressional Research Service (CRS) have been expanded, and new arms including the Office of Technology Assessment (OTA) and the Congressional Budget Office (CBO) have been created.

These legislative analysis offices, exclusive of the professional staff of the Congress itself, now number more than 6,600 employees and have a combined budget in excess of 184 million dollars. Their professional staffs are well paid, talented, and highly qualified experts. The problem of focusing this analytical power upon critical policy choices, however, remains unsolved.

The GAO primarily monitors executive agencies and ongoing activities. Its auditing, both financial and administrative, most often acts as a substitute for, rather than an adjunct to, legislative oversight by committees of the Congress.

The CRS enjoys a much closer liaison with congressional members and committees and serves as an extension of the staff capability. It is called upon for a variety of factual studies, both cursory and in depth. Some of its products can be described as policy research.

The CRS, however, has learned the pitfalls of contributing judgmental opinions to political controversies. As a matter of policy, its formal reports on controversial issues are confined to facts and the cited views of others. The ultimate judgment is left to political adversaries who sometimes can find support for both sides of an argument in a CRS report.

Two more recent experiments in congressional policy analysis, the OTA and the CBO, cannot yet be evaluated.

OTA was conceived almost entirely to be a policy research organization dealing with technology-related issues. With organizational competence in transportation, world trade, health, energy, materials, oceans, and food, it would appear to be capable of involvement in a large share of major congressional decisions.

Thus far, OTA has performed as a technological CRS. It has made factual inputs to such congressional staff work as drafting of coastal zone legislation and review of the energy research and development budget. It has not yet had the time, or perhaps the temerity, to offer a policy judgment on such politically charged emerging issues as the advisability of breeder reactors.

If OTA does not step forward with judgmental analysis of critical technological issues, it will take its place with the GAO and CRS; another vast reservoir of undigested factual knowledge, largely untapped and untappable by the handful of political actors and aides who must choose between yea and nay on critical votes. If OTA does throw its expert opinion behind one side of congressional debate on a controversial issue, the other side—by definition nearly half of the Congress—will be obliged to try to discredit it. It will be interesting to watch the evolution of OTA in either situation.

Congressional budgeting is a unique case of policy research. CBO must share the dilemma facing the whole concept. Wherever budgeting is done, it involves a process of winnowing out of proposed uses of scarce resources. It is not usually a question of eliminating unworthy proposals; it is more often a delicate judgment among desirable alternatives. Budgeting also is typically a sequential process. The final, most difficult choices are based upon unmeasurable values and are reserved for the chief executive.

It is difficult to know how such final choices can ever be made by a collegiate body of equals with disparate views. It is equally difficult to know how the CBO can offer analyses of fiscal policy that can be useful for the more conservative Republicans and the more liberal Democrats alike.

Fiscal policy, after all, implies a set of values against which the economic and financial impacts of programs can be measured. Everyone can agree that budget deficits and unemployment are both bad, but there may be important differences in judgment about which is worse.

CBO can easily provide an accounting service. It can be the "number monger" to the Congress, but when it provides policy analysis, can it remain nonpartisan and professional or will it become an advocate providing detailed justifications for a particular dominant political viewpoint? Again, it will be interesting to see.

Even if all of the political and administrative problems of policy research were solved and if objective, comprehensive, and timely analyses could be produced within the legislative establishment when major issues were under consideration, there would still remain the question of how much new information do the real political decisionmakers need. How much, in fact, can they cope with? Senator Buckley has stated the problem well:

What needs to be understood is that the Congress by its nature operates under an unavoidable limitation. Whereas the Executive Branch can build new buildings to house and hire specialists to man the new agencies created by the Congress under the supervision of a new department of the Cabinet, each member of the Congress is expected to cast an independent judgment on every matter that comes before the body as a whole. The Congress can only try to cope with the ever-expanding number and variety of federal activities by dividing ever thinner the amount of time its members can devote to any one.[7]

Conclusions

The observations that have been made strongly suggest the futility of attempting to introduce sophisticated policy research into the congressional decision process. Where congressional decisions involve legislative oversight and policy adjustment, such analysis is simply superfluous to the summary role that Congress plays. Major policy decisions, alternatively, frustrate the timely preparation and introduction of independent policy research because of the very nature of the congressional decision process.

Experience thus far with efforts to attach policy research capabilities to the legislative branch tend to reinforce these contentions. Although there is no practical limit to the technical or professional staff that could be attached to the Congress directly or through appendages such as the Congressional Research Service and the Office of Technology Assessment, the research and analysis such resources produce will remain sterile of personalized political insight. The last, often crucial judgment must be made by the chosen few whose ranks cannot be expanded. The energies, comprehension, and time of those few impose a practical limit upon the research and analysis that can effectively be brought to bear upon congressional decisions.

This discussion is not a rejection of policy research in federal decision making. Rather, it questions the feasibility and the need of making the legislative process a focal point of such research. Masses of data and corps of analysts are best managed by the executive. Watergate paranoia notwithstanding, most options and viewpoints on national issues can be adequately developed outside of the Congress.

An open congressional process, a vigilant press, and active interest groups will guarantee abundant information to feed debate. The Congress should weigh the final contentions, remain sensitive to the tastes and demands of society, and act upon its collective political instincts. Then it will provide responsive and responsible decisions. We should not, and fortunately we probably cannot, overwhelm the political judgment of the Congress with masses of factual data and technical analysis.

Notes

1. Mark J. Green, James M. Fallows, and David R. Zwick, *Who Runs Congress?* Ralph Nader Congress Project (New York: Bantam Books, 1972), p. 119.

2. For example, the Nader study approvingly quotes Joseph Califano writing in the *Washington Post* as follows: "The stark fact is that neither the Congress nor any of its committees has the consistent capability—without almost total reliance on the information and analytical resources of the executive branch—of developing coherent, large-scale federal programs" (ibid., p. 129).

3. Dror speaks of "mega policy" as being decision making that results in changes in the policy-making system itself. Yehezkel Dror, *Ventures in Policy Sciences: Concepts and Applications* (New York: American Elsevier, 1971). Redford differentiates between "micropolitics" or routine decision making and "macropolitics" that "arises when the community at large and the leaders of the government as a whole are brought into the decision." Emmette S. Redford, *Democracy in the Administrative State* (New York: Oxford University Press, 1969), p. 107.

4. For example, Robert V. Head divides management decisions into three broad levels of significance: strategic planning, management control, and operational control. The latter is so routine as to be amenable to automated or programmed decisionmaking. Robert V. Head, "The Elusive MIS," *Datamation*, September 1, 1970, pp. 22-27.

5. Aaron Wildavsky, *The Politics of the Budgetary Process* (Boston: Little, Brown, 1964).

6. James L. Buckley, *If Men Were Angels: A View From the Senate* (New York: G.P. Putnam's Sons, 1975), p. 127.

7. Ibid., p. 137.

Social Science and Judicial Policy Making

Paul L. Rosen

The impact of social science in judicial policy making, while of growing importance, has for a number of reasons been relatively modest in comparison to its uses in other areas. Not the least of these reasons is the long-standing reluctance of the Supreme Court to concede in the first instance that it makes law, much less public policy, and when indeed it does so, to make law formally on the basis of social science research. But whereas adjudication in America has been transformed into a surrogate form of politics, thereby making good Tocqueville's prescient observation that "scarcely any political question arises in the United States that is not resolved sooner or later into a judicial question,"[1] the selective making of law and policy has become an indisputable though somewhat controversial function of the judiciary. As early as 1908 the Supreme Court recognized the relevance and utility of social science data in the judicial decision-making process. But given the internal restraints and limitations of this process, the decisive use of social science by the Court did not occur until nearly a half century later.

Needless to say, the Supreme Court has been making law and policy ever since it determined in 1803 that it possessed the far reaching power of judicial review.[2] Throughout the nineteenth century the Court for the most part drew its policy-making facts from history, doctrines of social Darwinism, and what was in effect judicial intuition. The relatively limited policy output of the Court during this time, coupled with the fact that its major decisions with few exceptions were in tandem with the exigencies of political and economic development, presented little reason for observers to question how the Court went about finding facts. For that matter the broader question of how the judicial decision-making process actually worked was scarcely raised at all.

The onset of judicial activism in the 1880s changed all this. The Court under its general economic policy of laissez faire began to strike down state legislation designed to ameliorate some of the excesses of industrialism. The heavy hand of the Court continued to discourage important social and economic reforms well into the New Deal period.

In the early part of the new century, the Court's negative social and economic policies prompted progressive jurists to react vigorously. They began to take a more critical look at the judicial decision-making process. It was not merely judicial activism as such that disturbed reform-minded jurists. What alarmed them most was the Court's method of reasoning and its general approach to jurisprudence. The Court was charged with practicing a mechanical jurisprudence. Instead of adjudicating a dispute open-mindedly—that is, applying legal principles to an objectively defined fact-situation—the Court tended strongly to begin with an abstract proposition of law such as "liberty to contract" and to proceed to reason syllogistically or through logical deduction to a conclusion often at wide variance with reasonable interpretation of the actual facts concerning the dispute in question.[3]

Such notable figures as Louis D. Brandeis, Roscoe Pound, and Benjamin N. Cardozo began a long-term campaign to change the Court's sterile pattern of legal reasoning and hopefully to curb its frequently reactionary decision making. In law review articles, public lectures, and legal argumentation, these progressive jurists along with others put together a case for a more factual or a sociological jurisprudence. Pound insisted, for example, that law was not simply an abstract concept and that there should be a keener awareness and interest in legal dynamics. He emphasized that law was a social institution and, more important-ly, one that could be changed. Pound suggested that jurists, instead of being preoccupied with penalties and sanctions, should show more concern for the social objectives of law. Cardozo made more explicit the then novel idea that law was a method of social engineering and even suggested that a judge ought to liken himself to a legislator. Both Pound and Cardozo emphasized that law should serve all citizens and not just those with vested property interests. Social justice, Brandeis argued, could be achieved by using law to reform society. But this could be done, he insisted, only if courts based their decisions on observable social facts instead of uncertain assumptions and intuitive guesses about the workings of society.

Brandeis figured prominently in helping to move American jurisprudence away from a conception of law colored by judicial bias and vested corporate interests towards a vision of law more sensitized and compatible with the public interest. He understood that law was a conservative institution and that judges by temperament and training were unlikely to hurry the slow course of legal change. Moreover, he realized that the judiciary had little incentive to change ingrained habits. It was clear to Brandeis that judges had neither the time nor the facilities to research the crucial factual questions on which important constitu-tional decisions often turned. Convinced that counsels' best option was to press empirical facts upon the Court, Brandeis in the 1908 case of *Muller* v. *Oregon*,[4] introduced a startling innovation in American legal procedure. In what might otherwise have been a routine case involving legislation that fixed a maximum ten-hour work day for women employed in Oregon laundries, Brandeis presented the Court with an unusual brief. Though 113 pages long, this brief contained only three pages of traditional legal argumentation. The bulk of this prototypic document, now commonly known as the Brandeis brief, was filled with numerous extracts of reports by physicians, economists, psychologists, factory inspectors, and various bureaus of statistics. These reports provided the Court with detailed descriptions of industrial conditions and particularly with an account of their physical, psychological, and moral effects on women. In short, Brandeis had assembled for the Court a vivid picture based on social science data of harsh realities in industrial society.

In upholding the Oregon statute, Justice Brewer speaking for the Court accorded formal recognition to Brandeis' social science data. "[It] . . . may not be amiss, in the present case," he observed, "to notice the course of legislation as well as expressions of opinions from other than judicial sources."[5] This data, Brewer wrote, "may not be technically speaking, [by legal] authorities, and in them is little or no discussion of the constitutional question presented to us for determination, yet they are significant of a widespread belief that women's physical structure, and the functions she performs in consequence thereof, justify special legislation restricting or qualifying the conditions under which she should be permitted to toil."[6] Most significantly, acknowledging the admiss-ability and relevance of social science data to the Court's critical fact-finding function, Brewer remarked: "When a question of fact is debated and debatable, and the extent to which a special constitutional limitation goes is affected by the truth in respect to that fact, a widespread and long continued belief concerning it is worthy of attention. We take judicial cognizance of all matters of general knowledge."[7]

Subsequent uses of the Brandeis brief did help to moderate the Court's fundamental hostility to social welfare legislation, and provided the justices with better factual insight for making constitutional decisions with broad policy import. But by no means did social science data overwhelm or have an irresistable influence on the Court.[8] It could ignore or dismiss social science data when it chose to do so. Thus, for example, when social science data was submitted in support of a federal minimum wage law applying to women, in order to show that there was a causal relationship between the earnings of women and their "moral" behavior, Justice Sutherland, although not in possession of facts to the contrary, found the data "interesting but only mildly persuasive." More importantly, with respect to the constitutionality of the act, ". . . the elucidation of that question," Sutherland quipped, "cannot be aided by counting heads."[9] Underscoring the Court's flippant attitude towards the voluminous data presented in this case, Chief Justice Edward D. White had remarked earlier in the proceedings, "Why, I could compile a brief twice as thick to prove that the legal profession ought to be abolished."[10]

Social Science as Modern Authority

The definitive break in the Court's occasionally irreverent attitude towards social science finally came in 1954 in the epoch-making school desegregation case of *Brown* v. *Board of Education*.[11] Racial segregation, especially in schools, had long been a matter of constitutional policy. The legal underpinning of this policy had been established in 1896 in the case of *Plessy* v. *Furguson.*[12] In this instance in order to justify racial segregation in railway cars, the Court had reasoned, on the basis of the "factual" assumption of the biological inferiority of Negroes, that segregation was not inconsistent with the equal protection clause of the Fourteenth Amendment. The Court's interpretation of the equal protection clause was clearly informed by the prevailing social Darwinist notions of race. "Legislation," Justice Henry B. Brown had concluded for the Court, "is powerless to eradicate racial instincts or to abolish distinctions based upon physical differences, and the attempt to do so can only result in accentuating the difficulties of the present situation."[13]

The Brown case was first heard by the Court in October 1952. The NAACP Legal Defense and Educational Fund had decided to base its case in part on social science findings that suggested that school segregation impaired the ability of black children to learn and had other harmful effects. In order to disabuse the law of the racist assumption of Negro inferiority, the NAACP social science statement presented as an appendix to its brief, informed the Court that ". . . enforced segregation is psychologically detrimental to the members of the segregated group."[14] The statement also advised the Court of the critical fact that ". . . much, perhaps all, of the observable differences among various racial and national groups may be adequately explained in terms of environmental differences."[15] After hearing oral argument the Court ordered further argumentation chiefly to the question of whether there was historical evidence that would suggest that the framers of the Fourteenth Amendment had intended or contemplated that school segregation might be proscribed.

In announcing its historic decision in May 1954, Chief Justice Earl Warren quickly concluded for the Court that history shed little light on the constitutionality of school segregation and for the Court's purpose was inconclusive. After discoursing on the role of education in contemporary society, Warren went to the heart of the question and asked whether school segregation deprived minority children of equal educational opportunities as guaranteed by the Fourteenth Amendment. In answering this constitutional question Warren first made a simple finding of fact. To separate children he wrote, ". . . from others of similar age and qualifications solely because of their race generates a feeling of inferiority as to their status in the community that may affect their hearts and minds in a way unlikely ever to be undone."[16] Emphasizing this crucial sociopsychological fact, Warren cited a lower court finding:

Segregation of white and colored children in public schools has a detrimental effect upon the colored children. The impact is greater when it has the sanction of the law; for the policy of separating the races is usually interpreted as denoting the inferiority of the negro group. A sense of inferiority affects the motivation of a child to learn. Segregation with the sanction of law, therefore, has a tendency to [retard] the educational and mental development of negro children and to deprive them of some of the benefits they would receive in a racial[ly] integrated school system.[17]

Warren then repudiated the pseudoscientific factual assumptions that governed the Plessy decision: "Whatever may have been the extent of psychological knowledge at the time of *Plessy* v. *Furguson*, this finding is amply supported by modern authority."[18] The modern authority referred to by the Chief Justice consisted of seven social science studies contained in what was to become the most controversial footnote in American constitutional law. Small wonder. The Court had used social science as the source of its finding of psychological harm, the factual underpinning of its legal holding that school segregation was intrinsically unequal and therefore unconstitutional.

The Court's use of social science elicited criticism from all sides. For those opposed flatly to the decision, social science was a convenient target of attack. That the decision, as some charged, was based on sociology and not law represented what was thought a horrendous constitutional aberration. Even some thoughtful legal critics were distressed that a great constitutional decision should be tied to the evolving knowledge of social science. If social science was to find another day that school segregation was salubrious, they asked, did that mean then that segregation ought to be constitutional? It was preferable instead they argued to base the decision on an unchanging legal principle that could always be taken to mean that racial segregation was abhorrent. Still others, including some social scientists less concerned with the propriety of segregation, claimed that the studies were methodologically unsound. For that matter, Southern politicians suggested that some of the social scientists whose works had been cited by the Court might even be politically unreliable. And amidst the wide-ranging debate, a few casual onlookers suggested that the Court's use of social science was mere window dressing.[19]

It should have been clear to observers who found the *Brown* decision to be sociological rather than legal, that many of the Court's sweeping constitutional decisions historically followed from extralegal assumptions of one kind or another. How else could the Court fashion constitutional policy without presuming the factual context that called for a given decision and the fact situation to which it was applied? Plainly enough law can neither be made or applied in a social vacuum. To see social science as an alien intrusion in the decision-making process was to take a myopic view of the place of the Brandeis brief in American constitutional law. Moreover, such a view of *Brown* ignored the factual development of constitutional law—that is, its overall tendency to move into increasingly clear congruence with the empirical facts of social reality.

Those who believed that the Constitution was explicit enough for the Court to outlaw racial segregation in schools without having to turn to social science did not explain how the Court had managed to overlook the precise meaning of the Constitution for so long. True enough, the findings of social science were amenable to change, but this simply indicated that the factual dimension of our understanding of racism would be constantly enlarged. The possibility and danger that social science would at some point in time suggest that racial segregation be reimposed in order to satisfy the functional prerequisites of the constitutional commitment to equality seemed greatly exaggerated. To be sure, some social scientists have suggested recently that school integration has been of dubious educational benefit to minority children. Even were this to be true, it might be a persuasive political argument against busing as a tactical integrative remedy, but far less than the indispensable element of a constitutional case for the establishment of a new system of school segregation based solely on the criterion of race.[20]

In a sense, the political opponents of *Brown* and the legal purists both overreacted to the Court's use of social science by attaching too much importance to the role played by social science in the decision. The Court's decision was not based solely on social science—that is, social science was not the source of the applicable legal principle. Social science, however, did document the Court's critical finding of fact: That racially segregated schools did not as a matter of factual record provide equal educational opportunities as required by the Fourteenth Amendment. Because the distinction between law and fact is a subtle one, inasmuch as the two are dialectically related with fact situations giving rise to the reinterpretation of legal principles, the role of social science was easily misunderstood.

There was better reason for methodological criticism of the seven social science studies used by the Court. The Clarks' well-known doll test, for example, presented some difficulties. Here two groups of black children, one from integrated schools in the North and the other from segregated schools in the South, were tested for positive and negative identifications with identical black and white dolls. In general, the Clarks found that black children more frequently preferred the white doll, which thus suggested a negative self-assessment on the part of black children.[21] Yet, the study left important questions unanswered. It was not adequately explained, for example, why southern children were less likely than their northern counterparts to react negatively to the black doll. Questions such as these did suggest an apparent weakness of the study.

Furthermore, none of the seven studies had actually determined that school segregation per se was the causal factor of the Court's finding of psychological harm. The studies relied on by the Court were not conspicuously strong in terms of hard data. Indeed, at that point in time, relatively little social science research had been done on the subject of race relations. The Court was aware, however, that the preponderant opinion of modern social science was that enforced segregation did have detrimental effects on black school children.[22] In citing that opinion, the Court was deciding a momentous question of law on the basis of the best evidence available. It is hard to see why the Court should have been faulted for doing so.

It is difficult, of course, to gauge the influence of social science as a decisional factor in the minds of the justices. At best, any estimate in this instance would be just that. The debate engendered by the Court's use of social science suggested that many citizens who studied the *Brown* opinion (all judicial opinions being intended as instruments of persuasion) were convinced that social science had been a significant factor in the Court's reasoning process. To be sure, the small group of racist social scientists who attempted thereafter to provide for judicial consumption evidence to prove the biological inferiority of Negroes, thus indicated their belief that social science had played a serious role in the decision.[23] That role can best be understood in terms of the function of the Court's opinion.

A judicial opinion obviously is intended to demonstrate to a possibly skeptical public that the Court's decision is the result of a reasoned process of deliberation and not simply an arbitrary act of will. In this sense, it could be said that the Court used social science to legitimate its decision. But the same might be said of the opinion in toto. More importantly, it should be noted that even if an opinion were to be crafted in a cynical fashion, given the rule of stare decisis, the Court must be prepared to live with it for some time, which is to say that the Court, as a model of the rational decisionmaker, must and usually does avoid making casual statements it does not mean because of their powerfully binding power.

In *Plessy*, the Court had condoned racial segregation on the assumed factual ground of Negro inferiority. Undoubtedly, many citizens in 1954 would not have disputed that belief. It was therefore important for the Court to refute explicitly the racial mythology that had long served the cause of white domination. By relying on modern social science, the Court was able to dismiss effectively the psychology and law represented by *Plessy*.

Factors Mitigating the Judicial Use of Social Science

Even though social science came of judicial age in the *Brown* case, it remains true in general that scientific method and law have had relatively little impact on each other.[24] The reasons for this go beyond the possible insufficiencies of social science and must be understood in terms of the divergent paths taken long ago by law and science. Moreover, though law cannot afford to contradict too flagrantly the dictates of empirical reality, social science must still be accepted and a proper place found for it in the judicial process, and not the other way around. This means social science must be adapted to the requirements of legal procedure if it is to influence law. There still remains some doubt as to whether differences between law and social science (and the underlying tension) can ever be successfully bridged in some consistent way.

Social science unlike law takes no command from society's need for political and social order. Law unlike social science is fundamentally opposed to change and seeks to contain and channel it into an orderly procedural mold. Law, theoretically speaking, serves the underlying polity and helps insulate society from the shock of unregulated change. Social science, on the other hand, remains open to revision and, theoretically speaking, follows the canons of scientific truth in whatever direction it should lead. This is what Rousseau meant when he suggested that society is a closed body animated by parochial teachings for the purpose of extracting through law obedience and conformity. Science, because it pursues truth, was for that reason potentially subversive.[25]

There is as well the problem of operating style or accustomed approaches and vocabularies for analyzing issues. These tend to clash and create mutual suspicion. Holmes said it well when he noted, "Judges commonly are elderly, and are more likely to hate at sight any analysis to which they are not accustomed, and which disturbs repose of mind, than to fall in love with novelties."[26] Even were judges and lawyers to seek out social scientists for mates, how well would they communicate? As one lawyer has complained, "A great deal of behavioral science is cult oriented rather than problem oriented and the behavioral scientists are more interested in sharing with each other niceties and displays of technical erudition rather than sharing with the larger community some useful disclosures."[27]

The problem of introducing or making social science findings available to the legal community is not small.[28] The attorney anxious to buttress his case with social science is not likely to know how to gain access to the findings he requires. In the absence of formal and practical channels of communication between the legal and social science disciplines, the lawyer without social science training must rely on his own necessarily limited resources in locating findings appropriate to his case. A recent handbook, *Sources and Uses of Social and Economic Data: A Manual for Lawyers*[29] is one step towards amelioration of this problem but also confirms how difficult the problem of information exchange actually is.

The judiciary also has severely limited resources for fact finding. This is an old problem that Cardozo noted as early as 1921. He suggested that a ministry of justice be established to gather facts from all sources, particularly from social science, which would be relevant to the judicial decision-making process.[30] Although the Court does appoint experts in some instances to make findings on technical matters, it is obviously very sensitive about its autonomy—which requires usually that it find facts for itself. Thus, the Brandeis brief remains the Court's best link to social science. The brief with its limitations also suggests that the ultimate responsibility for insuring that the Court is informed of apposite social science findings rests with counsel. "There are many things that courts would notice if brought before them that beforehand they do not know," Justice Holmes once remarked. "It rests with counsel to take the proper steps, and if they deliberately omit them, we do not feel called upon to institute inquiries on our own account."[31] This attitude, of course, underlines the special factual problem of judicial policy making.

When social science does find its way into the courtroom, there are still numerous problems to be overcome. There is the possibility that certain kinds of data may be regarded as inadmissible hearsay. Since courts presume challenged statutes to be constitutional until proven otherwise, lawyers must be sure to introduce findings that "overwhelmingly" support their cases, or else the judiciary is not likely to dispute the legislative statements of fact. With this in mind, one observer has remarked: "... live expert testimony is potentially dangerous if the expert either hedges on cross-examination, or if the state can introduce contrary evidence. Plaintiffs are not likely to prevail if there is even a small 'battle of the experts'."[32]

Further complications arise when, because of procedural necessity, social science is presented in the courtroom within the framework of the adversary mode. Here opposing counsel produce highly partisan versions of the facts, and the Court is left to find the true facts for itself by choosing between or selecting from two one-sided and necessarily conflicting statements.[33] Counsel's objective is to win for his client a favorable verdict rather than to establish a record of scholarly detachment and commitment to truth. Thus, there is present within the adversary system a positive incentive for lawyers to manipulate social science data or to use it with less than a scrupulous concern for scientific method. Social scientists too may be tempted to stray from the canons of their disciplines when they put their learning at the service of a worthwhile but nonetheless partisan cause. One sociologist familiar with this problem has written: "The social science researcher has a fear of his being captured subtly, and even unconsciously, by the desire to prove his case, to show the kinds of evidence he believes and wants to believe exists."[34] Social science may well be used simply because its findings are credible, but findings can be credible without necessarily being scientific. This is not to say that social science will necessarily be abused, but to point out that the courtroom is hardly an ideal forum for the discussion and advancement of scientific knowledge.

Clearly social science cannot produce easy solutions or in some instances any solutions to the multiple problems of judicial policy making. There simply may, for example, be no findings applicable to the problem at hand. Even if some mechanism were to be established to stimulate social science research on problems of immediate judicial concern, such research could be very expensive and not necessarily complete when needed at the moment of decision. Moreover, social science in the main is concerned with general problems of theoretical interest. Most findings, therefore, that deal with groups and classes are not likely to apply precisely to a specific legal dispute involving specific parties. The application of general social science principles can lead to controversy about the adequacy of data and hypotheses. The judiciary, for the most part lacking the necessary expertise, is then left to make final determinations on these matters or simply to skirt such issues altogether.

Finally, it needs to be emphasized that the Supreme Court is a cautious policymaker. Judicial authority and the Court's mandate to write law in bold letters is uncertain and will be measured carefully each time it is exercised. The Court, moreover, is a passive decisionmaker. It does not initiate cases but must wait as they do, or do not, slowly wind their way up the judicial ladder. In the meantime, public attitudes and positions may harden, and the Court may find itself asked to solve the very issues that political branches of government have already found too intractable to handle. If the law is to resolve this kind of conflict, it must do so in its own way, which means that the Court as a policymaker is governed by a special set of restrictions. The Court must consider the practical exigencies that are of concern to all policymakers, but it must above all oblige the legal principles that are the fundamental rationale of its existence. This process may require at times that some legal principles hang in abeyance in order that the whole fabric of law is better served. Thus, if social science findings indicate some striking abuse of law, the Court may wish to ignore those facts in order to decide a case on some other or more narrow ground. Perhaps, the Court may not wish to decide such a case at all. Where social science clarifies and explains the sobering conditions of life, and even points to policies for ameliorating some of them, the paramount question for the Court will always be one of law. Justice Frankfurter remarked during the oral proceedings of the *Brown* case in regard to the question of whether race was a legally permissible criterion for the statutory classification of citizens: "I do not care what any associate or full professor in sociology tells me. If it is in the Constitution, I do not care about what they say. But the question is, is it in the Constitution?"[35]

Judicial Uses of Social Science

Despite some of the factors that limit the judicial use of social science, it has nonetheless made an appreciable contribution to the factual development of American jurisprudence during the past half century. Not all jurists of course are enamored of social science. But there is presently in the juristic community a more acute perception of the interrelationship between law and social science than in the social science community.[36] Political scientists, for example, have expended much energy in the task of psyching-out, explaining, and predicting the judicial mind. They have not paid much attention, however, to the practical ways social science may be used to improve the judicial decision-making process. More social scientists clearly need to address themselves to this problem.

Doing so will not enable social scientists to impose their findings on a reluctant Court, because ultimately the criteria for using social science will remain a matter for judicial determination. As one observer, though, points out, "It is not for the social sciences to tell courts what criteria should govern their decisions, but it is not for judges to posit subjective or naive armchair notions of social science in the course of decisions conditioned on attitudes or behavior of people."[37]

Courts, to be sure, are playing an ever increasing role in American society.

The upsurge of judicial influence is not due simply to the revolution of the Warren Court that broadly extended the procedural and substantive guarantees of the Bill of Rights. As government at all levels inevitably expands its operation in a society constantly becoming more complex, it stands to reason, though to the consternation of some, that courts necessarily will increase their orbit of operation.[38] The Supreme Court as in the past will be asked to review the constitutionality of the policy decisions of myriad governmental and quasi-governmental agencies. The Court, whose main concern is after all to provide relief from arbitrary government, will thus be making legal decisions on issues inextricably tied to considerations affecting policy making. The grounds on which policy decisions are made will help determine whether given policies pass constitutional muster under such infinitely flexible legal principles as due process of law. Social science could be very helpful to the Court in determining whether governmental policies rest on rational or reasonable factual assumptions. On the other hand, when the Court proceeds to review statutes or administrative policy decisions on the basis of dubious factual assumptions, justice is not likely to be well served.

So much can be seen in the case of *United States* v. *Krass,*[39] where the Court reversed a district court ruling that invalidated the fee system of the Bankruptcy Act. Under the Act, Congress had established fees in order that those who availed themselves of the benefits of the Act would pay the costs instead of the taxpayers at large. Krass argued that he was unable to pay the fifty-dollar filing fee. The Supreme Court, however, assumed otherwise. Justice Blackmun, speaking for the Court, showed a dim factual appreciation of the grinding conditions of poverty. The fee he observed could be broken into installments of $1.92 weekly or even as low as $1.28 per week. And such payments were "less than the price of a movie and a little more than the cost of a pack or two of cigarettes."[40] In Blackmun's estimation any able-bodied man should have no difficulty in paying such trifling sums. Justice Marshall in a dissenting opinion disputed the Court's middle-class understanding of poverty: "It may be easy for some people to think that weekly savings of less than $2.00 are no burden. But no one who has close contact with poor people can fail to understand how close to the margin of survival many of them are."[41]

Poverty law, particularly because of the breadth of its reach and the wide gap between members of the legal profession and the poor, is an area where social science evidence can be very enlightening for courts. A case in point is a successful challenge to New York State regulations that provided for an automatic reduction in welfare payments to families with dependent children who housed noncontributing lodgers.[42] In this instance, New York welfare authorities deprived the families of a portion of their housing allotment because male lodgers made no formal contribution to the upkeep of the household. The New York Code of Rules and Regulations in question was based on "irrebuttable presumptions" that the presence of a noncontributing lodger proved a welfare family had excess living space, and so required less public assistance to help it pay its rent. Counsel for the plaintiffs, in order to demonstrate the irrational and unreasonable nature of these factual presumptions, introduced the testimony of sociologist Herbert Gans and urban planner Paul Davidoff.

Gans explained the subculture of the poor and their precarious style of life that creates a strong incentive for patterns of cooperation not characteristic of the middle-class family. Gans also stated that among the poor there was a relationship between lowness of income and the tendency ". . . to have people other than spouse and children living in the household."[43] Most importantly, Gans outlined the role of the surrogate father, usually played by the male lodger. In this role, Gans explained, the male lodger contributed far more to the well-being of the family than the small monetary payment required from him by welfare authorities. Davidoff testified to the various standards for measuring the adequacy of living space and made clear the arbitrary nature of the state's presumption that the presence of the lodger proved the family had excess living space. These expert testimonies helped the Court to find that the state's "irrebuttable presumptions" lacked a factual foundation. Social science was thus used to define a fact-situation that middle-class judicial intuition may not properly have grasped. It convinced the Court of facts apparently beyond the pale of understanding of the state. As District Judge Weinstein noted in his opinion, "The poor do not necessarily cohabit on a bed of roses."

Statutes based on "irrebuttable" factual presumptions seem almost to invite the judicial use of social science. Justice Harlan once noted, "A statute based upon a legislative declaration of facts is subject to constitutional attack on the ground that the facts no longer exist; in ruling upon such a challenge a court must, of course be free to re-examine the factual declaration."[44] Social science findings can be employed by the Court to help determine a wide spectrum of issues ranging from such technical questions as economic standing to sue to such broader policy questions as multifaceted discrimination based on sex.[45] There would seem to be no limit to the number of issues on which social science findings can be potentially useful to courts. The adjudication of questions involving housing, busing, abortion, obscenity, criminal responsibility, sentencing procedures, capital punishment, and other great public issues call for resolution on the basis of empirical understanding. Traditionally, certain categories of people, such as minority groups, women, children, homosexuals, and mental patients, because of factual assumptions made about them have enjoyed less than the full protection of the law. Similarly, in total institutions like the army, schools, hospitals, and prisons, the Bill of Rights has operated in a very restricted fashion.

Legal change is generally inhibited by precedent, and for this reason policy decisions of the Court on questions concerning due process and equal protection, the most frequently invoked legal principles, will not be based ". . . on abstract logic but on empirical foundations."[46] Whether the Supreme Court ventures to make policy on troublesome public issues will depend on many factors. Judges may be rare animals but are no less concerned than other policymakers with the results of their decisions. Two kinds of judges—those who are ". . . result-orientated, and those who are also result-orientated but either do not know it or decline for various purposes to admit it."[47]—should be able to look to social science for understanding of the probable impact of decisions and the likelihood of compliance. Social science, which often teaches that things are not as they seem, can influence judicial assumptions in all these respects, but this requires an improved dialogue between the two disciplines.

Notes

1. Alexis de Tocqueville, *Democracy in America*, ed. Phillips Bradley (New York: Vintage Books, 1961), vol. 1, p. 290.

2. *Marbury* v. *Madison*, 1 Cranch 137 (1803).

3. Paul L. Rosen, *The Supreme Court and Social Science* (Urbana: The University of Illinois Press, 1972), pp. 23-66.

4. *Muller* v. *Oregon*, 208 U.S. 412 (1908).

5. Ibid., p. 412.

6. Ibid., p. 420.

7. Ibid., pp. 420-21.

8. Rosen, *The Supreme Court*, pp. 87-98.

9. *Adkins* v. *Children's Hospital*, 261 U.S. 525, 560 (1923).

10. Quoted in Alpheus T. Mason, *The Supreme Court From Taft to Warren* (New York: W.W. Norton, 1964), p. 31.

11. *Brown* v. *Board of Education*, 347 U.S. 483 (1954).

12. *Plessy* v. *Ferguson,* 163 U.S. 537 (1896).

13. Ibid., pp. 199-200.

14. "Appendix to Appellants' Briefs: Statements by Social Scientists," reprinted in *Social Problems* 2 (1955), pp. 227, 230.

15. Ibid., p. 231.

16. *Brown* v. *Board of Education*, 347 U.S. 483, 494 (1954).

17. Ibid.

18. Ibid.

19. Rosen, *The Supreme Court*, pp. 173-96.

20. "Lawyers, Sociologists Debate Busing," *The New York Times*, December 7, 1975, p. 62. Cf. also Eleanor P. Wolf, "Social Science and the Courts: The Detroit Schools Case," *The Public Interest* 42 (1976), p. 102.

21. Kenneth B. Clark and Mamie Clark, "Racial Identification and Prefer-

ence in Negro Children," in Newcomb et al. (eds.), *Readings in Social Psychology* (New York: Henry Holt, 1947), pp. 169-78.

22. Max Deutscher and Isidor Chein, "The Psychological Effects of Enforced Segregation: A Survey of Social Science Opinion," *Journal of Psychology* 26 (1948), p. 259.

23. See I.A. Newby, *Challenge to the Court: Social Scientists and the Defense of Segregation, 1954-1966* (Baton Rouge: Louisiana State University Press, 1967).

24. James Marshall, *Law and Psychology in Conflict* (Garden City: Anchor Books, 1969), p. ix.

25. Jean-Jacques Rousseau, "Discourse on the Sciences and Arts," in R.D. Masters (ed.), *The First and Second Discourses* (New York: St. Martin's Press, 1964).

26. Oliver Wendell Holmes, *Collected Legal Papers* (New York: Peter Smith, 1952), p. 230.

27. Geoffrey C. Hazard, "Limitations on the Uses of Behavioral Science in the Law," *Case Western Reserve Law Review* 19 (1967), p. 71.

28. I am indebted to Martin A. Schwartz, attorney with the Legal Aid Society of Westchester County, for his valuable discussion of this matter and some of the material that follows.

29. *Sources and Uses of Social and Economic Data: A Manual for Lawyers* (Washington, D.C.: Bureau of Social Science Research, Inc., 1973).

30. Benjamin Cardozo, "A Ministry of Justice," *Harvard Law Review* 35 (1921), p. 113.

31. *Quong Wing* v. *Kirkendall*, 223 U.S. 59, 64 (1921).

32. Martin A. Schwartz, letter to author, February 20, 1976.

33. Mirjan Damaska, "Presentation of Evidence and Fact Finding Precision," *University of Pennsylvania Law Review* 123 (1975), pp. 1083, 1091.

34. Marvin E. Wolfgang, "The Social Scientist in Court," *The Journal of Criminal Law and Criminology* 65 (1974), pp. 239, 241.

35. "Oral Argument," in Leon Friedman (ed.), *Argument: The Oral Argument before the Supreme Court in Brown v. Board of Education of Topeka, 1952-55* (New York: Chelsea House, 1969), p. 65.

36. Cf. Manfred Rehbinder, "The Development and Present State of Fact Research in Law in the United States," *Journal of Legal Education* 24 (1972), p. 567.

37. Victor G. Rosenblum, "A Place for Social Science Along the Judiciary's Constitutional Frontier," *Northwestern University Law Review* 66 (1971), p. 455.

38. Nathan Glazer, "Towards an Imperial Judiciary?" *The Public Interest* 41 (1975), pp. 104, 116.

39. *United States* v. *Krass*, 409 U.S. 434 (1973).

40. Ibid., p. 449.

41. Ibid., p. 460.

42. *Hurley* v. *Van Lare*, 380 F. Supp. 167 (S. and E.D.N.Y. 1974). Currently under review by the Supreme Court.

43. Ibid., trial transcript, p. 56.

44. *Leary* v. *United States*, 395 U.S. 6, 55 (1969).

45. Rosenblum, "A Place for Social Science," pp. 463-78.

46. *Katzenbach* v. *Morgan*, 384 U.S. 641, 688 (1966).

47. J. Braxton Craven, Jr., "Paean to Pragmatism," *North Carolina Law Review* 50 (1972), p. 977.

10

Research Funds and Advisers: The Relationship between Academic Social Science and the Federal Government

Michael Useem

The national government relies extensively on the private sector for the conduct of state business. Defense firms produce armaments for the military, private medicine assists in the delivery of state-supported health services, and community organizations conduct federally funded antipoverty programs.[1] Government strategy for the production of social knowledge has been no different. Although some research is administered internally, federal agencies have generally depended on the private sector, notably academic social science, for the delivery of needed social research.[2] Of the $329 million invested in social research by the government in 1970, for instance, 43 percent went to investigators in academic settings.[3]

While the "... behavioral sciences ... are an essential and increasingly relevant instrument of modern government,"[4] academic social science is not oriented toward serving as an "instrument" of state administration. If there is a dominant orientation to its activities and organization, it is the advance of basic social scientific knowledge. The divergence in the research goals of the government and academic social science poses serious problems for federal efforts to mobilize the resources of academic social research for state ends.

An initial barrier to mobilization—reluctance of academic investigators to consider engaging in applied social research—has been largely overcome by academe's condition of economic dependency. The standards of modern research dictate sophisticated designs with costs far above those that can be met through self-financing. At the same time, relatively generous sums of research money have been made available by the federal government. Indeed, in recent years the national government has acquired a near-monopoly position in the external finance market faced by academic investigators. In 1970, two-fifths of all expenditures for social research conducted in colleges and universities were obtained from federal agencies.[5] Academic social science has had little choice but to enter a dialogue with the government.

A willingness to consider accepting federal sponsorship does not inherently carry with it an acceptance of government research objectives. A second barrier to government mobilization is the academic community's preexisting commitment to the pursuit of academic questions rather than policy issues. Academic

This chapter is based on a larger research project supported in part by grants from the U.S. Office of Education/National Institute of Education and the Spencer Foundation. The research assistance of Pamela Bulloch, Harriet Gluckman, and Priscilla John, and Norma Panico is gratefully acknowledged.

125

social science would allocate available research resources to the advance of the academic disciplines, not the promotion of government programs. The government would invest its money in the pursuit of government interests, not the assistance of social science for its own sake. However, the mutual interdependence of government and academe ensures that some compromise among these conflicting objectives will be sought. Whether the solution is more favorable to the interests of one party or the other is a matter of their relative political strengths and the bargaining strategies available.[6]

Observation of the actual distribution of federal research funds can indicate whether the political relationship is more favorable to government agencies or the academic disciplines. The first would imply that the government is securing a useful return on its investment in academe, while the latter would imply that academic social science has successfully diverted state resources to its own purposes.

A critical institutionalized link between federal agencies and the academic community is the government advisory system. Academic social scientists serve in a variety of formal advisory positions with the government, and their recommendations and evaluations often play an important role in the allocation of federal research funds and the application of research results.[7] Academic social science would select advisers who are likely to protect its interests, while the government would choose advisers who are prone to advance the government's interests. Study of the actual distribution of government advisory positions among academic social scientists can, therefore, also help establish whether the government-academe relationship is more advantageous to the former or the latter. Certain types of advisers would assist the government's mobilization of the academic social sciences for its research objectives. Other kinds of advisers would aid the social science disciplines' mobilization of government resources for their own ends.

Research Design

The primary data are from a questionnaire survey of social scientists in the disciplines of anthropology, economics, political science, and psychology. The population consists of the academic members listed in the most recent directory of the major professional associations representing the four disciplines.[8] A random sample of 500 was drawn from each of the discipline directories, and an initial twelve-page form was sent in December 1973. Four months later, after a second mailing of the questionnaire and a final follow-up letter, 1,079 usable responses had been obtained, for a return rate of 54 percent.[9] Comparison of the respondents and nonrespondents revealed no significant association between likelihood of response and the faculty member's rank, sex, year and type of graduate degree, professional status of the department of current appointment, and rate of citation to one's work. Profiles of the respondents and nonrespondents are sufficiently similar to warrant the assumption that respondents are reasonably representative of the study's population.

Principles of Research Money Allocation

Government agencies and academic disciplines would distribute research funds to different sets of people. Government strategy would be to support investigators likely to deliver results applicable to government policy formulation and program assessment. Academic discipline strategy would be to support researchers who will produce findings of greatest value to the advance of the discipline's scientific paradigm.

Discipline-Oriented Research

A social scientist's contribution to the development of the discipline's paradigm is a matter of the judgment to the discipline. Collegial evaluation is assessed through two indices.

The frequency with which a social scientist's research is referred to in the scholarly papers of other investigators can be viewed as a reflection of the social scientist's impact on the field. Highly cited authors are contributing more to the discipline's advance than are seldom-cited investigators. The frequency-of-citation is measured here by the number of citations a social scientist received in several hundred major social science journals during a recent twenty-month period. This index is labeled *citation rate.*[10]

A second indicator of the discipline's collective opinion is the number of professional society offices, journal editorships, and scholarly awards the discipline has bestowed on a social scientist. Summarizing these signs of professional recognition, a *professional achievement* index is constructed as an unweighted sum of the number of eight types of discipline decision-making positions and scholarly distinctions held or received by the social scientist.[11]

Government-Oriented Research

A social scientist's likely contribution to the formulation and execution of government policy is assessed through two other indicators. One is the social scientist's evaluation of the potential utility of his or her own research to the federal government. This indicator is assessed by a survey item inquiring whether the social scientist expected his or her research to benefit a variety of groups and institutions. A dichotomous *policy-relevance* index is based on whether the federal government was identified as one of the institutions likely to find the research useful. The proportion identifying the government as a potential beneficiary ranges from 15 percent in psychology to 39 percent in economics.[12]

A second measure assesses the quantitative orientation of the social scientist's research. Research based on large data sets collected under rigorous procedures and providing quantitative indicators of manipulable social factors is likely to be of greater value to federal agencies than would other types of social research.[13] The social scientists were asked whether their research during the past five years involved the "analysis of quantitative evidence," "statistical tests," or "computer aided analysis." The number of items reported forms a *quantitative-orientation* index.

The Distribution of Federal Funds

If the government is allocating research funds to academic social scientists according to its own priorities rather than those of the academic disciplines, sponsorship should be disproportionately received by those involved in policy-relevant quantitatively oriented investigations. Conversely, if academic social science has been effective in reorienting this federal resource to its own ends, highly cited and professionally recognized social scientists should be disproportionately funded.

The receipt of federal research funds is measured here by the scale of the largest research grant or contract, if any, the social scientist obtained from a federal agency during the previous five years. *Federal funds* is the log of the dollar amount of the largest government sponsorship, with no support coded as zero. Excluded from the following analysis were those social scientists who had not been engaged in any research or scholarly writing during the same five-year period (ranging from 2 percent of the anthropologists to 16 percent of the economists).

Simple correlations between the social scientist's research-orientation variables and obtaining federal funds are presented in Table 10-1. Coefficients are reported for each discipline separately and, using variables standardized by discipline, for all disciplines combined. It is apparent that all four research variables are substantially associated with the receipt of government under-writing in each discipline. The correlations range from .22 to .50 for citation rate, from .13 to .34 for professional achievement, from .25 to .33 for policy relevance, and from .25 to .42 for quantitative orientation.

The simultaneous influence of the research-orientation factors on receipt of federal funding is examined through multiple regression. The standardized regression coefficients are shown in Table 10-1. These beta coefficients indicate that both sets of factors independently structure the distribution of federal research money. Although the magnitude of the coefficients varies among the

Table 10-1
Simple Correlations and Standardized Regression Coefficients of Receipt of Federal Funds with the Research Orientations of Social Scientists

Research Orientations (Independent Variables)	Academic Discipline								All Disciplines[a]	
	Anthropology		Economics		Political Science		Psychology			
	r	β	r	β	r	β	r	β	r	β
Discipline-oriented research										
Citation rate	.416[c]	.352[c]	.268[c]	.174	.224[c]	.148	.502[c]	.400[c]	.358[c]	.265[c]
Professional achievement	.249[c]	.055	.221[b]	.187	.128[b]	.069	.343[c]	.103[b]	.236[c]	.099[b]
Government-oriented research										
Policy relevance	.260[c]	.189[c]	.334[c]	.265[c]	.250[c]	.192[b]	.301[c]	.210[c]	.282[c]	.206[c]
Quantitative orientation	.420[c]	.328[c]	.299[c]	.290[c]	.375[c]	.349[c]	.255[c]	.105	.341[c]	.275[c]
Multiple correlation coefficients	.589[c]		.513[c]		.460[c]		.571[c]		.520[c]	
Number of cases	(227)		(157)		(234)		(227)		(845)	

[a]Variables are standardized by discipline.
[b]Statistically significant at the .01 level.
[c]Statistically significant at the .001 level.

Note: The means, standard deviations, and intercorrelations of the four independent variables, with the disciplines combined, are as follows:

	Mean	S.D.	C	P	R	Q
C) Citation rate	1.67	1.76	—	.374	.100	.129
P) Professional achievement	1.78	1.46		—	.128	.040
R) Policy relevance	0.29	0.46			—	.132
Q) Quantitative orientation	1.65	1.30				—

disciplines, all coefficients are positive, with professional achievement showing the weakest independent influence and quantitative orientation demonstrating the strongest independent effect. For all disciplines combined, the beta value is .27 for citation rate, .10 for professional achievement, .21 for policy relevance, and .28 for quantitative orientation. The substantial predictive power of the four factors combined is reflected in the multiple correlation value of .52. The standardized regression coefficients are nearly the same even if those social scientists who had not applied for federal support during the previous five years are excluded from the analysis.

Significant variations in the structure of federal support for academic social science are possibly obscured by the aggregate character of the federal funds variable. This possibility can be tested by considering several divisions in the federal funding system that are presumably strongly related to whether the support is oriented toward producing knowledge for the discipline or for the government. One such division is that between research grants and contracts. Grants involve considerable latitude in problem selection and research design for the interested faculty member, while the government preestablishes many of the research parameters in the contract. Another comparable division is between financing by the National Science Foundation (NSF) and by other federal agencies. The central mandate of the National Science Foundation has been the support of basic scientific research, and it alone among the granting agencies has had no major social programs of its own.

To examine the possible variation between NSF and non-NSF support, the federal funds variable is divided into NSF money versus that of all other agencies, and all disciplines are combined for the analysis (all variables are standardized by discipline). In the case of NSF financing, the discipline-oriented research factors together are, as expected, stronger independent predictors of funding than are the government-oriented research factors. The standardized regression coefficients for the impact of citation rate and professional achievement are .22 and $-.02$; the coefficients for the impact of policy relevance and quantitative orientation are .05 and .14. Also, as anticipated, the reverse holds for non-NSF federal financing. The beta coefficients for the citation rate and professional achievement variables are .13 and .12, while the coefficients for policy relevance and quantitative orientation variables are both .18. Thus, the National Science Foundation places less of a premium on applied research for the government than on basic research in allocating its money, but at least the quantitative orientation remains a significant consideration. Similarly, other agencies give greater emphasis to criteria of government utility than discipline utility in allocating their funds, but even here basic research is not ignored.

The possibly variant methods of allocating grants and contracts are examined for sponsorship by federal agencies other than the National Science Foundation. Though the precise shape of the distribution varies by discipline, contract recipients are somewhat more likely to be involved in policy-relevant research than are grant recipients. There are no systematic differences in the citation rate, professional achievement, and quantitative orientation of the two groups. Furthermore, grantees and contractors are more similar to each other than to nonrecipients. With all disciplines combined, the proportion of nonrecipients, grant recipients, and contract recipients with one or more citations are 49, 71, and 65 percent, respectively; the corresponding proportions with two or more professional distinctions are 44, 62, and 66 percent. Similarly, the proportion of nonrecipients, grant recipients, and contract recipients involved in policy-oriented research are 23, 33, and 54 percent, respectively; and the corresponding proportions scoring the highest level of quantitative orientation are 30, 54, and 53 percent.

It appears that there are important differences in the allocation of NSF and non-NSF money and in the dispensing of grant and contract support. Nonetheless, the differences are generally overshadowed by a relatively invariant preferential funding of academic social scientists whose work facilitates either state planning or discipline advancement. The evidence indicates that the national government is distributing research funds among academic social scientists in a fashion likely to produce research of utility to both federal agencies and academic disciplines.

Principles of Advisory Position Allocation

Federal agencies draw on the advisory services of a large number of academic social scientists. Faculty members serve on formal advisory boards, as regular and occasional consultants, and on panels that review research proposals. Academic social scientists who serve in any of these capacities are termed *advisers*. Government agencies select their advisers, though normally not without some informal consultation with members of the academic disciplines.[14] From the standpoint of the research objectives of the government and academic social science, different types of advisers are preferable. Effective advisers for the government are those who maximize mobilization of the academic research capacity for federal ends. By contrast, effective advisers for academic social science are those who mobilize government resources for the advance of basic social research.

Discipline-Oriented Adviser

The interests of the academic disciplines would be advanced if the advisers are drawn from the ranks of academics who are best informed on the research frontiers of the field. Their input on the topics and individual researchers the government should support would be highly congruent with the priorities of the disciplinary paradigms. A social scientist's ability to offer a sensitive and discriminating judgment of these issues is likely to be a function of his or her involvement in the leading research of the discipline. This likelihood can be assessed through the previously described indices of citation rate and professional achievement.

Government-Oriented Adviser

From the government's vantage point, useful advisers are those who can provide detailed information on the areas and individuals in academic social science that are most likely to yield policy-related research if funded. Those who can help translate research findings into social policy would be valued as well. The input of such advisers would contribute to the realization of government research priorities.

Social scientists best prepared to offer informed opinion on the government-related research potential of academe are those whose own research is similar to that which finds application in government programs. Compared with other academics, social scientists engaged in government-oriented research are more able to render a discerning judgment on the people and proposals that should receive backing, the areas and methods that deserve additional investment, and the policy implications of existing research. Engagement in government-related research is assessed by the previously developed policy-relevance and quantitative-orientation indices.

The government faces an additional problem in mobilizing academic research that dictates another consideration in the selection of advisers. The system of government research financing requires at least a modicum of legitimacy within the recipient community. The purposes, administration, and impact of government sponsorship must be perceived by academics as relatively desirable, fair, and appropriate, especially in light of the divergence in government and academic research objectives. The appointment of prominent and respected members of the discipline would help achieve this goal. Their advisory service creates the appearance that government research policies and funding decisions are receiving significant input from academic social science, thereby making acceptance of a government grant and the denial of a grant request more palatable. Elite cooperation with the government sanctions rank-and-file cooperation and thus facilitates federal enlistment of academics who might otherwise resist working on applied topics.

The professional achievement index would be a suitable measure of the stature of a social scientist, but it is already serving as a measure of an academic's discipline-oriented advisory potential. However, it has been seen in the case of funding allocation that professional achievement played a comparatively minor role compared to citation rate. Professional achievement, relative to citation rate, if proven to be a relatively small predictor of advisory service, would indicate little tendency for advisers to be selected for their legitimizing function. On the other hand, professional achievement, if shown significantly greater in strength in the distribution of advisory positions than in the allocation of funds, would imply that the symbolic value of an academic's high stature is emphasized in the selection process.

The Distribution of Federal Advisory Positions

Service as a government adviser is represented by the variable *federal adviser*, which is based on whether the social scientist served during the previous five years as a member of a federal grant review panel or study group, a member of an advisory board or group, a regular consultant, or an occasional consultant (e.g., field reviewer of a grant proposal). The social scientists are divided into those holding none, one, and two or more advisory positions; the percentages with at least one advisory capacity are 43 in anthropology, 22 in economics and political science, and 33 in psychology.

The simple correlations of the four predictor variables with federal adviser are shown in Table 10-2. Citation rate and professional achievement are generally more strongly associated with federal adviser than are policy relevance and quantitative orientation. Standardized regression coefficients for the independent effects of the predictor variables are also shown in Table 10-2. All coefficients are positive, thereby indicating that the four factors independently structure the distribution of advisory positions in the expected direction. Although there is some variation by discipline, citation rate and professional achievement are generally the two strongest factors; their beta coefficients with all disciplines combined are .21 and .25, respectively. Policy relevance and quantitative orientation are considerably weaker predictors, though their role is not insignificant; the beta values for the combined disciplines are .10 and .08. The multiple correlation of .42 indicates that these four factors together are substantially discriminating between those asked to serve as advisers and those not invited.

The distribution of advisory positions is similar to the distribution of research funds, though there are differences in emphasis. Three of the variables prove less important in the case of advisory positions than funds: citation rate (betas of .21 and .27), policy relevance (.10 and .21), and quantitative orientation (.08 and .28). By contrast, professional achievement is more important in the selection of advisers than in the selection of grant and contract recipients (.25 and .10). It would appear that a social scientist's involvement in government-related research is only a moderate consideration in inviting the person to serve as an adviser. More important is the engagement of the social scientist in discipline-related research, although this factor is less salient in

Table 10-2
Simple Correlations and Standardized Regression Coefficients of Federal Adviser Service with Four Social Scientist Attributes

Social Scientist Attributes	Academic Discipline								All Disciplines[a]	
	Anthropology		Economics		Political Science		Psychology			
(Independent Variables)	r	β	r	β	r	β	r	β	r	β
Citation rate	.298[c]	.207[c]	.350[c]	.275[c]	.313[c]	.204[c]	.327[c]	.187[b]	.320[c]	.212[c]
Professional achievement	.302[c]	.204[b]	.291[c]	.223[b]	.361[c]	.271[c]	.389[c]	.289[c]	.340[c]	.248[c]
Policy relevance	.118	.080	.150	.082	.192[c]	.137	.162[b]	.063	.156[c]	.097[b]
Quantitative orientation	.182[b]	.130	.123	.142	.031	.031	.120	.036	.113[c]	.076
Multiple correlation coefficient	.396[c]		.437[c]		.434[c]		.434[c]		.420[c]	
Number of Cases	(259)		(183)		(264)		(261)		(967)	

[a]Variables are standardized by discipline.
[b]Statistically significant at the .01 level.
[c]Statistically significant at the .001 level.

selecting advisers than in funding investigators. Of particular salience in choosing advisers, compared with selecting grant and contract recipients, is the social scientist's professional stature.[15] Overall, these patterns suggest that the national government is distributing its advisory positions among academic social scientists such that the advisory system input furthers the research goals of both the government and academic disciplines.

It also appears that the advisory system will help legitimize the federal funding system in the academic community. In an extension of this study not detailed here, it is found that among social scientists not serving as advisers, respect for those who do serve is associated with confidence in the programs of government sponsorship. Nonadviser social scientists who see advisers as effectively representing their discipline's interests also tend to view the government funding system as furthering the interests of basic social science and as an institution with which collaborative work is appropriate. It would thus appear that placement of high status academics in advisory positions tends to increase the legitimacy of government's underwriting of academic research. Confidence in the sponsorship system is found to be even more prevalent among the advisers than nonadvisers, and if the advisers' attitudes are widely communicated, as is likely given their eminence and visible association with the government, confidence in the system will be further enhanced.

The problem of retaining academic confidence is a product of the divergence between academic and government research objectives. This gap is less pronounced in the case of the National Science Foundation than for other agencies. It has already been noted that NSF research funds are more likely to be received by discipline-oriented investigators than are non-NSF funds. Compared with citation rate, then, professional achievement is expected to be a more significant element in the allocation of non-NSF advisory positions than NSF posts. This expectation is examined by combining all disciplines and dividing the federal adviser variable into NSF and non-NSF components. The standardized regression coefficients for the effect of citation rate are .21 for NSF and .14 for non-NSF advisory positions, while the corresponding figures for professional achievement are .15 and .23. As expected, the professional achievement dimension is weaker than the citation rate in the selection of NSF advisers but is stronger in the selection of non-NSF advisers.

Discussion

The allocation of advisory positions follows principles similar to those structuring the distribution of research funds. The relative importance of these principles differs by discipline, agency, and whether the resource is money or positions, but at least some application of the principles is evident in all areas. These patterns suggest that the government is obtaining a useful return on its considerable investment in academic research. Yet, this reliance on the private sector for the delivery of needed social research is not without its costs. Substantial government funds are skewed toward academic investigators whose research is valued by professional colleagues, but is of little interest to policymakers. Similarly, advisory positions are often filled with social scientists whose loyalties lie more with the academic discipline than the federal agency.

Although losses for the government, these allocations constitute gains for the social science community. Essential resources not otherwise available are acquired by academic social science on its own terms. But there are disadvantages for the academic disciplines as well. A substantial fraction of their research capacity is oriented toward government-related research of marginal relevance to the central concerns of basic social science. Moreover, the external financial stimulus expands government-related fields and reduces others. This process leads to the gradual and largely irreversible incorporation of political criteria into the discipline's paradigms. There are likely to be more permanent and far-reaching changes in the character of the social science disciplines than in the government.

The academic community generally weighs these considerations in favor of continuing its relationship with the government. Among the social scientists included in this study, over two-thirds supported the government's involvement in financing the production, distribution, and utilization of social science knowledge. This involvement is endorsed despite the implication of a government voice in the research affairs of the academic discipline. Indeed, only a small minority of the social scientists felt that their discipline would be best served by excluding the government from any role in setting research priorities. Half agreed with the view that their field would be best advanced if the government and discipline actively collaborated in establishing research goals. And strong majorities of the social scientists felt that it was important for federal agencies to fund grant applicants in part according to the relevance of the proposals to agency interests. The government-academic exchange relationship is far from universally accepted in academe, but there is a relatively favorable climate of opinion. Despite the intrusion of political considerations into scientific decision making, academic social scientists generally hold that their relationship with the state is desirable in principle and acceptable in the form practiced during recent years.

Federal agencies apparently also conclude that the advantages of contracting with a private institution for the production of needed research outweigh the costs. It is possible that what seems disadvantageous—the investment of resources in irrelevant research—is not so in fact. This investment could stem from the view that valuable applied research is only produced if a viable fundamental research tradition exists, as is often claimed as a reason for federal underwriting of basic physical science research. It is also possible that the government's role in American society is to ensure the availability of public goods that private institutions are incapable of producing if left to their own means. Government sponsorship of basic social research, then, simply represents a state commitment to maintain a valuable cultural institution that would otherwise languish.

On careful examination, however, such explanations prove less adequate than an alternative interpretation based on the premise that the backing of social science for its own sake represents a cost to the government but one that is necessitated by its dependence on academe. College-based social scientists possess the latent power of threatening to withhold their services from the government. Unlike organized labor, this threat is not explicitly articulated in the form of union-sanctioned strikes. But it need not be, for social scientists may simply refrain from entering the government finance market if the conditions are too unattractive. Generally, they can do so without reprisals, termination of academic employment, or loss of the capacity to conduct at least inexpensive research. Moreover, noncooperation is encouraged by the social science paradigms that prescribe research topics advancing the paradigm and that proscribe other lines of investigation. This resistance, however, can be undermined by improving the conditions that characterize the government-academe exchange relationship. Placing a significant fraction of the government's resources at the disposal of academe represents a fundamental improvement in conditions. In exchange for the opportunity to pursue funded research areas of its own choosing, the academic community is then prepared to take on funded research topics of the government's choosing. Support of social science for its own sake is the price of mobilizing academic research for the government's sake.

Notes

1. Bruce L.R. Smith and D.C. Hague, *The Dilemma of Accountability in Modern Government: Independence versus Control* (New York: St. Martin's Press, 1971). State contracting for the private production of science and art in the United States is discussed in Michael Useem, "Government Patronage of Science and Art in America," *American Behavioral Scientist* 19 (July 1976), pp. 785-804.

2. Gene M. Lyons, *The Uneasy Partnership: Social Science and the Government in the Twentieth Century* (New York: Russell Sage, 1969); Harold Orlans, *Contracting for Knowledge: Values and Limitations of Social Science Research* (San Francisco: Jossey-Bass, 1973).

3. Derived from National Science Foundation, *Federal Funds for Research, Development and Other Scientific Activities, Fiscal Years 1970, 1971, and 1972* (Washington, D.C.: U.S. Government Printing Office), and National Science Foundation, *Resources for Scientific Activities at Universities and Colleges, 1971* (Washington, D.C.: U.S. Government Printing Office, 1972).

4. National Research Council, *The Behavioral Sciences and the Federal Government* (Washington, D.C.: National Academy of Sciences, 1968), p. 17.

138

5. National Science Foundation, *Resources for Scientific Activities at Universities and Colleges, 1971* (Washington, D.C.: U.S. Government Printing Office, 1972), pp. 46, 83.

6. Richard M. Emerson, "Power-Dependence Relations," *American Sociological Review* 27 (February 1962), pp. 31-41.

7. Thane Gustafson, "The Controversy over Peer Review," *Science* 190 (December 12, 1975), pp. 1060-66.

8. American Anthropological Association, 1973; American Economic Association, 1970; American Political Science Association, 1973; American Psychological Association, 1973.

9. The response rate was 43, 44, 58, and 61 percent in anthropology, economics, political science, and psychology, respectively. The overall response rate of 54 percent is comparable to response rates obtained in other studies of similar populations using similar instruments and follow-up procedures. See, for instance, Alan E. Bayer, "Teaching Faculty in Academe: 1972-1973," *ACE Research Reports* 8 (Washington, D.C.: American Council on Education, 1973).

10. The period is 1972 and the first eight months of 1973. The citation rate is based on the Social Science Citation Index, which covers over 440 journals in the social sciences. The validity of the citation rate index as a measure of scholarly contribution is well established; see, for instance, Jonathan R. Cole and Stephen Cole, "Measuring the Quality of Sociological Research: Problems in the Use of the Science Citation Index," *American Sociologist* 6 (February 1971), pp. 23-29; Daryl Chubin, "On the Use of the Science Citation Index in Sociology," *American Sociologist* 8 (November 1973), pp. 187-91.

11. Four or more positions or honors are scored as four.

12. The question was: "Apart from your own discipline, do you hope that your research and publishing over the past five years will directly or indirectly benefit any of the following: [17 potential beneficiaries are listed, including 'The Federal Government']." The validity of this measure is established in Michael Useem, "State Production of Social Knowledge: Patterns in Government Financing of Academic Social Research," *American Sociological Review* 41 (August 1976), pp. 613-29.

13. E.M. Allen, "Why Are Research Grant Applications Disapproved?" *Science* 132 (November 25, 1969), pp. 1532-34; John F. Galliher and James L. McCartney, "The Influence of Funding Agencies on Juvenile Delinquency Research," *Social Problems* 21 (Summer 1973), pp. 77-90; James L. McCartney, "On Being Scientific: Changing Styles of Presentation of Sociological Research," *American Sociologist* 5 (February 1970), pp. 30-35.

14. National Research Council, *The Science Committee* (Washington, D.C.: National Academy of Sciences, 1972), Appendix E.

15. Other studies of scientific advisers with the National Science Foundation, Public Health Service, and National Research Council reveal a similar

emphasis on professional stature. Advisers with these organizations are considerably older than other members of their disciplines (age is related to professional distinction), and they are disproportionately located on the faculties of a small number of elite universities. National Research Council, *The Science Committee* (Washington, D.C.: National Academy of Sciences, 1972), and Lyle Groeneveld, Normal Koller, and Nicholas C. Mullins, "The Advisors of the United States National Science Foundation," *Social Studies of Science* 5 (August 1975), pp. 343-54.

11

In Search of Impact: An Analysis of the Utilization of Federal Health Evaluation Research

Michael Q. Patton, Patricia Smith Grimes, Kathryn M. Guthrie, Nancy J. Brennan, Barbara Dickey French, and Dale A. Blyth

The Issue of Nonutilization

The problem of the nonutilization or the underutilization of evaluation research has been discussed frequently in the evaluation literature. There seems to be a consensus that the impact of evaluative research on program decision making has been less than substantial. Carol Weiss (1972) lists underutilization as one of the foremost problems in evaluation research:

Evaluation research is meant for immediate and direct use in improving the quality of social programming. Yet a review of evaluation experience suggests that evaluation results have not exerted significant influence on program decisions [pp. 10, 11].

Other prominent reviewers have reached a similar conclusion. Ernest House (1972, p. 412) put it this way: "Producing data is one thing! Getting it used is quite another." Williams and Evans (1969, p. 453) write that ". . . in the final analysis, the test of the effectiveness of outcome data is its impact on implemented policy. By this standard, there is a dearth of successful evaluation studies." Wholey (1971, p. 46) concluded that ". . . the recent literature is unanimous in announcing the general failure of evaluation to affect decision-making in a significant way." He goes on to note that his own study ". . . found the same absence of successful evaluations noted by other authors" (p. 48). David Cohen (1975, p. 19) finds that ". . . there is little evidence to indicate that government planning offices have succeeded in linking social research and decisionmaking." Alkin (1974) found that Title VII evaluations were useful to project directors but were not useful at the federal level because the results were not timely in terms of funding decisions. Weidman et al. (1973, p. 15) concluded that on those rare occasions when evaluation studies have been used, ". . . the little use that has occurred [has been] fortuitous rather than planned."

This research was conducted as part of an NIMH-supported training program in evaluation methodology at the University of Minnesota. Trainees worked through the Minnesota Center for Social Research, University of Minnesota. The following trainees, in addition to the authors, participated in the project: James Cleary, Joan Dreyer, James Fitzsimmons, Steve Froman, Kathy Gilder, David Jones, Leah Harvey, Gary Miller, Gail Nordheim, Julia Nutter, Darla Sandhofer, Jerome Segal, and John Townsend. In addition, the following Minnesota faculty made helpful comments on an earlier draft of this chapter: John Brandl, Director, School of Public Affairs; Martha Burt, Tom Dewar, and Ron Geizer. Neala Yount transcribed over one hundred hours of interviews with unusual diligence and care.

Decisionmakers continue to lament the disappointing results of evaluation research, complaining that the findings don't tell them what they need to know. And evaluators continue to complain about many things, ". . . but their most common complaint is that their findings are ignored" (Weiss, 1972, p. 319).

The issue at this time is not the search for a single formula of utilization success, nor the generation of ever-longer lists of possible factors affecting utilization. *The task for the present is to identify and refine a few key variables that may make a major difference in a significant number of evaluation cases* (cf. Weiss, 1972, p. 325). The research on utilization of evaluations described in this chapter is a modest effort to move a bit further along that path of refinement.

This chapter is based on a follow-up of twenty federal health evaluations. We attempted to assess the degree to which these evaluations had been used and to identify the factors that affected varying degrees of utilization. Given the pessimistic nature of most writings on utilization, we began our study fully expecting our major problem would be to find even one evaluation that had had a significant impact on program decisions. What we found was considerably more complex and less dismal than our original impressions led us to expect. Evaluation research is used but not in the ways we had anticipated. Moreover, we found that the factors we had expected would be important in explaining variations in utilization were less important than a new factor that emerged from our analysis. After reviewing our sample and methodology, we shall report these findings and discuss their implications.

The Sample

The twenty case studies that constitute the sample in this study are national health program evaluations. They were selected from among 170 evaluations on file in the Office of Health Evaluation, HEW.[1] We excluded policy pieces, think pieces, and arm-chair reflections from our analysis. We also eliminated studies that did not examine national programs and any studies completed before 1971 or after 1973. We did this to enable a follow-up of evaluations that were recent enough to be remembered and at the same time had been completed far enough in the past to allow time for utilization to occur. These control variables reduced the number of abstracts from 170 to 76 and gave us a more homogeneous group of abstracts consisting of (1) program evaluation studies of (2) national scope where (3) some systematic data collection was done and (4) where the study was completed no earlier than 1971 and no later than 1973.

A stratified random sample of twenty studies was then drawn from among the remaining seventy-six abstracts. They consist of four evaluations of various community mental health center program activities, four health training programs, two national assessments of laboratory proficiency, two evaluations of neighborhood health center programs, studies of two health services delivery system programs, a training program on alcoholism, a health regulatory program, a federal loan forgiveness program, a training workshop evaluation, and two evaluations of specialized health facilities.

Since it is impossible to specify the universe of evaluation research studies, it is not possible to specify the degree to which this sample of twenty cases is representative of evaluation research in general. The sample is diverse in its inclusion of a broad range of evaluations. We feel that this heterogeneity increases the meaningfulness of those patterns of utilization that actually emerged in our follow-up interviews because those patterns were not systematically related to specific types of evaluations.

Data on Utilization: The Interviews

The first purpose of this study is to examine the nature and degree of *utilization* of federal evaluation research. Very limited resources allowed for interviewing only three key informants about the utilization of each of the twenty cases in the final sample. These key informants were (1) the project officer[2] for the study, (2) the person *identified by the project officer* as being either the decisionmaker for the program evaluated or the person most knowledgeable about the study's impact.[3] and (3) the evaluator who had major responsibility for the study.

The project officer interviews were conducted primarily to identify informants, decisionmakers, and evaluators who would be interviewed. This snowball sampling technique resulted in considerable variation in whom we interviewed as the "decisionmakers" in each case. Most of the government informants had been or now are office directors (and deputy directors), division heads, or bureau chiefs. Overall, these decisionmakers each represent an average of over fourteen years' experience in the federal government. Evaluators in our sample each represent an average of nearly fourteen years' experience in conducting evaluative research.

Two forms of the interview were developed: one for government decisionmakers and one for evaluators. Both interviews were open-ended and ranged in length from one to six hours, with an average of about two hours.[4]

Impact of Evaluation Research

The conceptualization and operationalization of the notion of *research impact* or *evaluation utilization* is no easy task. We began with an ideal-typical construct of utilization as *immediate and concrete effect on specific decisions and program activities resulting directly from evaluative research findings*. Yet, as noted earlier, the consensus in the evaluation literature is that instances of such impact are relatively rare. Because we expected little evidence of impact and because of our inability to agree on an operational definition of utilization, we adopted an open-ended strategy in our interviewing that allowed respondents to define utilization in terms meaningful to them. Our question was as follows:

Now we'd like to focus on the *actual* impact of this evaluation study. We'd like to get at *any* ways in which the study may have had an impact—an impact on program operations, on planning, on funding, on policy, on decisions, on thinking about the program, and so forth. From your point of view, what was the impact of this evaluation study on the program we've been discussing?

Following a set of probes and additional questions, depending upon the respondents' initial answers, we asked a question about the nonprogram impacts of the evaluation:

We've been focusing mainly on the study's impact on the program itself. Sometimes studies have a broader impact on things beyond an immediate program, things like *general thinking on issues that arise from a study*, or *position papers*, or *legislation.* . . . Did this evaluation have an impact on any of these kinds of things?

What we found in response to these questions on impact was considerably more complex and less dismal than our original thinking had led us to expect. We found that evaluation research *is used* by decisionmakers but not in the clear-cut and organization-shaking ways that social scientists sometimes believe research should be used. The problem we have come to feel may well lie more in many social scientists' overly grand expectations about their own importance to policy decisions than in the intransience of federal bureaucrats. The results of our interviews suggest that what is typically characterized as underutilization or nonutilization of evaluation research can be attributed in substantial degrees to a definition of utilization that is too narrow and fails to take into consideration the nature of actual decision-making processes in most programs.

The Findings on Impact

In response to the first question on impact, fourteen of eighteen responding decisionmakers and thirteen of fourteen responding evaluators felt that the evaluation had had an impact on the program. (Two of the decisionmakers and six of the evaluators felt that they had too little direct knowledge of actual use to comment.) Moreover, thirteen of sixteen responding decisionmakers and nine of thirteen responding evaluators felt these specific evaluation studies had had identifiable nonprogram impacts.

The number of positive responses to the questions on impact are quite striking when one considers the predominance of the theme of nonutilization in the evaluation literature. The main difference here, however, may be that the actual participants in each specific evaluation process were asked to define impact in terms that were meaningful to them and their situations. Thus, none of the impacts described was of the type where new findings from an evaluation led directly and immediately to the making of major, concrete program decisions. *The more typical impact was one where the evaluation findings provided additional pieces of information in the difficult puzzle of program action, thereby permitting some reduction in the uncertainty within which any federal decisionmaker inevitably operates.*

The most dramatic example of utilization reported in our sample was the case of an evaluation of a pilot program. The program administrator had been favorable to the program in principle, was uncertain what the results would be, but was "hoping the results would be positive." The evaluation proved to be negative. The administrator was "surprised, but not alarmingly so. . . . We had expected a more positive finding or we would not have engaged in the pilot studies" (DM367:13).[5] The program was subsequently ended with the evaluation carrying "about a third of the weight of the total decision" (DM367:8).

This relatively dramatic impact stood out as a clear exception to the more typical pattern where evaluation findings constitute an additional input into an ongoing, evolutionary process of program action. One decisionmaker with twenty-nine years' experience in the federal government, much of that time directing research, gave the following report on the impact of the evaluation study about which he was interviewed:

It served two purposes. One is that it resolved a lot of doubts and confusions and misunderstandings that the advisory committee had. . . . And the second one was that it gave me additional knowledge to support facts that I already knew, and, as I say, broadened the scope more than I realized. In other words, the perceptions of where the organization was going and what it was accomplishing were a lot worse than I had anticipated . . . , but I was somewhat startled to find out that they were worse, yet it wasn't very hard because it was partly confirming things that I was observing [DM232:17].

He goes on to say that following the evaluation:

. . . we changed our whole functional approach to looking at the identification of what we should be working on. But again I have a hard time because these things, *none of these things occurred overnight, and in an evolutionary process it's hard to say, you know, at what point it made a significant difference or what point did it merely verify and strengthen the resolve that you already had"* [DM232:17].

His overall assessment of the actual impact of the evaluation was quite constrained: "It filled in the gaps and pieces that various ones really had in their orientation to the program" (DM232:12), and "It verified my suspicions" (DM232:24).

Respondents frequently had difficulty assessing the degree to which an evaluation study actually affected decisions. This was true, for example, in the case of a large-scale evaluation effort that had been extremely expensive and had taken place over several years' time. The evaluation found some deficiencies in the program, but the overall findings were quite positive. Changes corresponding to those recommended in the study occurred when the report was published, but those changes could not be directly and simply attributed to the evaluation:

The staff was aware that the activities in the centers were deficient from other studies that we had done, and they were beefing up these budgets and providing technical assistance to some of the projects and improving health activities. Now I can't link this finding and that activity. Again that confirms that finding and you say, eureka, I have found ____ deficient, therefore I will [change] the program. That didn't happen. [The] deficiency was previously noted. A lot of studies like this confirmed what close-by people know and they were already taking actions before the findings. *So you can't link the finding to the action, that's just confirmation. ... The direct link between the finding and the program decision is very diffuse.* [Its major impact was] confirming our setting, a credibility, a tone of additional credibility to the program [DM361:12,13].

Moreover, this decisionmaker felt that additional credibility for the program became one part of an overall process of information flow that helped to some degree reduce the uncertainty faced by decisionmakers responsible for the program: "People in the budget channels at OMB were, I guess, eager for and interested in any data that would help them make decisions, and this was certainly one useful bit of data" (DM361:13).

The kind of impact we found, then, was that evaluation research provides some additional information that is judged and used in the context of other available information to help reduce the unknowns in the making of difficult decisions. The impact ranges from "it sort of confirmed our impressions ... , confirming some other anecdotal or impression that we had" (DM209:7,1) to providing a new awareness that can carry over into other programs:

Some of our subsequent decisions on some of our other programs were probably based on information that came out of this study. ... The most significant information from this study that we really had not realized ... made an impact on future decisions with regard to other programs that we carry on [DM209:7].

And why did it have this impact?

Well I guess I'll go back to the points I've already made, that it confirmed some impressionistic feelings and anecdotal information that we had about certain kinds of things. At least it gave us some hard data on which to base some future programming decisions. It may not have been the only data, but it was confirming data, and I think that's important.... And you know at the time this study was conceived, and even by the time it was reported to us, we really had very little data, and you know, probably *when you don't have any data, every little bit helps* [DM209:15].

This reduction of uncertainty emerged as highly important to decision-makers. In some cases it simply made them more confident and determined. On the other hand, where the need for change is indicated, an evaluation study can help speed up the process of change or provide an impetus for finally getting things rolling:

Well I think that all we did was probably speed up the process. I think that they were getting there anyhow. They knew that their performance was being criticized by various parts of the government and the private sector. As I said earlier, we didn't enter this study thinking that we were going to break any new ground, and when we got finished, we knew that we hadn't. All we did was document what the people have been saying for a long time—that _____ are doing a lousy job, so what else is new? But we were able to show just how poor a job they were doing [EV268:12].

Reducing uncertainty, speeding things up, and getting things finally started are real impacts—not revolutionary, organization-shaking impacts—but important impacts in the opinion of the people we interviewed. One administrator summarized this view both on the specific evaluation in question and about evaluation in general as follows:

Myself I have a favorable view toward evaluating. If nothing else it precipitates activity many times that could not be precipitated without someone taking a hard look at an organization. It did precipitate activity in [this program]. Some of it was not positive. Some of it was negative. *At least something occurred that wouldn't have occurred if the evaluation hadn't taken place* [DM312:21].

Another evaluator made it quite clear that simply reducing the enormous uncertainty facing many program administrators is a major purpose of evaluative research:

One of the things I think often is that the government itself gets scared ... of whatever kinds of new venture that they want to go into, and they're quite uncertain as to what steps they want to take next. So then they say, okay, let's have some outside person do this for us, or maybe an inside person do this, so at least we have some "data" to base some of our policies on [EV283:34].

The image that emerges in our interviews is that there are few major, direction-changing decisions in most programming and that evaluation research is used as one piece of information that feeds into a slow, evolutionary process of program development. Program development is a process of "muddling through" (Lindblom, 1959; Allison, 1971; Steinbruner, 1974) and evaluation research is part of the muddling.

Further, we did not find much expectation that government decision making could be or should be otherwise. One person with thirty-five years' experience in the federal government (twenty of those years in evaluation) put it like this: "I don't think an evaluation's ever totally used. That was true whether I was using them as an administrator or doing them myself" (EV346:11). Later in the interview he said:

I don't think the government should go out and use every evaluation it gets. I think sometimes just the insights of the evaluation feed over to the next administrative reiteration, maybe just the right way to do it. That is, [decisions aren't] clearly the result of evaluation. There's a feedback in some way . . . , upgrading or a shifting of direction because of it. [Change] it is, you know, small and slow . . . [EV346:16].

An evaluator expressed a similar view:

I think it's just like everything else in life, if you're at the right place at the right time, it can be useful, but it's obviously only probably one ingredient in the information process. It's rather naive and presumptuous on the part of the evaluation community [to think otherwise] and also it presumes a rationality that in no way fits [EV264:18].

Our findings, then, suggest that the predominant image of nonutilization that characterizes much of the commentary on evaluation research can be attributed in substantial degree to a definition of utilization that is too narrow in its emphasis on seeing immediate, direct, and concrete impact on program decisions. Such a narrow definition fails to take into account the nature of most actual program development processes.

The impact of most basic research seems quite similar. Researchers in any field of specialization can count the studies of major impact on one hand. Most science falls into that great amorphous activity called "normal science." Changes come slowly. Individual researchers contribute a bit here and a bit there and thus reduce uncertainty gradually over time. Scientific revolutions are infrequent and slow in coming (Kuhn, 1972).

The situation is the same in applied research. Evaluation research is one part of the "normal science" of government decision making. Research impacts in ripples not in waves. Occasionally a major study emerges with great impact. But most applied research can be expected to have no more than a small and momentary effect on the operations of a given program. The epitaph for most studies will read something like this:

[We expected that it would be used] but in a way of providing background information around the consequences of certain kinds of federal decision-making options. But not necessarily in and of itself determining those decisions. In other words you might have some idea of what the consequences of the decision are, but there might be a lot of other factors you'd take into account in how you would decide . . . [DM264:8].

[It had a particular impact in that] it contributed to the general information context of what was going on at the time, rather than in itself. . . . It contributes to that background of understanding one of the policy issues, rather than resulting in one option versus another of policy being adopted [DM264:11].

Factors Affecting Utilization

We took a dual approach to the problem of identifying the factors that affect utilization. Once the respondents had discussed their perceptions about the nature and degree of utilization of the specific evaluation study under investigation, we asked the following open-ended question:

Okay, you've described the impact of the study. Now we'd like you to think about *why* this study was used in the ways you've just described. . . . What do you feel were the important reasons why this study had the level of impact it did?

Following a set of probes and follow-up questions, we asked respondents to comment on the relevance and importance of eleven factors extracted from the literature on utilization: methodological quality, methodological appropriateness, timeliness, lateness of report, positive-negative findings, surprise of findings, central-peripheral program objectives evaluated, presence-absence of related studies, political factors, government-evaluator interactions, and resources available for the study. Finally, we asked respondents to "pick out the single factor you feel had the greatest effect on how this study was used."

Two related factors emerged as important in our interview: (1) a political considerations factor and (2) a factor we have called the personal factor. This latter factor was unexpected and its clear importance to our respondents has, we believe, substantial implications for the utilization of evaluation research. *None of the other specific literature factors about which we asked questions emerged as important with any consistency.* Moreover, when these specific factors were important in explaining the utilization or nonutilization of a particular study, it was virtually always in the context of a larger set of circumstances related to the issues and decisions at hand.

Lateness of Study Completion

We wanted to examine the allegation that much evaluation research is under-utilized because studies are completed too late to be used for making a specific decision, particularly budgetary decisions. This problem is based to a large extent on the notion that the purpose of evaluation research is to serve as the basis for the making of specific, identifiable, and concrete decisions. Inasmuch as we have already argued that most evaluation research does not serve such a narrow function and is not intended to serve such a narrow function, it is not surprising that lateness in the completion of studies was not an important factor in explaining utilization of the studies in our sample.

In four of our twenty cases, decisionmakers indicated that the final research reports were completed late, but in all four cases preliminary information was available to a sufficient extent to be used at the time the study should have been completed. In no case was lateness considered the critical factor in explaining the limited utilization of the studies. Rather, the information was viewed as feeding into a longer-term process of program development and decision making. Several decisionmakers commented that it was helpful to have the information on time, but had the final report been late the impact of the study would not likely have been different, partly because few issues become one-time decisions. As one decisionmaker put it:

[The] study was too late for the immediate budget that it was supposed to impact on, but it wasn't too late in terms of the fact that the same issue was occurring every year after that anyway [DM264:16].

Methodological Quality and Appropriateness

A major factor often identified as the reason for nonutilization is the poor quality of much evaluation research. Of the fifteen decisionmakers who rated methodological quality of the study about which they were interviewed, five rated the methodological quality as "high," eight said it was "medium," and only two gave the study a "low" rating. Of seventeen responding evaluators, seven gave "high" ratings, six "medium" responses, and four "low" ratings. No decisionmaker and only one evaluator felt that the methodology used was inappropriate for researching the question at issue.

More to the point, only four decisionmakers felt that methodological quality was "very important" in explaining the study's utilization. Further probing, however, revealed that "methodological quality" meant different things to different decisionmakers. For some, it meant the reputation of the evaluators; for others it meant asking the right question. In no case was methodological quality identified as the most important factor explaining either utilization or nonutilization.

The relevance of methodological quality must be understood in the full context of a study, the political environment, the degree of uncertainty with which the decisionmaker is faced and thus his/her relative need for any and all clarifying information. If information is scarce, then new information of even dubious quality may be somewhat helpful. For example, one administrator admitted that the evaluation's methodological rigor could be seriously questioned, but the study was highly useful in policy discussions:

The quality and the methodology were not even considered. All that was considered was that management didn't know what was going on, the terms, the procedures, the program was foreign to their background. And they did not have expertise in it, so they were relying on somebody else who had the expertise to translate to them what was going on in terms that they would understand and what the problems were [DM312:17].

Social scientists may lament this situation and may well feel that the methodology of evaluation research *ought* to be of high quality for value reasons—that is, because *poor quality studies ought not be used. But there is little in our data to suggest that improving methodological quality in and of itself will have much effect on increasing the utilization of evaluation research.*

Again, the importance of methodological quality as a factor explaining utilization is tempered by the nature of the utilization we found. Were evaluations being used as the major piece of information in making critical one-time decisions, methodological rigor might be paramount. But where evaluation research is one part, often a small part, in a larger whole, decisionmakers displayed less than burning interest in methodological quality. One highly experienced administrator viewed methodology as part of the political process of utilization:

Well, let me put it in another context. If it were negative findings programmatically we would have hit very hard on the methodology and tried to discredit it. You know, from the program standpoint. But since it was kind of positive findings, we said, "Okay, here it is." If anybody asked us about the methodological deficiencies we were never reluctant to tell them what we thought they were. *Not many people asked* [DM361:13].

Political Factors

This last quote on methodological quality makes it clear that methodology, like everything else in evaluation research, can become partly a political question. The political nature of evaluation research has been well documented. The decisionmakers and evaluators in our sample demonstrated an acute awareness of the fact that social science research rarely produces clear-cut findings. Findings must be interpreted, and interpretation is partly a political process—a value-laden process where truth is partially a matter of whose priorities are being reviewed.

Of the eleven specific factors about which we asked respondents to comment, political considerations were identified more often than any of the others as important in explaining how study findings were used. In fifteen of the twenty cases, at least one person felt that politics had entered into the utilization process. Nine decisionmakers and seven evaluators felt that political considerations had been "very important" as a factor explaining utilization. On the other hand, nine decisionmakers and five evaluators reported that political considerations played no part in the utilization process.

The political factors mentioned include intra- and interagency rivalries; budgetary fights with OMB, the administration, and Congress; power struggles between Washington administrators and local program personnel; and internal debates about the purpose and/or accomplishments of pet programs. Budgetary battles seemed to be the most political.

We did not find, however, that political factors suddenly and unexpectedly surfaced once a study was completed. In almost every case, both the decision-makers and evaluators were well aware of the political context at the outset. Moreover, our respondents seemed to feel that political awareness on the part of everyone involved was the best one could expect. Social scientists will not change the political nature of the world, and while several respondents were quite cynical on this point, the more predominant view seemed to be that government would not be government without politics. One particularly articulate decisionmaker expressed this view quite explicitly:

This is not a cynical statement. . . . A substantial number of people have an improper concept of how politics works and what its mission is. And its mission is not to make logical decisions, unfortunately for those of us who think program considerations are important. Its mission is to detect the will of the governed group and express that will in some type of legislation or government action. And that will is very rarely, when it's pooled nationally, a rational will. It will have moral and ethical overtones, or have all kinds of emotional loads. . . .

It's not rational in the sense that a good scientific study would allow you to sit down and plan everybody's life, and I'm glad it's not, by the way. Because I would be very tired very early of something that ran only by the numbers. Somebody'd forget part of the numbers, so I'm not fighting the system, but I am saying that you have to be careful of what you expect from a rational study when you insert it into the system. It has a tremendous impact. . . . It is a political, not a rational process. . . . Life is not a very simple thing [DM328:18-19].

The importance of political considerations in much (though clearly not all) evaluation research can be partly understood in terms of our emphasis on the role of evaluation in reducing uncertainty for decisionmakers. Several organizational theorists (e.g., Thompson, 1967; Crozier, 1964) have come to view power and relationships within and between organizations as a matter of gaining control through the reduction of uncertainty.

More directly, James Thompson (1967) describes evaluation research as one major organizational mechanism for reducing internal as well as environmental uncertainty. He argues that the methodological design of much evaluation research can be predicted directly from the political function that assessment plays. We believe that our data directly support this viewpoint. Evaluations are undertaken as a mechanism for helping decisionmakers cope with the complexity of the programs for which they have responsibility. As one weapon or tool in the struggle to gain control over organizational and program processes evaluation research can fully be expected to take on a political character. Indeed, as Thompson argues, it is completely *rational* for decisionmakers to use evaluations in a political fashion for control and reduction of uncertainty.

It would appear to us that it behooves social scientists to inform themselves fully about the political context of the evaluations on which they work. It is precisely through such a heightened awareness of the political implications and consequences of their research that social scientists can reduce their own uncertainty about the uses to which their work is put without impairing their ability to state their "truth" as they see it.

Other Factors Affecting Utilization

None of the other factors about which we asked specific questions emerged as consistently important in explaining utilization. When these other factors were important, their importance stemmed directly from the particular circumstances surrounding that evaluation and its purpose, particularly its political purpose. For example, the amount of resources devoted to a study might add to the credibility and clout of a study, but more costly evaluations did not show any discernible patterns of utilization different from less costly evaluation. The resources available for the study were judged inadequate for the task at hand by only two decisionmakers and five evaluators.

Whether or not findings were positive or negative had no demonstrable effect on utilization. We had studies in our sample in which the findings were rated by respondents as predominantly negative; other studies were predominantly positive in their conclusions; and still others had mixed findings. This variation was evenly distributed in our sample. Interestingly enough, the decisionmaker and evaluator on the same study often differed on whether findings were "positive" or "negative," but despite such disagreements, neither rated the positive or negative nature of the findings as particularly important in explaining either utilization or nonutilization of the evaluation.

Furthermore, the negative or positive nature of an evaluation report was unimportant as a factor explaining utilization partially because such findings, in either direction, were virtually never surprising. Only four decisionmakers expressed surprise at the findings of the study. Only one decisionmaker felt this surprise had an important effect on utilization. There was considerable consensus that surprises are not well received. Surprises are more likely to increase uncertainty rather than reduce uncertainty.

One decisionmaker took this notion a step further and made the point that a "good" evaluation process should build-in feedback mechanisms that guarantee the relative predictability of the content of the final report:

If you're a good evaluator you don't want surprises. The last thing in the world you want to do is surprise people, because the . . . chances are surprises are not going to be well received. . . . Now you could come up with findings contrary to the conventional wisdom, but you ought to be sharing those ideas, if you will, with the people being evaluated during the evaluation process . . . , but if you present a surprise, it will tend to get rejected. See, we don't want surprises. We don't like surprises around here [DM346:30-31].

The evaluator for this project expressed the same opinion: "If there's a surprising finding it should be rare. I mean, *everybody's missed this insight except this great evaluator? Nonsense!"* (EV346:13).

It is sometimes suggested that evaluations aren't used because they concentrate on minor issues. But only two decisionmakers and one evaluator felt that the evaluation in question dealt with peripheral program objectives. On the other hand nine decisionmakers and eight evaluators felt that a major factor in utilization was whether or not the evaluation examined central program objectives. The most useful evaluations were those that focused on central objectives, but these were also precisely the kinds of evaluations that would not produce information that in and of itself could change a major policy direction. The reason may have been because by focusing on major objectives the studies in our sample became one part in the larger policy process; an evaluation aimed at some peripheral, easily-changed policy component might have had more potential for immediate, concrete impact. We lacked sufficient cases of the latter type, however, to explore this possibility more fully.

Another factor of interest to us concerned the point in the life of the program when the evaluation took place. Our sample contained studies that were done at all stages in the lives of programs. The key point that emerged with regard to this factor was that different questions emerge at different points in the life of a program. Early in the program the most useful information concerns procedures and implementation. Outcomes become important only after the program has been operating for a reasonable period. Budget and cost issues become central late in the program's life. Our respondents generally felt that in each case the questions examined had been appropriate to the point in the life of the program when the evaluation had taken place. The point in the program's history when the evaluation occurred was not a factor in explaining utilization in our data.

A factor that did emerge as somewhat important was the presence or absence of other studies on the same issue. Studies that broke new ground were particularly helpful because their potential for reducing uncertainty was greater. Nevertheless, such studies were viewed with some caution because our decision-makers clearly favored the accumulation of as much information from as many sources as possible. Thus, those studies that could be related to other studies had a clearly cumulative impact. On the whole, however, studies that broke new ground appeared to have somewhat greater identifiable impact. About half of the studies in our sample were of this latter type.

Finally, we asked our respondents about evaluator-government interactions. Interactions were almost universally described as cooperative, helpful, and frequent. Many respondents could offer horror stories about poor interactions on other studies, but with regard to the specific study on which we were conducting the follow-up, there appeared to be few problems. There was no indication that utilization would have been increased by greater government-evaluator interaction than that which actually occurred, though the degree of interaction that did occur was considered quite important.

We have reviewed eleven factors frequently identified in the evaluation literature as affecting utilization. The descriptions of the importance of these factors that emerged in the interviews clearly reinforced the definition of utilization as that of information feeding into an evolutionary process of program development—that is, information used in conjunction with other information to reduce uncertainty in decision making. None of these factors, at least as we were able to explore them, helped us a great deal in explaining variations in utilization. Nevertheless, there was one other factor that did consistently arise in the comments of decisionmakers, evaluators, and project officers—a factor so crucial that respondents repeatedly pointed to it as the single most important element in the utilization process.

The Personal Factor

For lack of a better term, we have simply called this new variable the personal factor. It is made up of equal parts of leadership, interest, enthusiasm, determination, commitment, aggressiveness, and caring. Where the personal factor emerges, evaluations have an impact; where it is absent, there is a marked absence of impact.

The personal factor emerged most dramatically in our interviews when, having asked respondents to comment on the importance of each of our eleven utilization factors, we asked them to identify the single factor that was most important in explaining the impact or lack of impact of that particular study. Time after time, the factor they identified was not on our list. Rather, they responded in terms of the importance of individual people:

I would rank as the most important factor this division director's interest, [his] interest in evaluation. Not all managers are that motivated toward evaluation [DM353:17].

[The single most important factor that had the greatest effect on how the study got used was] the principal investigator. . . . If I have to pick a single factor, I'll pick people any time [DM328:20].

That it came from the Office of the Director—that's the most important factor. . . . The proposal came from the Office of the Director. It had had his attention and he was interested in it, and he implemented many of the things [DM312:21].

[The single most important factor was that] the people at the same level of decision making in [the new office] were not interested in making decisions of the kind that the people [in the old office] were, I think that probably had the greatest impact. The fact that there was no one at [the new office] after the transfer who was making programmatic decisions [EV361:27].

Probably the single factor that had the greatest effect on how it was used was the insistence of the person responsible for the initiating the study that the Director of ____ become familiar with its findings and arrive at a judgment on it [DM369:25].

[The most important factor was] the real involvement of the top decision-makers in the conceptualization and design of the study, and their commitment to the study [DM268:9].

While these comments concern the importance of interested and committed persons in studies that were actually used, studies that were *not* used stand out in that there was often a clear absence of the personal factor. One evaluator, who was not sure about how his study was used but suspected it had not been used, remarked: "I think that since the client wasn't terribly interested . . . and the whole issue had shifted to other topics, and since we weren't interested in doing it from a research point of view . . . , nobody was interested" (EV264:14).

Another evaluator was particularly adamant and articulate on the theory that the major factor affecting utilization is the personal energy, interests, abilities, and contacts of specific individuals. This person had had thirty-five years' experience in government, with twenty of those years spent directly involved in research and evaluation. Throughout his responses to our questions on the importance of various specific factors in affecting utilization, he returned to the theme of individual actions. When asked to identify the one factor that is most important in whether a study gets used he summarized his viewpoint:

The most important factor is desire on the part of the managers, both the central federal managers and the site managers. I don't think there's [any doubt], you know, that evaluation should be responsive to their needs, and if they have a real desire to get on with whatever it is they're supposed to do, they'll apply it. And if the evaluations don't meet their needs they won't. About as simple as you can get it. *I think the whole process is far more dependent on the skills of the people who use it than it is on the sort of peripheral issues of politics, resources. . . . Institutions are tough as hell to change. You can't change an institution by coming and doing an evaluation with a halo. Institutions are changed by people, in time, with a constant plugging away at the purpose you want to accomplish. And if you don't watch out, it slides back* [EV346:15-16].

He did not view this emphasis on the individual as meaning evaluation was simply a political tool. When asked how political considerations affected evaluations, he replied:

I don't think it's political at all. Oh, there's some pressures every once in a while to try and get more efficient, more money attributes, but I don't think that's the main course. The basic thing is how the administrators of the program view themselves, their responsibilities. That's the controlling factor. I don't think it's political in any way [EV346:8].

Later he commented:

It always falls back to the view of the administrator and his view of where his prerogatives are, his responsibilities. A good manager can manage with or without evaluations and a poor one can't, with or without evaluations. It just gives him some insights into what he should or shouldn't be doing, if he's a good manager. If they're poor managers, well . . . [EV346:11].

Earlier we described one project where the impact of the evaluation was unusually direct and concrete. After the evaluation had been completed, program funding was ended with the evaluation carrying "about a third of the weight of the total decision" [DM367:8]. The question then becomes why this study had such significant utilization. The answer from the decisionmaker was brief and to the point:

Well, [the evaluation had an impact] because we designed the project with an evaluation component in it, so we were expected to use it and we did. . . . Not just the fact that [evaluation] was built in, but the fact that *we* built it in on purpose. This is, *the agency head and myself had broad responsibilities for this, wanted the evaluation study results and we expected to use them. Therefore they were used. That's my point.* If someone else had built it in because they thought it was needed, and we didn't care, I'm sure the use of the study results would have been different [DM367:12].

The evaluator, (an external agent selected through an open RFP process), completely agreed that:

The principal reason [for utilization] was because the decisionmaker was the guy who requested the evaluation and who used its results. That is, the organizational distance between the policy maker and the evaluator was almost zero in this instance. That's the most important reason it had an impact [EV367:12].

What emerges here is a picture of a decisionmaker who knew what information he wanted, an evaluator committed to answering the decisionmaker's question, and a decisionmaker committed to using that information. The result was a high level of utilization in making a decision contrary to the decisionmaker's initial personal hopes.

This point was made often in the interviews. One highly placed and highly experienced administrator from yet a different project offered the following advice at the end of a four hour interview:

Win over the program people. Make sure you're hooked into the person who's going to make the decision in six months from the time you're doing the study, and make sure that he feels it's his study, that these are his ideas, and that it's focused on his values.... I'm sure it enters into personality things ... [DM283:40].

The personal factor applied not just to utilization but to the whole evaluation process. Several of the studies in our sample were initiated completely by a single person because of his personal interests and information needs. One study in particular stands out because it was initiated by a new office director with no support internally and considerable opposition from other affected agencies. The director found an interested and committed evaluator. The two worked closely together. The findings were initially ignored because there was no political heat at the time, but over the ensuing four years the director and evaluator worked personally to get the attention of key congressmen. They were finally successful in using personal contacts. The evaluation contributed to the eventual passing of significant legislation in a new area of federal control. From beginning to end, the story was one of personal human effort to get evaluation results used.

The specifics vary from study to study but the pattern is markedly clear: Where the personal factor emerges, where some person takes direct, personal responsibility for getting the information to the right people, evaluations have an impact. Where the personal factor is absent, there is a marked absence of impact. Utilization is not simply determined by some configuration of abstract factors; it is determined in large part by real, live, caring human beings.

Implications of the Personal Factor in Evaluation

If, indeed, utilization is to a large extent dependent upon the interests, capabilities, and initiative of individuals, then there are some profound implications for evaluators. First, evaluators who care about seeing their results utilized must take more seriously *their* responsibility for identifying *relevant* decisionmakers. Relevance in the context of the personal factor means finding decisionmakers who have a genuine interest in evaluation information—that is, persons who know what questions they want answered and who know how they can use evaluation information once findings are available. Such people are willing to take the time and effort to interact with evaluators about their information needs and interests.

Secondly, formal position and authority are only partial guides in identifying relevant decisionmakers. Evaluators must find a strategically located person (or persons) who is enthusiastic, committed, competent, interested, and aggressive. Our data suggest that more may be accomplished by working with a lower-level person displaying these characteristics than in working with a passive, disinterested person in a higher position.

Third, regardless of what an RFP calls for, the most valuable information with the highest potential for utilization is that information that directly answers the questions of the person(s) identified as the relevant decisionmaker(s). Requests for proposals (RFPs) may be written by individuals other than the decisionmakers who really need and want the evaluation information. It behooves evaluators to clarify the degree to which an RFP fully reflects the information needs of interested government officials.

Fourth, attention to the personal factor may assist not only evaluators in their efforts to increase the utilization of their research, but attention to the personal factor can also aid decisionmakers in their effort to find evaluators who will provide them with relevant and useful information. Evaluators who are interested in and knowledgeable about what they're doing, and evaluators who are committed to seeing their findings utilized in answering decisionmaker's questions will provide the most useful information to decisionmakers.

Fifth, there are political implications for both evaluators and decisionmakers in explicitly recognizing and acting on the importance of the personal factor. To do so is also to accept the assumption that decision making in government is likely to continue to be a largely personal and political process rather than a rationalized and scientific process. This assumption means that neither the decisionmaker nor the evaluator is merely a technician at any stage in the evaluation process. The personal factor is important from initiation of the study through design and data collection stages as well as in the final report and dissemination parts of the process. If decisionmakers have shown little interest in the study in its earlier stages, our data suggest that they are not likely to suddenly show an interest in using the findings at the end of the study. Utilization considerations are important throughout a study not just at the stage where study findings are disseminated.

Finally, the importance of the personal factor suggests that one of the major contributing reasons for underutilization of evaluation research is the high degree of instability in federal program operations. This instability, based on our data, is of three kinds: (1) high turnover rates among senior government staff so that the person initially interested in an evaluation may be in an entirely different office before the study is completed; (2) reorganization of government offices so that decision-making patterns are unstable, personnel are frequently rearranged, and responsibilities are almost constantly changing; and (3) program mobility as programs move from office to office (e.g., OEO to HEW) even if no formal, structural reorganization occurs.

We found the instability of federal organizational charts and the turnover among staff to be substantial. In trying to retrace the history of evaluations we frequently got a response like the following: "I've had so many changes in organizational assignments since then, I don't remember" (EV201:6). Asked about utilization of evaluation, the same person responded:

Well since you're not going to identify me and my name, I'll tell you what I really think, and that is, I think these plans go up to the planning office and the rotation of personnel up there in the ____'s office is so fast and so furious, that they never get a chance to react to them. [It] just sits. We know that happens sometimes, because the guy who asked for it is gone by the time it gets up there [EV201:8].

The problem of instability appears to be particularly critical in actually implementing recommended changes:

It was easier to get recommendations through with senior management approval. I mean, they read it and they could easily implement some of the areas, and they, I mean, at least they could implement them in theory anyhow. But still the problem, in any study or anything of this caliber, it's up to the people in the operating unit to make the change. And there's no way for senior management to measure that change. There's no way to see that it was even done. You know it's the old thing, of, you know, they tell people to do things, but in areas that require technical expertise there's no way to see that the change was done. *And so people in the operating area many times would just wait out the person, you know, some of these people have been through three directors, five associate directors, you know, and, they don't want to do something. They have tenure, and they know that if they sit long enough that that person will pass and someone else will come in with brand new ideas and . . .* [DM312:15].

Evaluators commented that it was common experience to go through several project officers on an evaluation.

Our own experience in trying to locate the respondents in the sample gave us a clear indication of this instability. Few of our interviewees were still in the same office at the time of the interview that they had been in at the time of the evaluation two to three years earlier. We still haven't been able to construct a meaningful organizational chart of HEW locating the various office changes and agency recommendations we encountered.

These structural conditions of mobility and instability make application of the personal factor in locating relevant decisionmakers or evaluators a risky business. That key person you locate may be gone by the time the study is completed. *Yet, these same structural conditions of mobility and instability may well be the underlying reasons why the decision-making process in the federal government has been and continues to be a highly personal and political process.*

Conclusion

Two major themes emerge from this study of the utilization of evaluation research. First, we found that much of the evaluation literature has focused on an overly narrow definition of evaluation research impacts and has thereby underestimated the actual utilization of evaluative research. Second, the importance of the personal factor in evaluation research, particularly the utilization process, has been considerably underestimated.

The two themes are directly linked. The impact of evaluation research is most often experienced as a reduction in the uncertainty faced by individual decisionmakers as they attempt to deal with the complexity of programming reality. Evaluation information is one piece of data available to decisionmakers. It must be assimilated and fitted into a contextual whole: "The results are never self-explanatory" (EV209:9). The translation, the interpretation, the meaning, the relevance are established through the interactions over time of individuals who care enough to take the time to make the contextual fit, and then are interested enough to act on the basis of that contextual fit.

It is an energy-consuming process. Energetic and interested people in government can and do use evaluation research, not for the making of grand decisions with immediate, concrete, and visible impacts, but in a more subtle, clarifying, reinforcing, and reorienting way. Evaluators, then, might do well to spend less time lamenting their lack of visible impact on major decisions and more of their time providing relevant information to those key persons of energy and vision whose thoughts and actions, to a substantial extent, determine the general direction in the evolutionary process of program development. It is in consciously working with such decisionmakers to answer their questions that the utilization of evaluation research can be enhanced.

Notes

1. The Office of Health Evaluation coordinates most evaluation research in the health division of HEW. In 1971 this office designed a new recordkeeping system that collected abstracts of all evaluations coming through that office. The 170 evaluations that were collected during the period 1971-73 became the population of evaluations from which we chose our final sample. We wish to

express our thanks to HEW officials for their assistance throughout this research project, particularly Harry Cain, Director, Office of Policy Development and Planning, Office of the Assistant Secretary for Health, and Isadore Seeman, Director, Office of Health Evaluation, Office of the Assistant Secretary for Planning and Evaluation, DHEW.

2. The term *project officer* refers to the person in the federal government who was identified as having primary responsibility for administering the evaluation. For studies that were done by organizations that are not a part of the federal government, the project officer was the person who administered the federal government's contract with that organization.

3. We identified decisionmakers by asking the project officers to name a person who would serve as an informant "about how the study was used in the government or elsewhere," and who "might be called a 'decisionmaker' vis-à-vis the study and its findings; who could tell us what decisions, if any, were made on the basis of information contained in the study."

4. This chapter represents the initial and general results of our analysis. A more extensive and detailed description of the sample, methodology, and analysis is presented in Nancy J. Brennan, "Variation in the Utilization of Evaluation Research in Decision Making," unpublished Ph.D. dissertation, University of Minnesota, 1976.

5. Citations for quotes taken from the interview transcripts will use the following format: (DM367;13) refers to the transcript of an interview with a decisionmaker about evaluation study number 367. The quote is taken from p. 13 of the transcript. Thus (EV201:10) and (PO201:6) refer to interviews about the same study; the former was an interview with the evaluator, the latter was an interview with the project officer.

References

Alkin, Marvin C., Jacqueline Kosecoff, Carol Fitz, Gibbon and Richard Seligman. 1974. *Evaluation and Decision-Making: The Title VII Experience.* Los Angeles: Center for the Study of Evaluation, University of California.

Brennan, Nancy J. 1976. "Variation in the Utilization of Evaluation Research in Decision-Making." School of Social Work, University of Montana, Unpublished thesis.

Cohen, David K., and Michael S. Garet. 1975. "Reforming Educational Policy with Applied Social Research." *Harvard Educational Review* 45, no. 1 (February), pp. 17-41.

Coleman, James S. 1972. "Policy Research in the Social Sciences." Morristown, N.J.: General Learning Press.

Crozier, Michael. 1974. *The Bureaucratic Phenomenon.* Chicago: University of Chicago Press.

Grimes, Patricia Smith. 1976. "Descriptive Analysis of 170 Health Evaluations." School of Public Affairs, University of Minnesota, Unpublished thesis.

House, Ernest R. 1972. "The Conscience of Educational Evaluation." *Teachers College Record* 73, no. 3, pp. 405-414.

Kuhn, Thomas. 1970. *Structure of Scientific Revolutions.* Chicago: University of Chicago Press.

Patton, Michael Quinn. 1975. *Alternative Evaluation Research Paradigm.* North Dakota Study Group on Evaluation Monograph, Center for Teaching and Learning, University of North Dakota, Grand Forks, North Dakota.

Thompson, James D. 1967. *Organizations in Action.* New York: McGraw Hill.

Weidman, Donald R., Pamela Horst, Grace M. Taher, and Joseph S. Wholey. 1973. "Design of an Evaluation System for NIMH." *Contract Report 962-7,* January 15. Washington, D.C.: The Urban Institute.

Weiss, Carol H. 1972. *Evaluation Research: Methods of Assessing Program Effectiveness.* Englewood Cliffs, N.J.: Prentice-Hall.

Wholey, Joseph S., John W. Scanlon, Hugh G. Duffy, James S. Fikumoto, and Leona M. Vogt. 1971. *Federal Evaluation Policy.* Washington, D.C.: The Urban Institute.

Williams, Walter, and John W. Evans. 1969. "The Politics of Evaluation: The Case of Headstart." *Annals of the American Academy of Political and Social Science* (September).

12 Policymakers' Use of Social Science Knowledge: Symbolic or Instrumental?

Karin D. Knorr

Introduction

In the literature on the utilization of social science knowledge, the concept of legitimation has long stood for the position that decisionmakers seek research results mainly to back up convictions they already hold and decisions they have already taken. A second equally popular position defines utilization in terms of the meaning it has in natural and technological sciences: It expects political decisions to be replaced by scientifically derived objective necessities (Schelsky, 1965). Both positions seem equally extreme in their interpretation of the utilization process, and both positions are equally speculative, since hardly any data are available to support one or the other thesis.

This chapter seeks to examine both assumptions by drawing from seventy face-to-face interviews done in 1974 with medium-level decisionmakers employed in Austrian federal and municipal government agencies (all located in Vienna) and directly involved with contract research. Since there are no lists of the universe of government officials who fund social science projects, the study cannot claim to be representative of the population; however, extensive search processes on the part of the project team suggest that the persons identified for the sample constitute a more-or-less complete set of government contractors in the city of Vienna, where more than 50 percent of Austrian social science government contract research is financed.[1] The study included only government officials who had (during the last few years) financed at least one project in a social science discipline that had been finished at the time of the interviewing. The distribution of projects over disciplines was as follows: sociology, 51 percent; economics, 24 percent; educational sciences, 13.5 percent; urban and regional planning, 4.5 percent; political sciences, 4.5 percent; and others 2.5 percent. The frequency of projects classified as sociological reflects the predominance of social research and opinion surveys in government contract research. This predominance should be kept in mind when reading the analysis that follows.

The study relied on both responses to taped, open-ended questions and answers given to standardized closed-ended questions. Furthermore, responses

Parts of this chapter have been published in German under the title "Politisches System und Sozialwissenschaften: Zur Plausibilität der Legitimationshypothese," in H. Strasser and K. Knorr (eds.), *Beiträge zur Theorie der Wissenschaftssteuerung* (Frankfurt am Main: Campus Verlag, 1976).

from government officials were supplemented in a few cases by data from a 1973-74 survey of 628 Austrian social scientists, which included a set of questions equivalent to those that were asked of the decisionmakers. Both surveys were done as part of one larger study; hence, certain parts of the questionnaires were constructed to match each other. The same definition of "social science," which centers around the disciplines mentioned above (including psychology, contemporary history, and business administration) was used in both cases. The population of social scientists analyzed for the present purpose excludes those researchers who had not done a contract research project during the previous few years.

Utilization Interests of Government-Sponsored Research: Four Functions of Social Science Knowledge

In trying to categorize the diversity of purposes[2] for which government officials had initiated or sponsored a project, we identified four functions that social science results seemed to serve: a census function, a motivation function, an acquisition function, and a rationalization function. All functions showed different patterns of characteristics with respect to the following dimensions:

Whether the definition of data to be supplied remained with the social scientist or was provided by the sponsoring agency;

Whether the data involved were "subjective" (opinions, attitudes, intentions, and so forth) or "objective" (mostly quantitative indicators that did not rely on the single subject as a source of information);

The level of methodological and technical requirements connected with the approach;

The degree of articulation and elaboration of cognitive interests on the part of the sponsoring agency;

The degree to which utilization responsibility was centralized in one person or office as opposed to being dispersed over several hierarchical levels and positions;

The role of the research results in actual decision-making processes.

With a view to those dimensions, the four predominant functions seemingly served by government-sponsored social science research can be described as follows:

1. The *census function* relates to all those cases in which the social scientist takes on the role of a census bureau because of a striking deficiency of the documentation and information infrastructure. In other words, the social scientist is more or less reduced to mere information-gathering activities to fill in the (mostly numeric) data blanks in specific planning and programming areas. By

implication, it follows that the cognitive interests of the sponsoring agency are articulated specifically and transmitted to the social scientist in the form of concretely defined information demands. In accordance with this pattern, the sponsoring agency sometimes supplies a ready-made questionnaire, in which case the methodological requirements of the project are very limited and center around a knowledge of interviewing procedures. The information gained is utilized by feeding it into a decision-establishing process or by simply distributing the documentation obtained to those who are concerned or interested. As an example, think of internationally standardized statistics on every educational science project done in a country—a set of information gathered, with slight variations, every year.

2. The *motivation function*[3] refers to the hypothesis that the social sciences in postindustrial societies take on the task of helping to motivate members of society to fulfill certain system requirements. By finding out motivating expectations, attitudes, and values, the social scientist assists in designing strategies and plans in such a way as to make the outcomes acceptable and attractive to society members. To show what we mean, let us cite a few lines from one of our respondents who described the project he initiated:

... we are doing traffic planning, and there it obviously is one of our greatest problems to find out how the potential user of the traffic system acts in relation to that system, how attractive traffic systems have to be in order to be accepted.... It is mainly the motivations of the users of different traffic systems which we want to get to know, and which we would like to take into account in the planning of those traffic systems, in order so to say to plan in accordance with the market, or in order to be able to control the behavior of the traffic participants through offering those traffic systems that seem to be viable for the city.

The following respondent's remarks illustrate that such utilization goals often constitute the exclusive interest in social science results on the part of government sponsors:

... [the goal of the sponsoring agency was] ... to establish a needs-oriented sponsoring program, focusing especially on surveys. Surveys of behavior patterns of the population, effects of planning measures taken, opinion polls as far as the degree of satisfaction with apartments, lodgings, is concerned, opinion polls on the degree of satisfaction with pedestrian regions....

There are several characteristic features of such projects. They are usually done by sociologists, psychologists, or political or educational scientists, who are allowed to determine the concrete definition of the desired information. Methodological requirements vary with the approach adopted, but they are typically not too high as far as the sponsoring agency's demands are concerned.

The sponsoring official wants to get out of the project at least some orientation or structuring of a complex problem area that he often does not know much about. The results are mainly utilized by being "softly" introduced into decision-preparation processes according to their perceived validity; they are almost never just "applied" as they stand. Utilization responsibility is typically difficult to localize because it is spread over several hierarchical levels and positions in the government bureaucracy. Finally, it should be noted that nearly 50 percent of the projects described here belong to the motivation function—a fact that may tell us something about both the ubiquity of the problems underlying this function and the adequacy of the social sciences for handling some as opposed to other problems.

3. The intentions underlying the third or *acquisition function* are in a way very similar to those covered by the motivation function. However, there is one special feature that warrants separate treatment of the projects relevant here: the typically direct translation of research results into practical measures.

To understand the goals of this kind of social science research, let us again cite one of our respondents:

All this [the project results] serves as the basic material for our acquisition policy, that is, it has to do with winning new clients and [with our] communication policy, [that is with] ways of addressing the target groups. As soon as I know what my target groups look like I can address them much better. . . .

This traditional problem area of commercial market research is related to the winning of voters, readers, voluntary helpers motivated to go to developing countries, and so forth. The definition of needed information typically remains with the sponsoring agency, which usually has quite specific cognitive and utilization interests: the development of a strategy that stimulates a specific response on the part of the target group. Together with the typically direct application of results, there is the fact that utilization responsibility is not dispersed over several hierarchical levels or positions, but remains with *one* person or one office. That office can be held accountable if application of the results is not successful. This is a crucial difference from all the other functions, where typically the career or position of the sponsoring official is not dependent upon the success of the research utilization strategy he adopts.

4. The term *rationalization function* has been chosen to characterize the last kind of utilization interest identified in our population. In general it can be described as an interest in increasing the planning and programming capacity of government agencies in order to deal more effectively with socioeconomic crises and impediments to growth while relying exclusively on "objective" data. In a sense the motivation function presented above can be considered as a subcategory of the present function, specializing in subjective motivations and expecta-

tions of society members. The problem areas included here range from the development of new accounting schemes to improvements in didactic technologies and prognoses of socioeconomic development trends. Economic interests predominate but do not exhaust the topics. As in the case of the motivation function, the final definition of the information sought is left to the social scientists, and utilization of results is marked by diffuse, selective inclusion in decision-preparation processes. In cases of routine prognoses based upon regular market observations, projects show some similarity to those classified under the "acquisition" heading. In contrast to the latter, the information gained is, however, usually not put into practice directly.

It is interesting to note that concentrating exclusively on factual "rationalization," without taking into account subjective motivations and expectations, creates problems when consumer interests of various groups of the population are directly involved. Some of the respondents sponsoring such projects were perfectly aware of this dysfunctionality, which is to a certain degree increased by discipline-oriented division of labor among scientists:

In a similar project in the future I would at any rate change my strategy: it seems to me essential to include the opinions of those who are hit by a planning measure, the opinions of target groups in a district and of their representatives. This has been lacking in the present study completely and now would not help any more. They [those concerned by political decisions] have to be directly confronted with it, that is, then it could be the case that goals and policies change, you have to face this, then goals and policies have to be more flexible.

Krause (1968) assumes that this requirement of flexibility of goals and policies might be the basic reason for decisionmakers' tendency to avoid participation strategies, even if anticipatory, as in the case of including subjective expectations and motivations in a rationalization project.

Table 12-1 summarizes the characteristics of the different utilization functions that social science results seem to serve. When interpreting the frequencies, keep in mind that more than one function may be served by one project and that only the predominant function has been counted. Correspondingly, the features listed characterize only the simple case in which there is only one function present. Furthermore, it should be noted that the frequencies reported are not representative for all social science *projects* initiated by government utilization interests. As an example, projects done by government-financed research units or research institutes are not included here. This omission may account for the fact that economic projects (mainly pertaining to the rationalization function) seem to be underrepresented here, while they constitute almost half of all social science projects currently done in Austria (cf. Knorr et al., 1975b). What is represented here is the distribution of interests of single government sponsors (or government agencies represented by single sponsors) who finance single social science projects because of certain utilization needs or expectations.

170

Table 12-1
Utilization Functions of Social Science Results and Their Characteristics, as Derived from Reports of Government Sponsors

Characteristic Feature	Census Function (N = 11)	Motivation Function (N = 30)	Acquisition Function (N = 5)	Rationalization Function (N = 19)
Level of methodical requirements	low	low	higher (precision)	higher (data manipulation)
Kind of data	subjective or objective	subjective	subjective	objective
Origin of the definition of the information	sponsoring agency	scientist	sponsoring agency	scientist
Degree of elaboration and articulation of cognitive interests	specific	vague	specific	vague; in case of routine market observations, specific
Localization of utilization responsibility	dispersed	dispersed	centralized	dispersed
Role of research results in decision processes	decision preparatory	decision preparatory	decision constitutive	decision preparatory
Function of research results	replacing a deficient infrastructure	anticipatory motivation and legitimation	target group-oriented communication	technical rationalization of planning
Percentage of cases[a]	17%	46%	8%	29%

[a]Five percent of the projects could not be subsumed under one of the functions isolated, mainly because there was no spelled out utilization interest.

The Role of Social Science Research Results
in Decision-Making Processes

From the results obtained so far, we are able to differentiate four different roles social science research results are apt to play in actual decision-making processes:

1. Social science results serve as an "information base" or "ground" for actual decisions to take place. In other words, the data (especially for the census function) or arguments (especially for the motivation and rationalization functions) supplied by the social scientist enter into the preparatory stage of a decision, where they influence the final outcome of the process to various degrees. We call this the *decision-preparatory role* of social science results.

2. Instead of entering the decision-preparatory stage, social science results can be directly translated into practical measures and action strategies. As noted by Caplan (1975, p. v), it is this kind of more-or-less direct application of knowledge that social scientists strive for. In the extreme case, the original decisionmaker in charge, even with all his decision experience and capacity, becomes redundant in the face of scientifically established proposals about what to do about a problem—a situation envisaged by earlier theories of technocracy.[4]

In our data, project results were typically used in such a *decision-constitutive* manner only where the acquisition function is concerned. Clearly, the most enthusiastic statements in our population with regard to the usefulness of social science results refer to marketing research and advertising strategies initiated by acquisition interests:

... those scientific disciplines are on the one hand underestimated; people believe that they achieve better results when relying on their intuition. They do not realize the true character of the social sciences, that is to assist in the solution of market oriented problems.

3. There is a third way in which social science research results play a role in the activities of government administrators: as a *substitute* for the decision or problem solution that is required. By initiating, distributing, and publishing a research report, the government official in this case tries to signal to those concerned that something is being done about the problem, while proper decisions and measures that should be taken are postponed or neglected altogether. This process is what is sometimes meant when we say that the social sciences play a key role in legitimating decisionmakers' activities at the same time that they are ignored in the actual decision-making process.

4. More often, however, the fourth function of social science research results established in our data is identified with the "legitimating" role of the social sciences: Here the social scientists' data and arguments are used selectively and often distortingly to publicly support a decision that has been taken on different grounds or that simply represents an opinion the decisionmaker already

holds. In this respect let us cite the thesis of Garfinkel (1967, p. 114) that the crucial difference between scientific and nonscientific (everyday life) rationality is the fact that in the latter case decisions are made intelligible and are legitimized only after the resolution, while in the former case the rationality of what is decided has to be established before a measure is taken. We call this the *legitimating role* of the social sciences and cite the judgment of one of our respondents, which is marked by cynicism and resignation resulting from some experiences with this kind of social science utilization:

> There is a kind of fiction in the whole thing which we all play, that policy is becoming "scientific" through research, that arguments and results from social science studies influence legislation. In reality this is not the case, because in the legislature such people are asked who are at any rate convinced they know what's going on, because one has to take seriously those who hold a chair on official committees and who speak for the record and out of the window and who bring with them all their prestige, the power of the organization from which they come, those who themselves ask for research results in order to back their arguments. But I believe it is always like this: You've got the argument, then you look for somebody to prove it for you. Then you stand up and say: Study XY shows, too, that . . . exactly as you think things are, etc.

Such a policy only superficially made scientific (Kreutz, 1970, p. 20) is, as Downey (1967) emphasizes correctly, an ideological means of domination. For a science-based policy, the *claim* of a science-based policy is substituted—a claim that is sufficient to enhance the development of the image of a modern and progressive government and at the same time to provide a means for effectively protecting and backing political action strategies.[5]

The Legitimating Capacity of the Social Sciences

The thesis that the main function of the social sciences is legitimation is heavily represented in the literature (compare Edelmann, 1964, 1971; Downey, 1967; Kreutz, 1970; Lécuyer, 1970; Offe, 1972; Daele and Weingart, 1974). It should be discussed in the light of the following arguments:

1. Claims made for the "scientific" basis of some measures or decisions derive their validity from a general acceptance of science as yielding objective information (not biased by personal interests) and cognitively valid information (logically consistent, of high empirical content and explanatory value). Needless to say, the current state of the social sciences allows for only very weak and limited fulfillment of both requirements. There is no consensus as to what constitutes social science "knowledge" among social scientists, and more important, there is no unquestioned acceptance of this "knowledge" on the part of clients and users of these sciences. Several of our respondents commented upon the uncertainty of social science results:

... in the social sciences one is confronted with results which one does not have to accept without question as in the case of natural sciences or in the case of technical or biological things; rather one can check or seemingly check them. One can say to oneself: just a moment, there he [the social scientist] is right, there he is not right ... that is the case, that is not the case. One does much more evaluate critically, can evaluate critically, what one gets. . . .

2. Another—social—aspect of the social sciences, in addition to their pre-paradigmatic (Kuhn, 1970), theoretical, and methodological inadequacies, influences their legitimation capacity. The public acceptance of social "science" disciplines, especially as far as sociology and political science are concerned, has suffered from their being identified with society-critical and revolutionary movements in the recent past. One of our respondents commented:

... I believe that the student movements of the sixties did have important impact on the further development of the social sciences; especially, I think, you have now got a rather general distrust against them. . . .

About 45 percent of the actual users of social science results interviewed by us did see a direct connection between the institutionalization and current situation of the social sciences on the one hand and the student movement on the other (Knorr et al., 1975a). Must it not be considered an indicator of the legitimative deficiency of the social sciences if they did not succeed so far to make their critical activities intelligible to the general public as a genuine and legitimate interest of their own?

3. In addition to the social sciences' cognitive inadequacy and their association with politically rebellious or anarchic groups in the mind of the public, a third factor should be taken into account when trying to assess the legitimation potential of the social sciences: The social sciences deal with phenomena about which the average citizen does have an "opinion" of his own and with which he deals in his everyday activities. In addition, the fact that social science concepts are deeply rooted in our everyday language creates a situation where—contrary to the natural and technical sciences—the nonexpert feels perfectly legitimized to interpret, criticize, and dismiss the results of the expert social scientist. If this is the case—and we believe that every social scientist who ever had anything to do with the user of his or her results will know this reaction—then the legitimating capacity of the social sciences must again be called into question.

The Motivation Function and Problems of Legitimation in Postindustrial Societies

It is our contention that the thesis of the primarily legitimative role of social science research results has to be replaced by the thesis of the instrumental use of social science results *for the purpose* of securing legitimacy for political decisions. It goes without saying that in the public relations work of government bureaucracies, social sciences are used to a certain degree instrumentally as a means of "ideology-planning" (Luhmann, 1969) as well as sometimes symbolically in the sense of mere claims made as to the scientific basis of the measures prescribed. The predominance of motivation problems as articulated by our respondents[6] and the fact of their being connected to decision-preparatory research utilization suggest that there is a special need for instrumentally applicable social science research *induced* by a growing lack of legitimation of political action. The causal chain starting with state interference and leading through a decrease in legitimation to motivation crises has been analyzed to a certain degree by current theories of postindustrial societies (cf. Offe, 1972; Habermas, 1973). According to them, there is an increasing consciousness as far as the growth of state interference with the concrete conditions of life is concerned. With the increase in government planning and the consequent crises in socioeconomic development, traditional norms and values increasingly lose their meaning and their motivating strength without being replaced by functional equivalents. There is a growing discrepancy between the motivation capacity of our sociocultural systems (especially regarding intrinsic achievement motivation, individual property values, and the free-market ideology) and the need for motives that guarantee the continuity of societal subsystems. The loss of meaning is replaced by consumer-oriented, controlled-by-success expectations that the political system has to fulfill while threatened by a loss of legitimacy in case of failure.

It is exactly here that the use of social science research studies enters the stage: As an instrument of *anticipatory legitimation*, they are used to identify and predict the above-mentioned expectations in order to have them included in planning and programming stages from the beginning. If our thesis is correct, then vast areas of social science have taken on the task of transplanting participation as an "early warning system" of democratic planning (Offe, 1972) from the level of communicative debate to the level of technical anticipation in order to reduce the dangers of overparticipation and organization of those concerned. At a second stage, the anticipatory legitimation function of the social sciences is continued in the form of the ideology-planning mentioned before—that is, an attempt to structure public opinion effectively with the help of market and opinion research. Both kinds of utilization—subsumed here under the motivation and acquisition functions—largely outnumber the mere symbolic use of social science results. In projects corresponding to the rationalization function, subjective expectations are ignored; hence, this area of social science research can only indirectly be subsumed under what we have called anticipatory legitimation. Here, too, however, the instrumental use of social science results seems to predominate. The instrumental use we are talking about, however, refers much more to the decision-preparing than to the decision-constituting role of social science knowledge.

Extent of Utilization Reported

The thesis of a primarily instrumental use of social science is in accordance not only with the utilization interests inferred from the responses of government officials, but also with the judgment of Austrian social scientists who worked on government-sponsored projects during the last few years. In their opinion, the demands for "data" and for "control" (van den Daele and Weingart, 1974) largely outnumber the symbolic legitimative utilization interests, as shown in Table 12-2.

Reports of the utilization interests of sponsors given by social scientists seem to be especially relevant to us since they are independent of the responses of the users themselves.[7]

Further indirect proof of the instrumental usefulness of social science results can be found in the responses of our government officials on the extent to which social science results changed their previous opinions and fulfilled their expectations (see Table 12-3). As can be seen from the table, almost three-fourths of the government sponsors considered that their expectations were widely or completely fulfilled. More important, about two-thirds of the respondents (65.5 percent) claimed to have at least slightly changed their

Table 12-2
Dominant Utilization Interest of Project Sponsoring Agency, as Reported by Social Scientists

Dominant Interest	Percentage of Respondents ($N = 259$)
Demand for data (decision preparatory function)	43.7
Demand for control (decision preparatory and decision constitutive functions)	19.0
Demand for symbolically "applicable" results (decision legitimative function)	11.1
Long-term financing or pure sponsoring	26.2
Total	100.0

Note: The wording of the question was as follows: "As far as you know, which interest predominated on the part of the financing organization?" The answer categories (1) sponsoring without utilization interests; (2) financing of research which could in the long run become relevant for the financing organization; (3) preparation of reports and situation analyses as a basis for decisions; (4) objective support for measures and programs intended; (5) proposal of solutions and alternatives for present problems; (6) derivation of practical action-prescriptions to solve detailed problems. Categories 1 and 2 have been combined into alternative 4 of the table; categories 5 and 6 into alternative 2; and category 4 was intended as an operationalization of legitimative interests.

Table 12-3

Extent to which Government Sponsors' Expectations Were Fulfilled and Opinions Changed by Social Science Research Results

Extent	Fulfillment of Expectations (% respondents) (N = 64)	Change of Opinion (% respondents) (N = 58)
Expectations not fulfilled or no change of opinion	1.6	34.5
Expectations only moderately fulfilled or slight change of opinion	6.2	22.4
Expectations fulfilled to a medium degree or medium change of opinion	18.8	34.5
Expectations widely to completely fulfilled or strong to very strong change of opinion[a]	73.4	8.6
Total	100.0	100.0

Note: The wording of the questions was as follows: "To what extent did the researchers fulfill—as far as you know—the expectations of the following persons with respect to the project?" One category referring to the respondent himself ("your personal expectations as to the project") was provided. The second question ran: "To what extent did the below mentioned change their opinion about the problem on account of the project results?" Again, there was one answer category ("you yourself") referring to the respondent. In both cases, answers were to be given on five-point Likert scales.

[a]It is interesting to compare the percentage of respondents whose expectations were widely or completely fulfilled (73.4 percent!) with the percentage that strongly or very strongly changed their opinion about the problem on the basis of the research results (8.6 percent!). The discrepancy suggests that expectations for social science research results are, from the very beginning, not too high.

opinion about the problem on the basis of the results of the social science project; somewhat more than one-third claim a medium degree of opinion change. It seems plausible that results that change the opinion of a client also influence the planning and decision process in a problem area in which he is involved. Let us look at the extent of self-reported use of social science results by government sponsors, as shown in Table 12-4. If responses of government sponsors can be believed—and depictions of utilization in the open-ended questions give the impression that they can—there is only a minor degree of nonutilization of results; indirect utilization of results as an information base or information support predominates, however. It is important to note that the first three kinds of utilization listed in Table 12-5 as well as the last two items correlate much more highly with each other than items from the first set with those of the second set. These data seem to imply two alternative action strategies of potential users: Social science results are *either* directly translated

Table 12-4

Extent of Utilization of Social Science Research Results, as Reported by Government Sponsors

Kind of Utilization	Extent of Utilization (%)				
	Not at All	Slight or Moderate	Strong or Very Strong	Total	(N)
Translation into significant practical action	37.9	37.9	24.1	100	(58)
Information base and support for measures and programs intended	14.3	26.8	59.0	100	(56)
Distribution of results within the organization of the sponsor	15.3	45.7	39.0	100	(59)
Sponsoring of further research	38.2	9.1	52.7	100	(55)
Invitation of the scientist for advising or consulting purposes	46.4	23.2	30.3	100	(56)
Other	82.0	10.0	8.0	100	(50)

Note: The wording of the question was as follows: "How much were the results of the project utilized in the following respects?" The respondent was provided with the categories included in the table and was supposed to answer on a five-point Likert scale running from "not at all" to "very strongly."

into practical measures *and* used as information support *and* made known in the organization in question, *or* they lead mainly to the sponsoring of further research and to further consulting of the scientist. If one assumes that direct translation into practical measures will be accompanied by decision-preparatory uses and internal publicity, but not vice versa, approximately 23 percent of the projects[8] were utilized in the latter sense but not "directly" applied. This percentage can be interpreted as an indicator of the potential extent of mere legitimative use of social science research results (or of a form of utilization in which mere symbolic use cannot be excluded) if one is willing to concede that the category "information base and support" allows for both post hoc rationalizations of decisions already taken and ex ante improvements of the understanding of a problem area before the actual measure is taken.

The Role of the Visibility of Consequences

Given the predominance of instrumental uses of social science results presented by us and backed by our data (and those of Caplan, 1975), the question arises as to why this use seems to be either ignored or replaced by too high or too low

Table 12-5

Intercorrelations among Types of Utilization of Social Science Results, as Reported by Government Sponsors

	Translation into Significant Practical Action	Information Base and Support for Measures and Programs	Distribution of Results within the Organization of the Sponsor	Sponsoring of Further Research	Invitation of the Scientist to Advise or Consult
Translation into significant practical action					
Information base and support for measures and programs	.71				
Distribution of results within the organization of the sponsor	.65	.69			
Sponsoring of further research	.36	.38	.30		
Invitation of the scientist to advise or consult	.31	.32	.21	.54	

Statistic = Pearson's *r*.

expectations. One of the main reasons is probably related to the *low visibility* of decision-preparatory utilization at issue here as against decision-constitutive and decision-legitimative utilization forms. It is obvious that a direct translation of research results into practical measures should be highly visible; the same holds for primarily symbolic utilization since it virtually consists in a *public* appeal to the scientific basis of what is proposed. There are several reasons why much less is known about research utilization in the decision-preparatory stage.

1. The relationship between the social scientist and the decisionmaker often ends with the delivery of the report. This leaves the social scientist largely ignorant of the evaluation or further utilization of his results. As an example, social scientists seem to vastly underestimate the extent to which government sponsors are critical of the results they get (cf. Knorr et al., 1975a).

2. A second reason seems to be that hard and visible facts about the inclusion of social science research results in a planning, programming, or decision-establishing process are difficult to establish even if there is continued communication between the researcher and the decisionmaker. In much scientific writing, in spite of the requirement of citation, it proves to be rather difficult to identify the origin of arguments or the extent to which one author had an influence on another.

3. A third reason for the low visibility of the decision-preparatory function of social science research results may lie in the fact that decisionmakers do have a second problem of legitimation (see our earlier discussion of this role of the social sciences): They have to prove their own activity, technical competence, and intellectual achievements in front of higher hierarchical levels and in front of the public. This requirement implies that the decisionmaker will tend to document his *own* decision capacity with the help of social science results in a way in which his own brilliance can no longer be differentiated from that of the social scientist. Lazarsfeld (e.g., 1969) has commented upon decisionmakers' fear of a loss or underestimation of their most valued attribute: their talent and skill in evaluating a situation correctly and in finding quick problem solutions.

Technical and Discursive Utilization of
Social Science Results

In addition to the low visibility of decision-preparatory utilization, a second reason might account for the frequent disappointment with regard to the use of social science knowledge. The current definition of what constitutes "utilization" of social science results follows the engineering model taken from the natural and technological sciences in which "technical" applications do not create any basic difficulties (compare Weiss, 1975b; Caplan 1975, p. v). Suffice it to say here that the cognitive and methodological inadequacy of the social sciences—if nothing else—does at present preclude them from providing hard and solid bases for decisions. What is discredited here is a primarily decision-constitutive role for social science results. This must not, however, be equated with the thesis that social science results are hardly ever or not at all used instrumentally. The social-technological or engineering model of the social sciences has long been debated and has usually been confronted with an "emancipatory" or "enlightening" model (e.g., Strasser, 1975). If one accepts the latter, one would have to replace the picture of a technical translation of research results into practical measures by a "discursive" (*diskursiv*) concept that takes into account the fact that social science results by their nature require further rational processing on the part of the political decisionmaker. It should prove more fruitful to find out which accompanying measures within the scientific and political systems might be adequate for this kind of discursive utilization than to search for the disconnection between the production and utilization of results, which currently seems to predominate.

Let us summarize this chapter by saying that the thesis of a primarily symbolic utilization of social science results—insofar as it refers to post hoc legitimations of decisions already taken—is not supported by our data nor by theoretical considerations. This finding does not mean that there is no symbolic use of social science results, but rather that instrumental utilization (with legitimative or motivating purposes) currently predominates. However, this kind of instrumental utilization does *not* follow the pattern of technical implementation of results established in the natural or technological sciences. Rather, the main area of utilization consists of an *indirect* (bound to undergo further decision processes), *diffuse* (taken into account to various degrees and at different positions), *difficult to localize* utilization responsibility (distributed over various decision levels), and possibly *delayed discursive processing* of the results in the stage of program development and decision preparation. The low visibility of this kind of utilization and the far too high expectations contribute to the popularity of the thesis that little utilization takes place. Its plausibility should be reexamined in the light of the present data and arguments.

Notes

1. Exact figures are not available at present.

2. The analysis presented in this and the following paragraph is based upon two general open-ended questions about how the sponsored project came about, how the project results were finally utilized, and whether this utilization was in accordance with original expectations. In the context of those general questions, a series of more detailed questions was asked of the respondent: What kind of interests played an essential role in initiating the project and what expectations did those supporting the project have; to what degree were expectations made clear to the researchers, or how specific were the demands made upon the researchers; how could the results of the project in fact be utilized; are there any practical measures that were taken on the basis of the project that would not have been taken otherwise; if yes, what were the effects; and similar questions.

3. The concept "motivation" function has been chosen in analogy to the motivation crisis described by Habermas (1973, pp. 106ff.) as one of the characteristic problems of late capitalism.

4. For such a theory of technocracy, the politician of our time is "not a decisionmaker or governor, but an analyzing, constructing, planning, realizing person. Policy in the sense of a normative consolidation of intentions is factually lost in this area" (Schelsky, 1965; translation by the author of this chapter).

5. We did not attempt to derive precise quantitative indicators for the various kinds of utilization presented here from the answers to our open-ended questions since the questionnaire included standardized, quantity-oriented questions for most of the "qualitative" topics (parts of the results of which will be presented later on). "Qualitative" answers were used mainly for deriving classifications, as background information to facilitate interpretations, and for discovering "grounded" theory.

6. This holds especially if a more narrow definition of *social sciences* excluding economics is applied.

181

7. Responses by government sponsors and social scientists did not refer to the same projects, but have been collected as independent opinions of the corresponding subsystems. The comparison of the opinions is based upon the assumption that there are no systematic biases in the selection of projects described by the sponsors and social scientists is concerned.

8. This follows if one subtracts from the 37.9 percent of project results not directly translated into practical measures the 14.3 percent of projects that are also not used as an information base or the 15.3 percent of project results not internally distributed.

References

Caplan, N., Morrison, A., and Stambaugh, R.J. 1975. *The Use of Social Science Knowledge in Policy Decisions at the National Level.* Ann Arbor, Mich.: Institute for Social Research.

Daele, W. van den, and Weingart, P. 1974. *Factors of Receptivity and Resistance of the Social Sciences toward Political Demands–Cases from the FRG.* Paris: OECD.

Downey, K.J. 1967. "Sociology and the Modern Scientific Revolution." *The Sociological Quarterly* 8, pp. 239-54.

Edelmann, M. 1967. *The Symbolic Uses of Politics.* Urbana: University of Illinois Press.

_____. 1971. *Politics as Symbolic Action: Mass Arousal and Quiescence.* Chicago: Markham.

Garfinkel, H. 1967. *Studies in Ethnomethodology.* Englewood Cliffs, N.J.: Prentice-Hall.

Glaser, B., and Strauss, A. 1967. *The Discovery of Grounded Theory.* Chicago: Aldine.

Habermas, J. 1968. *Wissenschaft und Technik als "Ideologie."* Frankfurt/Main: Suhrkamp.

_____. 1974. *Legitimationsprobleme im Spätkapitalismus.* Frankfurt/Main: Suhrkamp.

Knorr, K.D. 1975. "The Nature of Scientific Consensus and the Case of the Social Sciences." In K.D. Knorr, H. Strasser, and H.G. Zilian (eds.), *Determinants and Controls of Scientific Development.* Dordrecht, Holland: Reidel.

Knorr, K.D., Zilian, H.G. et al. 1975a. *Sozialforschung als Auftragsforschung öffentlicher Instanzen.* Wien: Forschungsmemorandum des Instituts für Höhere Studien.

_____. 1975b. *Der Produktions- und Verwertungszusammenhang sozialwissenschaftlicher Forschung.* Wein: Forschungsmemorandum des Instituts für Höhere Studien.

_____. 1975c. *Die politische Instrumentalisierung der Sozialwissenschaft.* Wien: Forschungsmemorandum des Instituts für Höhere Studien.

Krause, E. 1968. "Functions of a Bureaucratic Ideology: Citizen Participation." *Social Problems* 16, pp. 129-43.

Kreutz, H. 1972. *Soziologie der empirischen Sozialforschung.* Stuttgart: Enke.

Kuhn, T.S. 1970. *The Structure of Scientific Revolutions.* Chicago: University of Chicago Press, 2nd ed.

Lazarsfeld, P. 1975. *An Introduction to Applied Sociology.* New York: American Elsevier.

Lecuyer, B.P. 1970. "Contributions of the Social Sciences to the Guidance of National Policy." In *International Social Science Journal* 22, pp. 264-300.

Luhman, N. 1969. *Legitimation durch Verfahren.* Neuwied, Berlin: Luchterhand.

Offe, Claus. 1972. *Strukturprobleme des kapitalistischen Staates.* Frankfurt/ Main: Suhrkamp.

Schaar, J.H. 1969. "Legitimacy in the Modern State." In P. Green and S. Levinson (eds.), *Power and Community: Dissenting Essays in Political Science.* New York: Random House.

Schelsky, H. 1965. *Auf der Suche nach der Wirklichkeit.* Düsseldorf: Diederichs.

Strasser, H. 1976. *The Normative Structure of Sociology: Conservative and Emancipatory Themes in Social Thought.* London: Routledge and Kegan Paul.

Weiss, C.H. 1975. *Improving the Linkage between Social Research and Public Policy.* Paper presented at the Vienna Roundtable on the Market for Policy Research.

13 A Minimal Set of Conditions Necessary for the Utilization of Social Science Knowledge in Policy Formulation at the National Level

Nathan Caplan

Knowledge utilization of any kind does not occur in a vacuum. The utilization of scientific information in the formulation of public policy, even under ideal conditions, is the result of a complex and often seemingly capricious set of circumstances. Some of these vicissitudes, however, are foreseeable, and it is my purpose to discuss certain of these factors and conditions on which social science knowledge utilization is contingent at the upper levels of governmental power and responsibility in the United States.

While the set of conditions to be discussed here operate in some way to influence knowledge use, they alone could not account for its occurrence. Undoubtedly, factors other than those discussed here are likely to produce a facilitating effect on the utilization of social science knowledge by policymakers. The generalizations discussed here are based on the findings of one study, and given the complexities of the utilization process and the formidable technical problems in measuring the direct and indirect impacts of informational inputs, it would be pretentious to argue that these findings represent anything more than a beginning in an area of accelerated interest in which empirical research so far has been meager and scanty.

In view of these considerations, the use of the word *minimal* in the title of this chapter may seem to imply the possession of more conclusive knowledge than is now available. Indeed, in the study that provides the basis for the generalizations to be discussed here, 575 instances of utilization of social science information by upper-level governmental officials in the United States government were identified, and many of these occurred under circumstances where few, and in some cases none, of these "minimal" conditions were present; utilization was often the result of an adventitious combination of events and a chain of circumstances in which chance factors and low probability events played the determining roles. Thus "minimal" is not used to imply that utilization will be guaranteed if all of these conditions are met, but to emphasize that, at a minimum, consideration must be given to this cluster of interrelated conditions, if we are even to begin to increase the probability for systematic and creative application of social science knowledge in the formulation of public policy.

This chapter was originally presented as a paper at the Conference on Social Values and Social Engineering of the International Sociological Association, Warsaw, April 18-19, 1975. The research was supported by the National Science Foundation through its RANN division. The interpretations and conclusions are those of the author and do not necessarily reflect the views of the funding source.

Before proceeding, let me briefly describe the study from which the main ideas discussed here are derived. During the period from October 1973 to March 1974, 204 interviews were conducted with persons holding important positions across the various departments and major agencies and commissions of the executive branch of the United States government. Thirty-one (15 percent) of these respondents were at the undersecretary, deputy undersecretary, assistant undersecretary, and assistant secretary levels. Fifty-four (27 percent) were institute directors and directors of commissions or other governmental units. Sixty-seven (33 percent) were deputy or assistant directors, upper-level administrators, and bureau or division chiefs. The remaining 52 respondents (25 percent) were agency personnel holding offices of somewhat lesser authority.

The interviews were conducted by professional interviewers and were carried out on a face-to-face basis. The average time required for each interview was about one and a half hours. The interviews were recorded on tape. During the course of the interview the interviewer wrote out the response to each item as completely as possible on the interview form. At the end of the interview, the tape was used by the interviewer to edit and complete the written narrative. These tapes have also proven valuable for coding difficult open-ended terms for computational purposes.

Perhaps more important, listening to these tapes has been an insight-provoking experience that made it possible to conceptualize the quantitative data in ways that extend beyond what could be inferred from the statistical analysis of the aggregate responses alone. To a large degree, the generalizations to be discussed here were the consequences of listening and relistening to the extensive, and often parenthetical, content contained in these tapes and then of interlacing these qualitative impressions with the results of the quantitative analysis.

The focus of the interview was the use of *empirically* based social science knowledge, other than orthodox economic research, in policy-related decision making. Routine use of purely economic data was excluded because its pervasive use would have required a study in its own right. Instances of economic data involving other behavioral dimensions, such as studies of consumer sentiment were coded as instances of utilization. As a result of this study, it was possible to identify 575 self-reported instances of social science knowledge uses that impacted on policy decisions. These instances of use were the basis for assigning a "utilization score" to each respondent, which, in turn, became the dependent variable for most of the statistical analyses. Further details of the study, procedures for analysis, and results can be found in *The Use of Social Science Knowledge in Policy Decisions at the National Level* by N. Caplan, A. Morrison, and R. Stambaugh.[1]

In the absence of longitudinal or crossnational data, it is impossible to say whether the identification of 575 instances of social science utilization supports or refutes the widely held opinion that social science research is inadequately utilized in policy making at the national level. It is worth noting that these 575 instances of utilization were located among governmental agencies with diverse missions and diverse target groups. Further, many of these instances involved creative and strategically important applications of policy-related social science utilization. Thus, there may be reason for modest satisfaction rather than the despair and cynicism so prevalent in the literature on the topic. Nonetheless, much can be done to foster utilization, and the discussion to follow is devoted to describing some considerations that should be instrumental in achieving this objective.

If one were to step back and take an overview of the data collected in this study of federal executives, a number of findings emerge as particularly important to successful utilization. At the risk of oversimplification, utilization is most likely to occur when:

1. The decision-making orientation of the policymaker is characterized by a reasoned appreciation of the scientific and the extrascientific aspects of the policy issue.
2. The ethical-scientific values of the policymaker carries with them a conscious sense of social direction and responsibility.
3. The policy issue is well defined and of such a nature that a "best" solution requires research knowledge.
4. The research findings share the following characteristics: (a) they are not counterintuitive; (b) they are believable on grounds of objectivity; and (c) their action implications are politically feasible.
5. The policymaker and knowledge producers are linked by information specialists capable of coupling scientific inputs to policy goals and objectives.

The Decision-Making Orientation

The ways in which policymakers process information appear to have different consequences in determining the amount and kinds of knowledge used in arriving at a policy decision even after variables such as rank and department are statistically controlled. Seventy percent of the respondents could be classified in one of the three information-processing styles—clinical, academic, or advocacy—on the bases of their descriptions of how they used knowledge pertaining to the scientific and the extrascientific aspects of the policy issue under consideration. The remaining 30 percent did not fall into these categories because either it was impossible to classify them, or they straddled two or more categories. Those who adopted the clinical style used empirically based knowledge to the greatest extent; those with an academic orientation exhibited the next highest level of use; and those who adopted the advocacy style exhibited the lowest level of utilization.

Before describing these three styles it is important to comment briefly on the kinds of information involved and their functions in decision making. While scientific and extrascientific are appropriate and proper labels for the issue under discussion, it will facilitate understanding if we think in functional terms: Consider "scientific" as referring to matters bearing on the *internal logic* of the policy issue—that is, pertaining to the gathering, processing, and analysis of the most objective information available to arrive at an unbiased diagnosis of the problem—and "extrascientific" as bearing on the *external logic* of the policy issue—that is, pertaining to the political, value-based, ideological, administrative, and economic considerations involved.

The Clinical Orientation

The federal officials who expressed this style, approximately 20 percent of those interviewed, are the most active users of scientific information. They combine two basic approaches to problem solving. First they gather and process the best available information they can obtain to make an unbiased diagnosis of the policy issue. They use knowledge in this way to deal with the "internal logic" of the problem. Next they gather information regarding the political and social ramifications of the policy issue to deal with the "external logic" of the problem. To reach a policy decision, they finally weigh and reconcile the conflicting dictates of the information.

The Academic Orientation

The largest group of social science information users, approximately 30 percent of those interviewed, processes information with an academic orientation. They are often experts in their fields and prefer to devote their major attention to the internal logic of the policy issue. They are much less willing, however, to cope with the external realities that confound this type of problem. Considerations of the external logic of the problem are likely viewed as a menace to the prestige and standing of their expertise. Consequently, they use scientific information in moderate amounts and in routine ways to formulate and evaluate policies largely on the basis of scientifically derived information.

The Advocacy Orientation

Comprising another 20 percent of the federal officials is the advocacy-orientation group, which is much at home in the world of social, political, and economic realities. Their use of social science information is limited, but when used, its use is almost exclusively dictated by extrascientific forces to the extent that the group will at times intentionally ignore valid information that does not fit the prevailing political climate. The preoccupation is with the external logic of a policy issue, and the function of scientific knowledge when used in that context is largely to rationalize a decision made on extrascientific grounds.

Respondents with a particular educational background or training tended to show an information-processing style highly reflective of that particular type of educational background. For example, medical doctors tended to favor the clinical style of processing information; Ph.Ds favored the academic style; and lawyers most frequently favored the advocacy style. Similarly, this pattern of differences is reflected in the correlations (gamma) between educational backgrounds and level of knowledge use as represented by the utilization scores of the respondents from the three educational backgrounds: M.D. degree, +.64; Ph.D. degree (social as well as nonsocial sciences) +.03; and LLB, LLD, or JD degree, $-.36$. It should be kept in mind, however, that the data base for these generalizations about differences in information processing orientations is the analysis of data from 70 percent of the respondents and therefore involves many more individuals than those who come from these particular backgrounds.

The Ethical-Scientific Values

An important characteristic of the more frequent users of social research is a quality of mind or what might be called a "social perspective," which, put simply, involves a sensitivity to contemporary social events and a desire for social reform: They react as if what is happening in the larger society were indistinguishable from what is happening within themselves.

It is evident to a large extent that many respondents failed to distinguish between objective social science information and subjective social sensitivity. Thus, most of the examples they offered to illustrate knowledge applications really involved the application of secondary source information, organized common sense, and social sensitivity, which as a mixture, might be called a "social perspective."

The importance of this social perspective is particularly evident from responses to the following item: "On the basis of your experiences in the federal government, can you think of instances where a new program, a major program alternative, a new social or administrative policy, a legislative proposal or a technical innovation could be traced to the social sciences?" The 82 percent of the respondents who replied "yes" to this question were asked to be specific and provide examples.

Among the approximately 350 examples given, the policy areas represented ranged widely and were as likely to be technological or medical issues as the more strictly social policy issues. To illustrate, the following decisions were offered as examples: to establish water and sewer construction assistance programs and highway construction projects such as the interstate system; to go to an all volunteer army; to select particular diseases such as sickle cell anemia and cancer for major governmental research funding; to establish the lead-base paint prevention program, compensatory educational programs, the Environmental Protection Agency, manpower and development programs, the GI Bill, consumer information programs, revenue sharing, and major programs to "humanize" management in government operations. All of these and many more programs involving governmental actions of considerable national importance were in some way traced by these respondents to the social sciences.

As respondents cited these examples, what seemed especially crucial in the decision-making process was the application of a value-laden appraisal of the possible social consequences of the policy decisions. This is not to deny that many respondents provided citations to specific social science information, particularly research, and emphasized its importance to the decision-making process. But such "hard" knowledge (research based, quantitative, and couched in scientific language) was usually only of some instrumental importance, and the final decision—whether or not to proceed with a particular policy—was more likely to depend upon an appraisal of "soft" knowledge (nonresearch based, qualitative, and couched in lay language) considerations of the possible social consequences of the policy decisions. Further, regardless of whether or not the relevant information was "hard" or "soft," these respondents were eclectic in their use of information sources and relied on newspapers, TV, and popular magazines as well as scientific government research reports and scientific journals sources. In fact, one gets the overall impression that social science knowledge, "hard" or "soft," is treated as news by these respondents—allowing its users to feel that their awareness of social issues does not lag behind the rest of society or the professionals who deal with the policymaker's field.

Regardless of whether the application of a social science perspective is scientifically objective or has scientific merit, the fact is that a very high level of sensitivity to social issues and a high level of effort to exhibit an empathic understanding of social events, and certainly a strong desire to be in close touch with contemporary social reality, existed among our respondents. Further, it should be pointed out that present knowledge utilization theories are often limited by their overreliance on an assumed pattern of knowledge use involving hard information (scientifically produced). This type of social science knowledge is used in a vast number of different contexts, and it is used often, but only rarely is policy formulation determined by a concrete, point-by-point reliance on empirically grounded data. Although the impact of soft (i.e., nonempirical) information on government functioning is extremely difficult to assess, there is widespread use of soft information, and its impact on policy, although often indirect, may be great or even greater than the impact of hard information.

The Policy Issue

Our third finding—that the policy issue is well defined and of such a nature that a "best" solution requires research knowledge—is a situation that is best understood if viewed from the standpoint of the policymaker and the setting in which he operates. Put simply, the policymaker dealing with macrolevel problems often finds himself beset with an overwhelming number of bewildering and complex responsibilities. This is especially true in social problem areas where terms suffer from considerable ambiguity and have accumulated a number of different meanings. Persons in such positions, particularly if they are political appointees and new to the job, often find themselves in a serious need of help to identify and understand the problem issues they face and the options available to deal with them. Often research is sponsored to help the policymaker find his way out of this conceptual mudhole; the purpose of such research, however, is rarely made explicit to the researcher.

It is conceivable that social scientists might be useful to help policymakers if the real purpose of the research were made explicit and if empirical data were really needed. But, without knowledge of the policymakers' difficulties, the researcher is unlikely to provide the policymaker with relevant and useful information. In the absence of a clear definition of the purposes to which the research will be addressed, the researcher creates his objectives, if for no other reason than to carry on within a framework in which he can operate.

This point is aptly illustrated by research in two areas representing major efforts to supply policymakers with useful knowledge; they are (a) the collection of social indicators and (b) program evaluation studies. My purpose here is not to go out of my way to fault the research efforts going on in these areas, but to argue that underutilization may result from a failure to clearly define research purposes in two areas where the federal government and the social science community have been most actively involved in efforts to increase the utility of social research.

In the present study, nine out of ten respondents reported that an index of social well-being was a good idea and that it represented a major opportunity for social science to contribute significantly to policy formulation. They were also able to name several measures relevant to their own operations that they would like to see included in such an index. But, when asked what use they would make of such data, the responses were so rambling and diverse that it was impossible to derive empirically based coding categories for purposes of quantification.

It is my opinion that this uncertainty results from the fact that a logically prior step in the policy formulation is lacking, namely, social indicators research would probably proceed more efficiently and its potential for policy use increased greatly, if the collection of data were based upon some previously agreed upon notion of what purposes were to be served by such indicators. But, instead, we witness a widespread and often desultory collection of data conducted with the implicit hope that, somehow, from this pragmatic but goalless effort, there will evolve some notions about what is the good life and how responsible government may help to achieve it. In short, the idea of social indicators and all of the activity currently associated with it is desirable and will probably result in a considerable amount of useful information. But it really cannot be considered to be an efficient activity simply because it started as and continues to be an activity where the "facts" are expected to provide answers to larger, essentially nonempirical issues.

Even a cursory examination of respondent comments on social indicators and other related research interests reveals a distinct tendency for top-level governmental officials to confuse extrascientific prescience and even prescience with science. The social scientist is expected to exhibit a kind of "knowing" that will tell the policymaker what values are right, what directions society should move in, and what is the good life. It is doubtful whether the social science researcher is in a better position to formulate such judgments than others. Further, it is even more doubtful if the products of social science research are better than nonresearch knowledge as a premise upon which to base such decisions. Yet, implicitly rather than explicitly, these are typical of the transcendent issues that social research is expected to illuminate, and when it fails in these matters, the expertise of social scientists and the appropriateness of their products in relation to the policymakers' interests and needs are discredited.

Perhaps evaluation research provides even better examples of these conceptual problems that hamper knowledge utilization. Here the criteria against which success and failure of program goals and strategies assessed by the evaluation researcher may bear little reference to what the sponsor "had in mind" and therefore, the findings, while not meaningless, may be viewed as irrelevant. The difficulty here appears to arise from the failure of research sponsors to be explicit with respect to the nature of the problems to be attacked, the nature of the treatment variables, or the criteria for evaluation. The research sponsor may well "know" what he means by mental health, and the like, but conceptualizing and then communicating that conceptualization may be difficult, and what he implicitly considers to be important may ultimately be quite different from the operational definitions imposed by the researcher for the purposes of obtaining measurable independent and dependent variables.

Many examples in the data show that well-conducted evaluations were judged useless by policymakers because the researchers' understanding of what was to be evaluated was not what the sponsor "had in mind." Often, however, the sponsor was unclear in his own mind about what he wanted, or was intentionally nonexplicit if he intended the research to serve latent political or administrative functions—evaluation objectives that the typical researcher would not likely assume if left to his own devices.

Some seriously disturbing consequences may have resulted from evaluations of Headstart and similar compensatory education programs. The original goals of these programs were far more broad based than allowed for by the scope of the measuring instruments used to evaluate their success. Initially, it was intended that social and emotional development were to be major components of efforts to increase academic adjustment among children from families in the lower economic ranges. This, however, was not made explicit to evaluators, who assumed the "obvious" and derived oversimplified characterizations of the program treatment and objectives. These researchers then went about evaluation almost exclusively in terms of intellective functioning and gave little more than passing attention to the broader issues. In consequence, as evaluations accumulated over time, policymakers and research evaluators lost sight of the original intent of the programs, and soon issues of race and intelligence replaced questions of emotional deprivation, sociological "damage," and educational achievement.

It is difficult to summarize these issues in any simple manner in a short chapter. The point to be made is that the policymaker has to know what he needs to know; he should have a good idea of use each piece of research will be to him; he must also understand that the formulation of a problem is at least as essential as its solution, because how a problem is defined determines what is done about it. Also, both the policymaker and the researcher must share a mutual understanding of the problems, the policy issues, and what kinds of knowledge are needed; and finally, the researcher, in particular, must understand which aspects of the problem are to be decided on the basis of data-based knowledge and which are to be based on nonresearch premises.

It is difficult enough to do policy relevant research without losing the sense of the problem even when we have explicit knowledge of the issues under investigation. But if the problem is not made explicit and if the kind of knowledge needed is beyond the range of social science research and analysis, then the conduct of research is very likely to be a wasteful and futile exercise.

Characteristics of the Research Findings

Counterintuitive Findings

Many respondents who rejected policy-relevant information did so because they found the result to contradict what they considered to be true. For example, they were impressed with the concepts of democratic leadership and organizational management and the data supporting these ideas, but given the nature and pressures of their situation, many upper-level officials were convinced that such approaches to management would probably fail. To illustrate further, although the evaluation of some governmental programs showed failure, program administrators and sponsors remain convinced that the programs had succeeded. Similar examples in research on criminal justice, welfare, work satisfaction, and education could be cited to illustrate the fact that officials are willing to accept findings that coincide with their beliefs, but unwilling to accept findings that are counterintuitive to their beliefs, quite apart from issues of scientific objectivity and political feasibility.

An additional finding is worth mentioning here. When asked about how worthwhile intuition is in understanding social behavior, the respondents who were high knowledge users answered differently from those who were low knowledge users. Low users were more likely than high users to agree that "a sensitive or intuitive person can know as much about social behavior as the social scientist can by doing research." Not only did respondents provide examples of the rejection of information because it was counterintuitive, but of equal concern were examples that indicated they often uncritically accept information that is intuitively satisfying.

Intuitive feelings about the correctness of social science research is probably a less important factor than either the issues of objectivity or political feasibility, but it nonetheless plays an influencing role in utilization. Surely one of the difficult tasks ahead for persons interested in advancing the use of social science information in the formulation of social policy is to find ways to increase the acceptability of counterintuitive findings and decrease the acceptability of findings simply because they are intuitively agreeable. It should also be added that many findings are counterintuitive not because they run contrary to the beliefs of a single person who occupies a policy position, but because they appear contrary to many of the sacred beliefs of society. A public official would be reluctant to defend actions premised on such information, even if it were politically feasible to do so. The supporting evidence for his actions would have no prima facie plausibility since the public would not be likely to be persuaded by any decisions made under these conditions and would interpret such information as political deception.

Objectivity

The following question was asked each respondent: "Have you for any reason purposely disregarded or rejected relevant social science information in making or influencing a policy decision?" Forty-four percent of the respondents indicated that they had intentionally chosen not to use certain social science information relevant to a policy issue. If they responded "yes," they were then asked to describe the rejected information and the circumstances under which it was disregarded. It was found that, first, there appeared to be no failure on the part of respondents to understand the meaning or relevance of their social science information policy. Indeed, in some instances it was clear that rejection arose because they understood only too well. Second, one of the most frequent reasons given for rejection was lack of objectivity, both in terms of methodology and interpretation.

Objectivity becomes an issue when the data base is viewed as weak and the study design as poor, or if in general the respondent is of the belief that objectivity is so lacking in the social sciences that valid findings are indiscernible from invalid findings especially when two studies in the same subject produce opposite findings. But perhaps more than for other reasons, careless, irresponsible, and shoddy program evaluations were cited by respondents to discredit social science research.

Evidence for objectivity as a factor affecting utilization is supported in other questionnaire items as well. The respondents were asked to rate various scientific disciplines on the basis of their objectivity, and it was found that the heavier users of social science information consistently rated the social science items higher than less frequent users or nonusers. These differences in ratings across utilization score levels were sizable and statistically significant.

Political Feasibility

The ultimate test of data acceptability is political, particularly in the area of domestic social policy. The reason given most frequently for rejecting relevant social science information is that the implications are politically unfeasible. Rarely are data in their own right of such compelling force as to override their political significance. While this issue is an ancient one, and much has been written on it, it remains important. We should note, however, that while operative in some way in almost all policy decisions, political considerations are rarely the sole basis for sponsoring research or for deriving action implications from its results. Moreover, we have found few instances where research was deliberately misused to serve political ends. The framework in which the policymaker seeks social science help is not, for example, one that simply looks for the "best" way to deal with welfare, but how to deal with it in such a way that what benefits recipients must also benefit the political givers.

Simply on ideological grounds it would be difficult for researchers to operate within such a framework. Moreover, even where no ideological conflicts exist, political events change at such speed that they would outpace the ability of researchers to orient themselves in accordance with the needs of policymakers who want relevant information quickly.

In fairness it should be pointed out that much of what is interpreted here as "political" would be interpreted "organizational" if this study had been conducted outside of a governmental setting. Which of these powerful and overriding "political" factors truly involve issues of political ideology and which involve considerations necessary for the management and survival of any large bureaucratic organization is difficult to say. This distinction is important, but a difficult one to make on the basis of empirical data and, in consequence, many factors labeled as "political" influences on utilization are probably more organizational than really political in that they operate in any large organization, irrespective of its goals and objectives.

The Policymaker and Knowledge Producers

In preparation for the interviews with the federal executives, a review of the literature on utilization and policymaking was conducted in order to frame questionnaire items specifically to test the most commonly held theoretical positions on the use and nonuse of scientific knowledge. Briefly, it was found that the most prevalent interpretations could be ordered into one of three classifications: (1) knowledge-specific theories, in which the essential idea is that the main reasons for nonutilization are the ways such information is gathered or the behaviors of the social scientists themselves; (2) two-communities theories, in which the argument is similar to the one C.P. Snow makes in *The Two Cultures* to explain the gap between the humanities and the hard sciences; and (3) policymaker-constraint theories, in which the chief idea is that nonutilization results mainly because of the constraints under which the policymaker operates.

Accordingly, one section of the interview was devoted to three sets of items, each of which represented one of these classifications of utilization theories. A multivariate analysis was conducted to determine the relationship between the attitudes of respondents to these theoretical positions and their self-reported use of social science information. In this process, the data were not simply aggregated by item to determine the degree of consensus among respondents about each classification of theories, but rather, to determine the relationship between the utilization scores of respondents and their responses to each of the three sets of items. The purpose was to determine the amount of variance, or utilization score differences, accounted for by the sets of items as they represented three different theoretical positions.

It was found that the items representing knowledge-specific and policymaker-constraint theories accounted for far less variance reduction than the items representing the two-communities theories. The attitudes of respondents toward the two-communities theories accounted for 14 percent of the variance compared with only 6 percent of the variance accounted for by the items representing the other two theoretical positions combined. Thus the set of items representing the two-communities theories clearly accounts for the largest proportion of explained variance.

The implication of this analysis is that theories of underutilization with the greatest degree of explanatory power are those emphasizing the existence of a gap between social scientists and policymakers due to differences in values, language, reward systems, and social and professional affiliations. More generally, it suggests that the factors responsible for the gap between the humanities and the hard sciences play a similar role in keeping the social science knowledge producers and knowledge users apart.

These three classifications of utilization theories are, of course, not meant to be mutually exclusive; it is likely that many factors work together to determine what use is made of social science information. But if the attitudes of these respondents accurately represent their experiences and their efforts to understand utilization, then these findings would strongly suggest that social scientists would be well advised to pay particularly close attention to the utilization theories that stress the lack of interaction among social scientists and policymakers as a major reason for nonuse.

It does not follow from these data, however, that an alliance of social scientists and policymakers is the appropriate recommendation to produce relevant research and to translate the results of scholarly analysis into terms of practical politics. The notion that more and better contact may result in improved understanding and greater utilization may be true, but there are also conditions where familiarity might well breed contempt rather than admiration. The need for reciprocal relations between knowledge producers in policy-making positions and knowledge users is clear, but the problem of achieving effective interaction of this sort necessarily involves value and ideological dimensions as well as technical.

Concluding Remarks

To a considerable degree the conditions described here overlap and to some extent appear to be contradictory. It is difficult, therefore, to say that one is more important than the others, or even to specify how they should work in combination. It does appear, however, that the major problems that hamper utilization are nontechnical—that is, the level of knowledge utilization is not so much the result of a slow flow of relevant and valid knowledge from knowledge producers to policymakers, but is due more to factors involving values, ideology, and decision-making styles. Thus, increased production of objective and policy-relevant data or further development and improvements in knowledge storage and retrieval systems are unlikely to advance utilization unless accompanied by success in influencing the policymaker's understanding of the problems he faces, increasing his awareness of what he needs from research, and increasing his willingness to balance scientific and extrascientific considerations.

If the key problems were more tangible and concrete, then the identification and application of appropriate technical solutions would be relatively simple. But because the problems are largely nontechnical and involve complicated extrascientific factors, the efforts at improving utilization will necessarily be more difficult and less certain in their consequence. The data suggest, however, that as a single step, what is needed to increase the level of utilization is to bridge social science and policymaker *perspectives*, but not necessarily increasing the amount of direct contact between social scientists and policymakers themselves.

This issue has not gone unrecognized. In fact, much attention has been given to training knowledge utilization experts and building knowledge retrieval systems to interlace social science knowledge production and policy information needs. These "linkage" efforts, however, have largely been based on oversimplified interpretations of the "gap" problem, and, in consequence, they have not been remarkably effective.

Insofar as the producer and user communities are comprised of people with differing abilities and inclinations to deal with the scientific and extrascientific aspects of policy issues, effective utilization probably will proceed best if it is pursued through a set of individuals representing different combinations of roles and skills located in an institutional arrangement that allows them to take into account the practical factors affecting both the production and the use of knowledge.

The precise roles played by such a group would vary substantially depending upon the informational and policy issues involved. But at a minimum the group must be capable of (a) making realistic and rational appraisals of the relative merit of the enormous amount of diversified information that abounds in the social sciences; (b) making appropriate reproductions of information from the universities to the policy setting so as to overcome problems of translation; (c) recasting policy issues into researchable terms; (d) recognizing and distinguishing between scientific and extrascientific knowledge needs; (e) dealing with the value issues and bureaucratic factors that influence the production and use of scientific knowledge; and finally (f) gaining the trust of policymakers as well as sufficient knowledge of the policy-making process to substantially introduce social science knowledge in usable form into the policy-making process at the key points where it will most likely be used.

These factors require a combination of individual and institutional characteristics that is not easily achieved. But the difficulties of effective utilization in governmental policy making should not be underestimated. Further, outlining these functions and their institutional requirements does not imply that the findings of this study will guarantee that they will work. If, however, government is serious in its intent to promote utilization, then I do mean to imply that the way to proceed toward that objective is by experimenting with (1) various forms of knowledge "transfer" groups designed with a view toward improving the capabilities of present utilization arrangements and (2) the development of new institutions designed specifically to couple scientific knowledge production to policy goals and objectives.

Note

1. N. Caplan, A. Morrison, and R. Stambaugh, *The Use of Social Science Knowledge in Policy Decisions at the National Level* (Ann Arbor, Mich.: Institute for Social Research, 1975).

14

Uses of Social Science Information by Federal Bureaucrats: Knowledge for Action versus Knowledge for Understanding

Robert F. Rich

Since World War II information concerning the attitudes and preferences of the public has become of increasing importance to political leaders and decision-makers. The Gallup and Harris poll reports became the subject of newspaper features, other news media reports, and presidential news conferences as well as books and articles. The importance assigned to public opinion information led to some proposals in the late 1960s for a council of social advisors (like the council of economic advisors) and/or a presidential public opinion advisor.

Recently, two congressional committees have begun examining the impact of public opinion data on policy making within the executive branch of the federal government. In relation to the use and impact of public opinion information (preferences and attitudes), it is clear that candidates for election feel that this input is critical for the conduct of a successful campaign. They continue to rely upon this input for guidance on how to maintain their popularity ratings. However, in terms of substantive policy making, it is not clear what importance, if any, policymakers assign to this particular information input. For what purpose is public opinion data used by policymakers? If it is used for policy making, what function or role is it a part of (e.g., problem formulation, general background or context setting, agenda setting, the formulation of legislation, and so forth)?

The Data

The questions raised above will be addressed by analyzing the experiences of the Continuous National Survey with clients in seven federal domestic service-oriented agencies. The National Opinion Research Center was given a grant by the National Science Foundation (Research Applied to National Needs Division [RANN]) to provide policymakers with policy-relevant public opinion data on a continuous basis.[1] Over the twelve-month period of the grant, thirteen different national surveys were conducted by NORC. Agency participants could ask different questions each time that were related to "hot issues," they could try to develop monitoring procedures through the use of time-series data, or they could

A version of this chapter was prepared for delivery at the 1976 Annual Meeting of the Midwest Political Science Association, April 29-May 1, 1976, Pick Congress Hotel, Chicago. The research used in preparation of this chapter was supported in part by a Russell Sage Foundation grant to Donald T. Campbell for "Methods for the Experimenting Society."

attempt to evaluate service delivery systems by integrating "objective data" on what services exist in a given area with subjective survey data on how often they are used and with what degree of client satisfaction.[2] NSF/RANN felt that if agency participants found this resource useful, then they would fund it out of their own on-line budgets after the grant period expired.[3]

In-depth interviews were conducted with (1) all agency participants involved with the administration and/or utilization of the research results of this experiment; (2) the "project staff" of NORC; and (3) those involved at NSF/RANN in administering the grant. Over the eighteen-month period in which the Continuous National Survey (CNS) was in the field, interviews were conducted with the same thirty-eight respondents on five different occasions. In addition, these respondents were also interviewed approximately nine months after the survey went "out of the field." Wherever possible, documentation (memos, letters, logs of telephone conversations) related to decisions concerning agency information handling was collected.

Definition of Concepts

In the analysis of these data, the policy or problem-solving area is the basic unit of analysis. The use of information is examined as it relates to a policy area as a whole. This approach is consonant with the operations of government. Single reports or memos tend not to be used by themselves. The available information resources on a given question are brought together before options are considered. For example, a report on the impact of diet drugs was written on the basis of four different surveys of public opinion; this report entered into policy discussion as opposed to a single memo written on the basis of one survey.[4] Upon the completion of this composite report, other information gathered on the same subject and the judgment of the experts also entered into the policy discussion. Our experience suggests that *information is used in groups or clusters and should be analyzed from that point of view.*

"Use" refers to information entering into the policy-making process. It comes to the desk of the decisionmaker, he reads it, and it influences the discussion of policy. The potential of influencing a decision is the critical component of our definition of utilization. If information is used, it is by definition "influencing" policy decisions.

Differentiation was also made between *instrumental* and *conceptual* utilization.[5] "Instrumental" use refers to those cases where respondents cited and could document (or it could be cross-validated) the specific way in which the CNS information was being used for decision-making or problem-solving purposes. "Conceptual" use refers to influencing a policymaker's thinking about an issue without putting information to any specific, documentable use. It also refers to planned uses of information "in the future." Both instrumental and conceptual use are tied to the policy-making process and are, therefore, to be distinguished from use of information exclusively for political purposes (e.g., campaign strategies) or for purposes of career advancement (e.g., journal articles).

Why Policymakers are Interested in
Public Opinion Information

In terms of understanding the importance of the Continuous National Survey to federal decisionmakers, it should be remembered that each participating agency (and its policymakers) could specify the questions and problem-solving areas they wanted to focus on. Unlike most external research funded by line agencies, the CNS was specifically designed to meet the needs of decisionmakers: It allowed policymakers to collect data on subjects they personally specified; it allowed them to collect information on timely topics of direct relevance to them; and it was designed to provide "fast turn around time" so that results from the surveys could be built into short-term problem-solving needs as well as long-range policy making and planning.

The documentation collected during the course of this research reveals that policymakers recognized the potential that this survey instrument offered to them and that they had the intention of applying it to their problem-solving needs. In writing about the questions that the CNS would be applied to, some of the memos stated:

The food program topic was ranked first for several reasons. First, though the program has grown rapidly over the past few years [over $3 billion budgeted for FY 1973], very little reliable information is available concerning the size of the program's target population, its performance in reaching that population, characteristics of participants, reason for nonparticipation, overlap with other forms of welfare assistance, etc. Furthermore, there is ample evidence that the survey information is wanted and would be used. The administrator of the agency has himself participated in the design of questions. Thus, the survey offers an opportunity to demonstrate that relevant information can be collected and made available for decision making in a relatively short span of time.

The questions on housing were given high priority for somewhat the same reasons, though in this case the questions originated within the secretary's office rather than within the administering agency. Again, this is a program that has grown rapidly over the past four or five years with loans in FY 1973 exceeding $2 billion. The problem this program is charged with addressing are formidable ... more so than most people appreciate. For example, though only 32 percent of the occupied housing units in the United States were located in areas served by this program in 1970, 68 percent of all units in the nation that lacked complete plumbing were located there. And when "substandard housing" is defined as incomplete plumbing and/or overcrowded units, rural areas account for just under half of the U.S. total. The questions included in the survey are designed to help determine: the opportunity for shifting program funds away from new housing starts and toward repair and renovation; attitudes toward mobile homes; the demand for rental housing in rural areas; citizen awareness of the Farmer's Home Administration housing loan program; and the relationship between residential mobility and the availability of housing. These are policy questions upon which decisions will be made within the coming months.

Those agency participants concerned with more general policy concerns were able to be more specific:

We propose to use two cycles of the RANN survey for questions about community control of public schools.

Ever since the controversy over Ocean Hill-Brownsville, the community control issue has entered into policy discussions at all levels of government. But our search of ERIC and other sources of educational research literature reveals little good evidence about how much "community control" people want, what are the characteristics of the people who support it, and how strongly the concern is felt in the general population.

We have designed a set of survey items to gather evidence from NORC's national sample on the following questions:

Do those who favor community control favor full operating control over the schools, full control over special aspects of school policy, or simply more influence than they have now (but not complete control of anything)?

How widespread is the opinion that citizens have too little influence in school policy? Are there some groups in which that opinion is especially prevalent?

These memos illustrate how policymakers intend to use survey data in the decision-making process. It is important to note that the CNS-generated information was seen as serving several different purposes in the policy-making process: (1) influencing decisions on concrete policy options; (2) helping to assess and/or anticipate future problems; and (3) helping to institutionalize this source of information as part of the regularly consulted decision-making inputs. Unlike other surveys available to policymakers, the Continuous National Survey represented a potential decision-making resource that policymakers (a) were interested in, (b) perceived as relevant to their concrete needs, and (c) had been involved in creating.

Patterns of Utilization

The data suggest that there were two waves or cycles of utilization associated with the participating agency's processing of the CNS-generated data. To some extent, they may be equated with long-term and short-term utilization.[6] The "intended uses" (i.e., the reasons for collecting the information) should take place in the short run, although some other uses may take place other than the one that was initially expected. The *first wave* seems to occur when information is initially received and for approximately three months thereafter. The three-month time period is tentative; in this case study, this span appears to be the maximum time an agency needs to digest the information and have it flow through the decision-making hierarchy if it is to be used on a short-term basis. The first wave can be characterized by the following profile: When information is used, the flow of information is upwards through the decision-making hierarchy and the utilization of information is primarily *instrumental.* Table 14-1 illustrates the breakdown between instrumental and conceptual uses for the first and second waves of utilization.

By way of interpretation, it should be noted: (1) In eleven of the policy areas to which the CNS was applied, no use of the information could be documented for the first wave of utilization; (2) the most common forms of instrumental use and/or dissemination were briefing the assistant secretary or secretary, briefing a joint level cabinet meeting, and writing memos to one's supervisors (dissemination); (3) the least common form of instrumental use was "regulation writing"; (4) the most common forms of conceptual use and/or dissemination were using the information for general background only and writing memos to one's counterparts; and (5) the least common forms of conceptual use were "methodological planning" and writing speeches or journal articles.

The second wave of utilization generally occurred from three to six months after the information was initially received, though it also might occur at a later time. The flow of information in this case was primarily lateral or downward in the decision-making hierarchy and the utilization of information was primarily conceptual (see Table 14-1), or traditional in the sense of the ways in which social science-related information has been used by federal policymakers in the past (e.g., for conferences, for journal papers, for general background only, and for purposes of writing new RFPs). For the second wave, we found that the CNS had a significant conceptual effect. As illustrated in Tables 14-1 and 14-2 the most prevalent form of utilization was memos written to subordinates in the

Table 14-1
Utilization of the Continuous National Survey: "Short-Term vs. Long-Term" Decision Making

Type of Use	First Wave		Second Wave		Totals	
	(N)	(%)	(N)	(%)	(N)	(%)
Instrumental	51	94	3	6	54	100
Conceptual	22	34	42	66	64	100
Totals	73	62	45	38	118	100

Note: Based on twenty-six policy areas in which the information was being applied.

Table 14-2
Specific Types of Utilization by "Short-Term/Long-Term"

Type of Use	First Wave	Second Wave	Totals
Instrumental			
Regulation writing	2	0	2
Writing memos to supervisors	16	1	17
Writing memos for congressional presentation	3	0	3
Briefing assistant secretary	11	0	11
Briefing secretary	10	2	12
Briefing joint cabinet-level meeting	9	0	9
Totals	51	3	54
Conceptual			
General background	6	6	12
Methodological planning	1	6	7
Writing memos counterparts	11	4	15
Writing memos downward	0	11	11
Writing new RFPs	0	6	6
Writing papers/journals	2	9	11
Speeches	2	0	2
Totals	22	42	64

Note: Based on twenty-six policy areas in which the CNS was being applied (fourteen were cases of nonuse).

decision-making hierarchy concerning general ideas that had been teased out of the CNS results.

As illustrated in Table 14-2, utilization and/or dissemination fell into three categories during the second wave: (1) writing memos downward in the decision-making hierarchy to one's subordinates; (2) planning future research and specifying what its dimensions (components) should be; and (3) writing papers or articles for purposes of career advancement. It is significant to note that it was only possible to document three instances of instrumental use.

The difference between the first and second waves of utilization can be viewed as a difference between information inputs oriented toward *action* in the policy sphere and inputs oriented toward gaining a better *understanding* of the policy context in which decision making takes place. "Understanding" represents the overall perspective developed by policymakers. Within this perspective, they are able to order diverse information inputs from several different sources. The action inputs represent the discrete bits of information that are used to fill in and support the overall perspective. Gaining an understanding of the policy context may also aid the decisionmaker in anticipating future needs and in learning from past experiences.

The types of questions requested by policymakers would have suggested distinctly different applications to short-term decision making in the agencies requesting the CNS data. The vast majority of questions asked were related to long-term monitoring of trends and program evaluation. If the information was used for its intended purpose, based on the types of questions asked and the responses of agency participants, more decision-making inputs related to (1) indicator construction, (2) program regulation, (3) the formulation of programmatic guidelines, and (4) short as well as long-range planning would have been documented. As the data indicate, only very few instances representing these kinds of decision-making inputs could actually be documented.

This finding reflects two realities of the actual versus "ideal" policy-making process. First, there is a propensity among lower-level policymakers and their staffs to cover all possible contingencies. Thus, information will be collected to meet short-term needs should they be put on the agenda. Information inputs, therefore, can enter into a *holding pattern*: uses that are planned for in the future. The documentation collected for this study reflects this type of future planning. For example, one respondent reported:

I collected this long-term trend information for the purpose of aiding the planning process and writing legislation in the area of facilitating travel between large cities. We just haven't had the time to get to it yet. I hope that within the next six to nine months that this will be possible.

Another respondent articulated the same concern:

Our staff have been told to work with other problems which have been assigned high priority. However, this information will be crucial in drafting legislation and regulations in this area.

Second, policy-related problems have priority over programmatic-related problems. The day-to-day problems on the immediate agenda of policymakers are more important than program evaluations that are viewed as a "long-term" adjustment. These data are consistent with this idea: Intended uses were met in 73.3 percent of the cases in policy-related areas and in only 16.6 percent of the cases in program-related areas.

Differences between Energy- and Nonenergy-Related Policy Areas

The most important difference we found in our study was the one between the energy-related and nonenergy-related areas. As illustrated in Table 14-3, the

206

Table 14-3
Utilization by Energy- vs. Nonenergy-Related Policy Areas

Type of Use	Energy Policy			Nonenergy		
	First Wave	Second Wave	Total	First Wave	Second Wave	Total
	%	%	% (N)	%	%	% (N)
Instrumental	100	0	100 (38)	81	19	100 (16)
Conceptual	41	59	100 (29)	29	71	100 (35)
Totals	75	25	100 (67)	45	55	100 (51)

Note: Based on twenty-six policy areas in which the CNS information was being applied.

information collected concerning the energy crisis in general and the impact of the Arab oil embargo in specific was used more consistently for instrumental purposes than the information collected in any of the other twenty-five policy areas. It is also in the energy-related areas that the information was put to the most diverse use and applications. In the energy areas, the generic differences between the first and second waves of utilization are still maintained. Relative to the energy-related areas, however, the other policy areas reflect very limited instrumental use.

By way of interpretation, it is important to note that energy-related problem/policy areas only represented 23 percent of the questions asked by agency participants in the CNS; yet, the instrumental (action-oriented) use made of the data represent 75 percent of all instrumental uses made of the information generated through the CNS. This finding raises the question of whether or not the uses made of the CNS in energy-related policy areas are representative of the potential or actual capacity of survey research to impact on public decision-making processes.[7]

In this same context, it is also important to highlight the conditions affecting the energy-related problem-solving areas: Upper-level policymakers were interested in receiving *any information* that could potentially be relevant to their *vast* and *immediate* decision-making responsibilities and needs. During the interviews, respondents said quite candidly that the CNS was in the "right place" at the "right time." Under "optimum, noncrisis conditions" policymakers might not have chosen survey methods to collect information relevant to their needs. Thus, it can be concluded that the decision-making processes affecting the use of the CNS in energy-related policy areas did not represent the typical conditions under which survey information is used at the national level. Instead, the nonenergy-related policy areas are probably far more typical of the ways in which survey information impacts upon decision making in domestic service-related problem-solving areas at the national level.

Discussion Conclusions

The literature in the areas of public policy, research utilization, and sociology of science suggests that social science knowledge is not effectively used, appreciated, or understood by policymakers. This is the basis for what C.P. Snow and others have called the two communities theory (see Horowitz, 1967; Caplan, 1975; Moynihan, 1973.) Thus, it is believed that *underutilization* and *nonutilization* are due to mistrust between researchers and decisionmakers; some feel that this reason is especially true for those researchers making use of surveys. In addition, some scientists believe that policymakers are unsophisticated about research methods and capabilities and would not be able to *effectively* utilize high-quality social science knowledge, if it were made available to them.

Within the context of the two-communities theory, several other assumptions are worth noting: (1) The social science community tends to assume that underutilization is due to a mismatch between their needs and constraints and those of policymakers; (2) social scientists tend to think of utilization strictly in terms of instrumental utilization (they do not see the "pay-off" if some action-oriented decision cannot be tied to the utilization of their research products); (3) if the two-communities perspective is accurate, policymakers would rather rely on their own intuition than take the risk of using information that they do not fully understand and value; and (4) as a result, there is a resistance within government to the development of new information sources that could be applied to decision making (Moynihan, 1969; Levine, 1972). It is also worth noting that these assumptions are based on a theoretical, anecdotal, case study, and experiential based literature.

This researcher's feeling is that the experiences of the Continuous National Survey serve as a suitable context in which to examine some of these assumptions. In its design, the National Science Foundation sought to take account of the assumptions made by the two-communities theory: (1) Social science information is irrelevant because it is not oriented toward the specific decision-making needs of policymakers (to counter this, participants could specify exactly what data they wanted collected); (2) researchers are not capable of providing information on a timely basis (to counter this, the CNS was constructed so as to guarantee the production of timely information—that is, one national survey was constantly in the field); and (3) researchers do not attempt to focus their research to fit into the overall information needs of agencies (to counter this, policymakers could construct questions so as to be integrated into overall agency information-gathering activities). Unlike most surveys available to policymakers, the CNS offered the opportunity for decision-makers within government to learn about the capabilities of survey methodology for problem-solving purposes.

Some of our findings are related to the assumptions associated with the two-communities theory. But our findings do not suggest that these assumptions are salient in explaining utilization patterns of decisionmakers. Although we discovered that some of these assumptions are present, other *important ones* were not documentable: (1) Policymakers *do value* survey research results and their potential to aid decisionmakers in the problem-solving process (this finding was verified in Caplan's recent survey of 204 federal executives); (2) policymakers are receptive to developing new information capacities within their agencies (this finding was verified by the support given to the CNS and the amount of time spent learning the strengths and weaknesses of survey methodology); (3) policymakers *do report* some feelings of mistrust toward researchers (this mistrust, however, does not appear to impede the utilization of the research results); (4) policymakers are aware of the needs, expectations, and constraints affecting the research community and are still anxious to avail themselves of the skills available in this community (Caplan found, for example, that upper-level policymakers feel that the best quality information is not available to them); and (5) policymakers do not appear to be unsophisticated about research methods and decisions related to the development of agency information capacities.

Given the findings from this analysis—that when survey research is used in a policy-making context, it is used conceptually—one would be tempted to conclude that survey research was not used for decision-making purposes, but, instead, merely influenced the way decisionmakers think about a particular problem, or the way they think about overall agency information needs. Thus, while action implications growing out of the CNS findings could not be documented, it was possible to document: (1) how the experiences of the CNS influenced decisionmakers' thinking about a problem (i.e., it helped them see a particular problem from another perspective or in a different way); (2) the experiences related to learning about the strengths and weaknesses of survey methodology helped to specify future RFPs designed to provide survey information to these agencies; and (3) the experiences with the CNS made policymakers more receptive to using survey results in the future. One policymaker, for example, commented to us: "We were not able to use the survey data intelligently at this time. But it is the wave of the future. You can be sure that we will have to make use of an instrument like the Continuous National Survey in the near future."

The results generated from this research project suggest that the conceptual uses of social science-related knowledge (e.g., survey data) should not be viewed as failures to translate research findings into action. This type of conclusion would be as short-sighted as the practice of some policymakers to collect information primarily for the purpose of "muddling through" on a day-to-day basis. A preoccupation with the action implications of social science knowledge overlooks the significance of other political and organizational functions that knowledge may serve: (1) organizational learning and planning, and (2) beginning to influence the way in which problems are defined and specified at the level of individual administrators.

If these findings can be shown to be generalizable across other methodologies and problem-solving areas, then these data underscore the necessity of rethinking our preoccupation with action implications in the application of scientific knowledge to public policy making.

Notes

1. For a full discussion of the details of this grant, see Robert F. Rich, "An Investigation of Information Gathering and Handling in Seven Federal Bureaucracies: A Case Study of the Continuous National Survey," unpublished doctoral dissertation, University of Chicago, 1975.

2. For details of the research design, see the NORC proposal to the National Science Foundation, Research Applied to National Needs Division, 1971.

3. This point was made to use in the interviews that were conducted as part of the research presented in this chapter. We promised respondents that their identities would not be revealed. Thus, we refer to the National Science Foundation and a position that it has taken. It is, of course, clear to us that the Foundation does not have one position. For purposes of confidentiality, however, this is the way we have chosen to protect individual people.

4. This type of information was drawn from the documents collected in connection with the interviews completed for this study.

5. For another discussion of the differences between instrumental and conceptual utilization, see Nathan Caplan et al., *The Use of Social Science Knowledge in Policy Decisions at the National Level: A Report to Respondents* (Ann Arbor, Mich.: Institute for Social Research, 1975), pp. 17-20. In this context, Caplan also makes a distinction between hard and soft knowledge.

6. For a more detailed discussion of two waves of utilization, see Robert F. Rich, "Selective Utilization of Social Science Related Information by Federal Policy-Makers," *Inquiry* 13, no. 3 (September 1975).

7. Ibid., for a more detailed discussion of the factors affecting utilization of energy related data.

References

Arrow, K.J. 1974. *The Limits of Organization.* New York: W.W. Norton.

Blau, P. 1955. *The Dynamics of Bureaucracy.* Chicago: University of Chicago Press.

Campbell, D.T. 1969. "Reforms as Experiments." *American Psychologist* 24, no. 4 (April), pp. 409-28.

Caplan, N. et al., 1975. *The Use of Social Science Knowledge in Policy Decisions at the National Level.* Ann Arbor, Mich.: Institute for Social Research.

Crozier, M. 1964. *The Bureaucratic Phenomenon: An Examination of Bureaucracy in Modern Organization and Its Cultural Setting in France.* Chicago: University of Chicago Press.

Hauser, P.M. 1972. *Statistics and Politics.* Paper prepared for the Annual Meeting of the American Statistical Association, August.

Horowitz, I.L. 1967. *The Rise and Fall of Project Camelot: Studies in the Relationship between Social Science and Practical Politics.* Cambridge, Mass.: M.I.T. Press.

Horowitz, I.L. (ed.). 1971. *The Use and Abuse of Social Science: Behavioral*

Science and National Policy-Making. New Brunswick, N.J.: Transaction Books.

Kitsuse, J., and Cicourel, A.V. 1969. "A Note on the Use of Official Statistics." *Social Problems* 11 (Fall), pp. 131-39.

Levine, R.A. 1972. *Public Planning: Failure and Redirection.* New York: Basic Books.

Likert, R. 1960. "The Dual Function of the Statistics." *Journal of the American Statistical Association* 55 (March), pp. 1-7.

March, J.G., and Simon, H.A. 1958. *Organizations.* New York: Wiley.

Moynihan, D.P. 1969. *Maximum Feasible Misunderstanding.* New York: The Free Press.

_____ . 1973. *Coping.* New York: Random House.

Shonfield, A., and Shaw, S. (eds.). 1972. *Social Indicators and Social Policy.* Social Science Research Council. (Especially Richard Rose's article on the market for policy indicators.)

Wilensky, H.I. 1967. *Organizational Intelligence.* New York: Basic Books.

15

The Challenge of Social Research to Decision Making

Carol H. Weiss
and
Michael J. Bucuvalas

So much rhetoric has been spilled on the subject of the use and nonuse of social science research for decision making that a yearning sets in for systematic evidence. How much use is made of social research? What are the obstacles to greater use? Does social research offer knowledge that *can* contribute to the making of decisions? When decisionmakers heed research, are their decisions wiser?

These are difficult questions, and most of them defy systematic analysis. The issues are too complex and soggy to yield readily to large-scale study.

In the last few years, however, several studies have been done that are making inroads on the morass.[1] We know several things that were not clear before. For one thing, it is now apparent that *how much* use government decisionmakers make of social research is largely a matter of definition. Nathan Caplan and his colleagues, for example, found from interviews with high-ranking U.S. federal administrators that the extent of research use *hinged* on the conceptualization of "use" and "research" (see Chapter 13 of this volume). If use was defined as the direct influence of study findings on pending decisions, it was not common. If it included the consideration of social science concepts and generalizations in formulating questions, setting agendas, and constructing images of policy, then it was not uncommon. We are thus alerted not only to the conceptual complexity of the questions we are raising, but also to the multiple conceptual complexities of the decision systems we want to study.

The study reported in this chapter was designed to answer one of the many questions in the area of research utilization: What are the characteristics of social science research studies that make them useful for decision making? This formulation avoids the concept of "use." We decided to finesse the collection of data on actual use of social research for a variety of reasons. First, it is exceedingly unclear what constitutes a use. Is "use" the adoption of research recommendations intact, the nudging of a decision in the direction suggested by research findings, the reinforcement of a likely decision by research, the consideration of research findings (even if these are overwhelmed by other considerations in the situation), rethinking the nature of the policy issue, redefining informational needs? What kind of use is a "real" use? And how much is enough? Second, the assumptions embedded in a study of the characteristics of those research studies that had proved to be used were troublesome. The presumption would be that the *right* kind of research, since it is worth its salt, would be used, and any studies that were disregarded would have something wrong with them. This is an unfair burden to put on research. Given the nature of the political decision-making system and its contingencies and perturbations, some excellent and apposite research is inevitably ignored. Therefore, the characteristics of utilized research might display little more than the quirks of fate.

Third, there were the methodological problems of respondent memory and bias. People do not always remember the source of their information and ideas. They don't maintain orderly reference files in their heads. Decisionmakers are also on occasion reluctant to acknowledge that they were influenced by other people's evidence or argument. So, the evidence we would collect might be incomplete and untrustworthy. Finally, if we were to undertake a quantitative study, it was possible that we would run up against a dearth of cases. We might find too few citations to specific utilized studies to allow investigation of their characteristics.

Aha, says the alert reader, you have only moved, not solved, the definitional problem. Now you have to conceptualize "useful," and you are still stuck with "research" and "decision making," too. True enough.

Some Definitions

In our study, "useful" research has two distinct features (and we keep them distinct). First, its content makes an intrinsic contribution to the work of the agency; it contains ideas or information that advance the decision-making process. Second, officials say that they are likely to take the research into account in their work. (Thus, we have also given a definition of research use. "Taking research into account" constitutes use.) Useful research then makes a substantive contribution and/or is likely to be considered.

"Research" was easier. We selected for our inquiry fifty actual research studies performed under government grant and contract funding and completed between 1970 and 1974. More about these studies appears in the next section on methods. Finally, "decision making" is defined as what people in top positions do. We found in pretests that officials, even those who head major agencies, tend to disavow making decisions. Responsibility is so widely shared within and between agencies that any individual person at best only "influences" decisions. Therefore, in selecting the sample of respondents, we chose people in positions of responsibility for policy and program decisions. Interview questions asked them about the intrinsic contribution that research makes and the likelihood that they would use it *in their work*.

Methods of the Study

The central feature of our research was the presentation of actual research studies (in abstract form) to occupants of decision-making positions. Interviews centered on their judgments of the usefulness of the proffered research and their ratings of that research on a series of descriptive dimensions. A good deal of additional information which helped to illuminate their responses was collected as well.

The substantive area of our investigation was mental health, defined in the broadest sense. We selected the research studies for analysis from research funded by the National Institute of Mental Health (NIMH), the National Institute of Alcoholism and Alcohol Abuse (NIAAA), and the National Institute of Drug Abuse (NIDA). We selected respondents from occupants of key positions in mental health decision making and research.

A stratified sample of 250 respondents was drawn from five positions. Of these, 150 were to be mental health decisionmakers. We actually interviewed 155, 51 of whom were from top federal positions within the Alcohol, Drug Abuse, and Mental Health Administration (ADAMHA) of the Department of Health, Education, and Welfare (DHEW) and its component institutes (NIMH, NIAAA, and NIDA). To redress the usual bias toward federal officeholders, we also included 52 state decisionmakers in the highest tier of positions in ten state departments of mental health and 52 local decisionmakers who administered mental health centers and mental hospitals and their component services. The other 100 respondents, whom we do not discuss in this chapter, were social science researchers engaged in government-funded research in mental health and members of ADAMHA research review committees who review research proposals for funding.

It may be worth mentioning something about the research studies that formed the focus of the interviews. We selected fifty social science research reports, completed between 1970 and 1974 under sponsorship by NIMH, NIAAA, and NIDA, that evidenced reasonable technical competence. We selected them to be representative of the spectrum of grant and contract research, with purposive variation on three dimensions: the manipulability of the major explanatory variables, the administrative feasibility of the implications, and the degree of congruence with prevailing beliefs in the mental health field. We also tried to vary such other factors as type of study, type and size of sample, and ambiguity of results.

For each of the fifty studies, our staff wrote a standard-format, two-page abstract. The abstracts covered the same information: objectives of the study, methods, major findings, and conclusions. Every abstract was assigned to two occupants of the five different positions in the sample. Each respondent read and discussed two of the abstracts during the interview. Since we found that decisionmakers often receive research results in summary form, the use of an abstract probably introduced more verisimilitude than artificiality into the event. We tried very hard to match the content of the study to the job responsibilities of the respondent, within the constraint of the design (i.e., assignment of abstracts to occupants of each position).

Respondents rated each research abstract on several measures of usefulness and on twenty-nine descriptive characteristics. The usefulness measures came from questions that asked the respondents (1) how likely he or she was to take the study results into account when making a decision on the issues discussed and (2) the extent to which the study contained ideas or information that could contribute to his or her agency's work. Respondents were also asked who the most appropriate user of the study would be, and then they were asked the same two questions for occupants of that position. A further question inquired about the types of purposes study results would serve: raising an issue to attention, formulating new policies or programs, improving existing programs, changing ways of thinking about the issues, and so forth.

The descriptive characteristics included items on research quality, feasibility of implementation, political acceptability of findings, and so forth. Appendix 15A contains the lists of usefulness measures and descriptive characteristics we used.

Expected Effects of Research Characteristics

We expected characteristics of the research studies to have an effect on their perceived usefulness. The premise was that some kinds of research stand a chance of being useful—and even of being used, despite all the external pressures on decision-making systems. Our task was to specify the characteristics that made some studies more useful than others.

We expected three clusters of items to affect the usability of research: its technical competence, the implementability of its conclusions, and its political acceptability. The set of items on the technical competence of the research would represent the degree to which it could be trusted because of its methodological soundness. We had eliminated seriously flawed studies from our inquiry since we did not want to lose our respondents' interest and respect by presenting them with outright tripe and since it appeared unnecessary to find out whether they would reject totally incompetent research from consideration. There was a wide enough range of research quality in the fifty studies included to allow analysis of differential effects. Items that we expected to fall in this cluster dealt with methodology, such as "Technical quality of the research is high," "Generalizable to equivalent populations," and "Statistically sophisticated." We did expect that methodological competence would play some part in a study's usability, although we were not sure how much. Perhaps it was only with methodological purists, or only below a certain cut-off point of technical capability, that this factor would make a difference.

A second set of characteristics that we thought would influence the usefulness of research had to do with the feasibility and practicality of its conclusions. Critics often note that much social research deals with issues in global form and makes grandiose recommendations. For example, a study on the crisis in city finances concludes with a call for fundamental redistribution of income in the United States. Or else research offers data but no interpretation of those data for action, so that busy executives are left to ferret out whatever guidance they can from the turgid prose and complex tables. Many studies deal with the effects of unbudgeable or sticky variables, such as race and socioeconomic status, that government decisionmakers cannot alter, but ignore the manipulable variables, such as program availability or eligibility for services, that they can change. Research is often late—arriving on the decisionmaker's desk after the decision that it might illumine has already been made. When social research studies do not match the decision needs and scope of authority of decisionmakers, then they are likely to have limited influence.

The third set of characteristics we envisioned had to do with a research study's compatibility with prevailing political arrangements. It seemed likely that research would be deemed more useful, and more likely to be used, when it accepted the value orientations of potential users, when its findings were compatible with the philosophy and program structures in operation, and when its problem formulation and its conclusions fit the political climate. It might be seen as particularly useful when it supported the position that potential users already held and could be used as ammunition in their cause. Research that challenged things-as-they-are seemed less likely to be judged useful by decisionmakers than research that confirmed and legitimated their positions.[2]

In addition to these three factors, we believed that relevance to the substantive content of one's work—its fit to the decisions the decisionmaker faced—was a sine qua non. We tried in several ways to ensure this fit. First, in assigning research studies to respondents, we made every effort to match topic to job responsibilities. Second, in the wording of the question about likelihood of use, we said, "Assuming your office had to consider the issues discussed in the study, how likely is it. . . ." And last, we asked each respondent to tell us who the most appropriate user of the study would be and to respond to questions about usefulness for occupants of that position.

Such were our expectations. We expected technical characteristics of the research to make a difference; we thought another effect would come from the practicality and implementability of the study; we expected political and value considerations to play a part. Each decisionmaker rated each study abstract on the characteristics listed in Appendix 15A, and we executed factor analysis on the ratings. It is time to see how the characteristics actually clustered.

Empirical Clustering of the Characteristics

Factor analysis as used here is more than a data reduction technique. It isolates those analytically separable dimensions of real studies that respondents use in their ratings. These dimensions summarize the patterns of covariation in respondents' descriptions, and as such, the factors represent underlying constructs that people use in describing research.

The total number of (analytic) cases for factor analysis was 510, which represents ratings of two studies by each of 255 respondents. From the factor analysis, we located four stable factors.[3] They are very much the same for the total sample, for the decisionmaker subsample, and for the researcher and review panel member subsamples. They represent dimensions of research that people distinguish as they assess research. Obviously, the factors derive from the list of research characteristics that we provided. Our list was developed from extensive study of the literature and from repeated pretests and attempted to be comprehensive.[4] In factor analyzing the data, we found that omission of some of the items left the factors unchanged. They appear to be tapping viable underlying constructs about research that tend to remain stable.

The four factors do not line up toe-to-toe with our three hypothesized dimensions. (See Appendix 15B for a listing of the items in each factor and their loadings.) Two of them, however, are very close. Factor I (research quality) is indeed the cluster of items about the intrinsic technical quality of the study. It contains the items about technical quality, statistical sophistication, objectivity, quantitative data, internal consistency of findings, comprehensive set of explanatory variables, support of recommendations by the data, generalizability, validity, and additions to descriptive, causal, or theoretical knowledge. Respondents went beyond the strictly methodological competence of design and analysis to include several other research essentials, such as lack of bias and the basing of recommendations directly on findings (rather than taking too great a leap into personal predilection). Moreover, two of the items have to do with how the results happened to turn out: the internal consistency and unambiguousness of findings (rather than the indeterminate, "on-the-one-hand-but-on-the-other" pattern) and the addition to descriptive or causal knowledge. These latter two items are in practice beyond the control of the researcher; they are the luck of the draw; but clearly they add to the authoritativeness of the research. Factor I then represents not only the methodological soundness usually associated with technical quality but also the cogency of the research.

The other factor that conforms to our expectations is Factor III (action orientation). This factor is very much like the implementability dimension. Studies that were rated high on Factor III contain explicit recommendations for action; they examined the effects of manipulable variables; they focus on a limited set of dependent variables; they have direct implications for action; and they add to *practical* knowledge. (The two items on our list about adding to knowledge divide in a sensible, sensitive way.) This is just the kind of research that administrators can put to use directly. Perhaps the only surprise is that the item "inexpensive to implement" did not load on this factor. "Inexpensive" did not load on any factor and in effect forms a separate factor of its own. An explanation is suggested by the fact that respondents had great difficulty rating this item; it had the highest number of missing answers. Ratings may have been unreliable because of the complexity involved in figuring how much implementation would cost and then deciding what scale of expense to apply in order to determine "inexpensiveness."

So far, so good. The pattern of abstract ratings has confirmed the two dimensions of research quality and administrative feasibility. However, the hypothesized political factor, it turns out, has separated into two factors. Factor II, which we call conformity to user expectations, contains the items: supports a position already held by the user, consistent with a body of previous knowledge, compatible with the ideas and values of the potential user, agrees with the respondent's sense of the situation, and (with a negative loading) findings are unexpected or novel. The emphasis here is on the *user*, rather than on the political system, and the theme is that the findings are compatible with what he or she believes. While there is certainly some sense that the research is congenial to the user's values and policy position, there is a more pervasive sense that it conforms with what he or she knows is so: that it supports his or her construction of reality. This factor then becomes grounds for believing the research, because research that is rated high on Factor II is consistent with one's own experience and knowledge. Factor I (research quality), provided technical grounds for faith in a study. The conformity factor appears to be an independent source of trust or distrust in research results.[5]

An experienced executive relies on his experience as an alternative source of information to that provided by social science research. When the two sources conflict, he may criticize the social research for its methodological inadequacy, not out of peevishness but because the research design yielded results contrary to his informed judgment and is therefore suspect. There is no particular reason to expect him to surrender his opinions without contest. As a rule, this type of behavior by a decisionmaker is labeled "political." The factor analysis suggests that responses to challenges to one's own opinions are not political in the same sense that are responses to assaults on agency philosophy, administration programs, or bureau organization.

The conformity factor dealt with support of the user's values and sense of reality, but it did not include such items as "implications of the findings are politically acceptable." The items that relate to the political system itself appear in Factor IV (challenge to the status quo). Items that load on the challenge factor are: challenges existing assumptions and institutional arrangements; implies the need for major change in philosophy, organization, or services; raises new issues or offers new perspectives; and (negatively) implications of the findings are politically acceptable. This factor is the most overtly political one—stripped down to assaults offered by research to the status quo. Research that rates high on this factor indicates disagreement with current institutional practice.

The challenge factor points toward change. In this respect, it has something in common with action orientation, which also represents a push to reform. Unlike action orientation, however, which has a practical bent, studies rated high on challenge tend to suggest fundamental reconceptualization and major change. There is a relationship, however. In the final oblique factor solution, challenge and action orientation are correlated (r = .30). There is some suggestion that studies that challenge also propose courses of action to bring change into effect.

Our hypothesized political factor has become two factors: conformity and challenge. Our respondents effectively separated their own beliefs from the beliefs and arrangements underlying the political and administrative systems. The implication is that they may (or may not) be in sympathy with findings that challenge institutional practice. The fact that conformity and challenge are not opposite ends of a continuum is demonstrated by the fact that they are not negatively correlated. They are essentially not correlated at all (r = .05). They vary independently.

A hypothetical example may clarify the distinction between conformity and challenge. In the 1960s a study that demonstrated the superiority of community-based day treatment over in-patient hospitalization of schizophrenics might have "conformed" to the beliefs of many mental health officials. At the same time, it would have "challenged" traditional and entrenched assumptions and arrangements and thus implied the need for major change. In this example, we can also see that the research quality factor could be an independent basis for finding the research useful. The action orientation of the research might provide a further and different basis for usefulness to the extent that the research explicitly spelled out the implications of the findings and provided feasible guidelines for application.

Before we leave the factor solution, let us note that four of the twenty-nine characteristics in the interview did not enter the four factors. We have indicated that inexpensiveness was only minimally correlated with any of the other variables. The other three items formed a cluster: relevance of the topic to the work of one's agency, high priority of the issue, and timeliness of the research for a pending decision. Our original hypothesis was that relevance of subject matter was a logical precondition for usability—a hurdle that had to be surmounted before a study could get into the game—and this tended to be supported. Therefore, it does not have the same theoretical interest as a dimension of usability as do the other factors. We therefore treated inexpensiveness, high priority, and timeliness as separate variables and discuss them further in the next section.

Given the empirical factors identified through analysis of respondents' ratings of fifty specific studies, it is time to revise our original hypotheses. We can now identify three types of factors that should affect the usefulness of research. First, relevance to decisions being made is a precondition for usefulness; the topic of the study, and perhaps something about the way the research problem is formulated, should fit the substantive concerns of the decisionmaker. Second, there are two factors that provide a basis for trust in the research. These are research quality, which helps to ensure the soundness and authoritativeness of the results, and conformity with user expectations, which provides the test of experience, judgment, and previous knowledge. We hypothesize that both these factors will be positively related to judgments of usefulness.

Finally, there are two factors that give direction. They have to do with implications for change. Action-oriented research, with its characteristics of practicality and explicitness, offers guidance for incremental change within existing programs. We hypothesize that it will be positively related to usefulness. Challenging research, on the other hand, which questions both intellectual and organizational perspectives and points toward fundamental change, runs counter to prevailing political feasibilities. We hypothesize that it will be negatively associated with judgments of usefulness. We now turn to the data.

Effects of Research Characteristics on Usefulness

To test the effects of the factors on usefulness, we employed multiple regression. The intent was to find out the relative importance of each dimension for the usability of research. As you may remember, we used four different measures of usefulness: (1) likelihood that the respondent would take the research into account if his or her office were considering the issue discussed; (2) the substantive contribution of the ideas or information in the study to the agency's work; and then for occupants of the position that was the most appropriate user of the study (3) the likelihood that they would take the research into account; and (4) the substantive contribution of the ideas or information to their work. These multiple measures are ungainly but they turn out to be revealing.

Table 15-1 shows the effects of the characteristics factors on each of the usefulness measures as derived from the responses of the 155 decisionmakers in the sample. For the ratings of the respondent about his own office, relevance of subject matter also appears. (Relevance is unnecessary for "most appropriate users," who are "appropriate" precisely because the subject matter is relevant to their work.) The table also shows the total variance in the usefulness measures explained (R^2) by the factors.

We find first of all that characteristics of research are important predictors of usefulness. They account for from 23 percent to 43 percent of the total variance in usefulness, depending on which measure we consider. Research characteristics clearly make a difference. If we add the other three variables (inexpensiveness, high priority issue, and timeliness), there is almost no addition to the variance explained. After the four factors and relevance are considered, these three variables together explain only about 1 percent of the remaining variance. Since the priority of the issue and timeliness are correlated with relevance, the implication is not necessarily that they are unimportant but that relevance is serving as a surrogate for them. Once relevance is taken into account, they add very little explanation.

Table 15-1

Effects of Research Characteristics on Measures of Usefulness: Standardized Regression Coefficients for Types of Usefulness Regressed on Characteristics of Research

Research Characteristics	Substantive Usefulness	Likelihood of Use
In the Work of Own Office		
Research quality	.24	.38
Conformity to user expectations	.11	.18
Action orientation	.19	.15
Challenge to status quo	.22	.19
Relevance to issues office deals with	.19	.14
R^2	.35	.43
In the Work of Most Appropriate User		
Research quality	.19	.13
Conformity to user expectations	.20	.20
Action orientation	.25	.22
Challenge to status quo	.32	.18
R^2	.38	.23

Note: All 310 cases (2 abstracts read by each of 155 decisionmakers) are used to construct a matrix of Pearson correlation coefficients with pairwise deletion of missing observations; 273 is the lowest N for a simple correlation and, therefore, the appropriate (conservative) N for computing degrees of freedom. In fact, however, most of the correlations are based on larger Ns, averaging about 290 of the 310 cases.

A second observation is equally apparent at first glance. All the factors have positive effects. The higher the score on each factor, the more useful the study. While the size and order of the standardized regression coefficients (betas) vary on the different usefulness measures, all of the factors contribute to usefulness. Further, the betas fall within a fairly narrow range. Since the positive consequences of the challenge factor are unexpected, we will return later to a discussion of this finding. As for the other factors, they all operate in the hypothesized direction.

Let us look first at the percentage of variance in usefulness explained by research characteristics. Respondents' ratings indicate that when it comes to the substantive usefulness of a research study—that is, the contribution that its ideas and information can make—research characteristics explain about the same amount of variance for their own work and for the work of others (35 percent and 38 percent, respectively). These figures suggest that the contribution that a study *can* make is dependent in a consistent way on its characteristics. However, for likelihood of use, there is a considerable difference. Research characteristics account for 43 percent of the variance in the respondent's own likelihood of using a study, but only 23 percent of the variance in others' use. The likelihood that other people will actually use research is far less predictable. It is dependent not only on the attributes of the research but also on factors outside the research: personal, situational, or political.

The major difference in the pattern of coefficients between one's own likelihood of use and others' likelihood of use is the salience of research quality. For oneself, research quality is the most important single factor ($\beta = .38$, which is twice as high as the next largest coefficient). If a decisionmaker is actually planning to take heed of research in his work, he apparently wants to be convinced of its validity and cogency. But respondents' ratings show that research quality has less effect on others' use of research ($\beta = .13$). The difference in the effects of this one factor largely accounts for the difference in the predictive power of all characteristics (R^2) on the likelihood of use. When it comes to the substantive usefulness of ideas and information, research quality has somewhat more effect for oneself ($\beta = .24$) than for others ($\beta = .19$), but it is nowhere as big as the difference that occurs for likelihood of use.

What accounts for the difference in the effects of research quality? One possibility is that the respondents, knowing the norms of social science, engaged in blatant idealization of their own conduct. We doubt that this is a convincing explanation.

Remember that the analysis is based on two different sets of ratings. We did not *ask* respondents how important any characteristic was for the usefulness of a study. Rather we asked each person to rate the usefulness of the study, then answer a set of open-ended questions, and then rate the study on the extent to which the descriptive characteristics applied. Interpretations here are based on the statistical relationships between characteristics and usefulness. To dissemble through this complicated rating scheme would have been possible, but difficult. Moreover, elsewhere in the interview, quite a few decisionmakers were outspoken about their "socially undesirable" skepticism regarding the utility of social research.

Nevertheless, what may be happening in the ratings of research quality and likelihood of use is that *for themselves* respondents reported what they would like to do—that is, their subjective disposition to give a hearing to research of good quality. They know themselves from the inside, with all their noble intentions, however much the good intentions are thwarted by events. For other people, they report what they observe. Their ratings may indicate that looking at other people's situation from the outside, they do not see a relationship between research quality and use. They judge other people by what they do.[6] Without deliberate misrepresentation, they may be giving themselves the benefit of the doubt.

If research quality is the most important attribute for the usefulness of research to their own work, action orientation turns out to be the most consequential factor for others' use of research. To judge from the regression coefficients, research with direct and practical implications for action and explicitly formulated recommendations appeals to other decisionmakers at a somewhat higher level than it does to the respondents themselves. But for their own offices, too, action orientation increases likelihood of use. Interestingly, this type of research, applicable within existing agencies and programs, also enhances substantive usefulness. The idea and information content can contribute to one's own work as well as to the decisions of other users when they confront the issues involved in the study.

Another question in the interview asked about the *purposes* that each research study could serve. It listed seven purposes, such as formulating new government policies or programs, improving existing programs, and mobilizing support for a position or point of view, and asked the respondent to rate how well the study, if it were used, could serve each purpose. (See Table 15-2 for the standardized regression coefficients when these seven purposes were regressed on the four factors of research characteristics.) In this analysis, conformity is of little moment. In fact, research that comes out in ways that people expect is of no use at all for such purposes as changing ways of thinking about an issue or planning new decision-relevant research. Research quality is of noticeable importance only for two functions: mobilizing support for a position or point of view (when it becomes handy to have solid evidence) and changing ways of thinking about an issue (where, too, resistance has to be overcome, whether one's own resistance or that of others). Thus, once it is decided that research will be used, the dimensions that lead to trust in the results are not especially important.

More useful for most purposes are research studies that provide direction. Action-oriented research, for instance, is particularly suited to improving existing programs. It is also useful for evaluating the merit of alternative proposals for action when decisions have to be made. Most valuable of all are studies that are high on challenge to the existing order of things. The betas for challenging studies range from a low of .28 (for mobilizing support) to a high of .40 for changing one's ways of thinking.

Which brings us back to what is probably the most exciting theme of the findings to date: the unexpected role of challenge to the status quo. As mentioned earlier, we had expected that research that suggested fundamental change in philosophy and policy—research that was out of phase with political realities—would be regarded as of little use and hardly likely to be used at all. Responses indicate otherwise. Challenge is a positive feature of research. As seen in Table 15-1, high scores on challenge are associated with substantive usefulness both for oneself ($\beta = .22$) and for other users ($\beta = .32$), and even show a moderate relationship to likelihood of the study's being used (self, $\beta = .19$; others, $\beta = .18$). An inspection of the total effects of each factor suggests that challenge to the status quo is perhaps the most favorable of all research characteristics for promoting usefulness. This conclusion is reinforced by the high ratings for challenge in Table 15-2.

Table 15-2
Effects of Research Characteristics on Appropriate Uses: Standardized Regression Coefficients for Appropriateness of Uses Regressed on Research Characteristics

Appropriate Uses	Research Quality	Conformity to User Expectations	Action Orientation	Challenge to the Status Quo	R^2
Raising an issue to the attention of government decisionmakers	.06	.10	.23	.34	.26
Formulating new government policies or programs	.06	.18	.21	.39	.32
Evaluating the merit of alternative proposals for action	.14	.10	.27	.29	.30
Improving existing programs	.06	.16	.34	.33	.38
Mobilizing support for a position or point of view	.25	.09	.20	.28	.30
Changing ways of thinking about an issue	.25	−.01	.18	.40	.36
Planning new decision-relevant research	.16	−.06	.16	.31	.20

Note: All 310 cases (2 abstracts read by each of 155 decision-makers) are used to construct a matrix of Pearson correlation coefficients with pairwise deletion of missing observations; 284 is the lowest N for a simple correlation and, therefore, the appropriate (conservative) N for computing degrees of freedom. In fact, however, most of the correlations are based on larger Ns, averaging about 295 of the 310 cases.

The implications of these results seem to be far-reaching. They suggest that research is useful not only when it helps to solve problems—when it provides ideas and information that can be instrumentally applied to recognized problems—but research is also useful when it questions existing perspectives and definitions of the problematic. These decisionmakers are indicating that research can make substantial contributions *to their work* by challenging the ideas currently in vogue and providing alternative cognitive maps. Even if the implications are not feasible or politically acceptable at present, such research helps to develop alternative constructions of reality. In time, these alternative images of reality can yield new ways of addressing policy problems and new programs and procedures for coping with needs.

Thus, the definition of research "use" is broadened. Research that challenges accepted ideas, arrangements, and programs obviously cannot be put to work in a direct and immediate way. It cannot be used instrumentally, particularly when it runs up against the antagonism of interests embodied within the current political balance. Yet, decisionmakers say it can contribute to their work and the work of other appropriate decisionmakers. It can *enlighten* them.[7] They make a distinction between research that is acceptable in the political decision-making system and research that they themselves will listen to and support. Their responses show that challenging research, whatever its political liabilities, is useful to them.

The Issue of Values

One of the reasons often alleged for decisionmakers' neglect of social research is that there are value cleavages between the social scientists who do research and the decisionmakers who are expected to use it. Value dissensus, it is said, precludes use. In the problem-solving or social-engineering model of research utilization, social researchers are expected to operate within the value frame of the decisionmakers. For practical purposes, in this view, researchers are expected to take off from decisionmakers' specification of what the problem is, what the social goals are, and which alternative means are feasible for moving toward the goals. To the extent that the researcher departs from the assumptions, goals, and priorities that decisionmakers adhere to, his or her research will be irrelevant to their needs and will go unheeded.

This is the conventional wisdom. The social researcher whose work is to enter the policy sphere should reach consensus with some important segment of decisionmakers on the value orientation of his or her work. For maximum research utility, the researcher should accept the fundamental perspectives—constructs of reality, values and myths, language and metaphors, goals, priorities, and political constraints—of the key decision-making group. In this way, his or her work will be useful for solving the problems as decisionmakers define them—and it will be used.

Our respondents did not denigrate problem-solving studies. On the contrary, action orientation is clearly an important element of usefulness. It can help them *instrumentally* to cope with specific problems they face.

But they gave even more weight to research with innovative implications. This kind of research presupposes a different model of use, an enlightenment model that does not make value consensus a prerequisite for useful research. On the contrary, the enlightenment model allows a role for research as social critic. It envisions research as providing the intellectual background of concepts, orientations, and empirical generalizations that filter into the decisionmakers' world. Research performs a *conceptual* function and in so doing introduces variant theories and orientations. As new perspectives come to attention, they affect the way that decisionmakers define issues, the priorities they set, and the elements they attempt to manipulate in seeking to cope with the problems reconceived.

It is easy to be carried away by the potential ramifications of policymakers' receptivity to challenging research. The finding seems to lend the support of government counterparts to social scientists' autonomous and critical stance. Merton years ago identified the basic function of sociology as revealing the "latent functions" that social patterns serve.[8] Deutscher makes the same point today: "It is a major responsibility of the sociologist to raise questions about what everyone else either fails to notice or takes for granted."[9] That policymakers endorse such critical and often iconoclastic perspectives is encouraging news indeed.

But as one anchor to reality, let it be noted that the research studies included in our inquiry were not excessively innovative. None of them raised questions about the basic institutions of the society or challenged fundamental economic arrangements. What the studies that were rated highest on challenge to the status quo did do was:

1. Show that current, accepted practices were not performing up to expectations (e.g., community care of the ex-mental patient);
2. Offer evidence supportive of emergent program schemes not yet put into practice (e.g., community control of care-giving facilities) or program schemes largely out-of-fashion (e.g., long-term hospitalization for schizophrenics);
3. Challenge basic intellectual assumptions in the field (e.g., the causal relation of stress to mental illness).

These were not *brand* new ideas. Looking at our factor solution, we see that the item "Findings are unexpected or novel" does not load high on the challenge factor. The ideas had been in circulation; some were being actively promoted. The research presented evidence that supported nonentrenched and controversial positions. In this sense, to the people responsible for policy and program, the research represented an alternative view, a reorientation. It challenged the existing scheme of things.

Special conditions of the study should be noted. As described earlier, our data derive from what people in decision-making positions say, not from what they do. With all the checks and multiple measures, we are dealing with simulated cases. We are not discussing actual use.

All our decisionmaker interviews were with officials in the field of mental health: in federal, state, and local positions. Decisionmakers in mental health may be a rather special breed. Most of them have training in psychology, psychiatry, or social work, and by the nature of their positions, many of them have contact with evaluation and analysis staffs or research grants offices. The history of the National Institute of Mental Health, where many of our federal respondents work, has been heavily oriented to research. Perhaps these people have a special affinity for research (although this is not a crucial crimp, since we are not concerned with the absolute levels of acceptance)[10] and a special receptivity to untraditional findings, particularly at a time when modes of treatment are in transition.

Analysis indicates that no personal characteristic of the decisionmaker that we have yet examined (e.g., age, field, highest degree, length of time on job, political orientation) affects his or her judgments of research usefulness. But we are working within the existent range and do not have data on people from other fields for comparison. Moreover, the style of mental health organizations may set a climate that affects all people working within them. So the question of generalizability remains.

Another limitation is that from all we know about research use, social research is seldom used one study at a time. However one defines "use," decisionmakers rarely latch on to one set of results and apply them to a decision at hand. (This is perhaps a reason why the characteristic of "timeliness" did not show up as important in our data.) Rather, they use the weight of the evidence from scores of studies, as these are filtered through their own experiential and political judgment. Even more commonly, they use the popularized generalizations (e.g., community care is better than institutionalization) without firm knowledge of where or how the generalization was derived. Or with greater attenuation still, they use social science orientations and concepts (e.g., the compatibility of services with ethnic subcultures) in structuring their thinking about policy and programs.

Our study investigated the usefulness of fifty discrete research studies. While we now know how people respond to the characteristics of individual studies, we do not yet know to what extent similar judgments apply to the diffuse social science knowledge that wends its way circuitously from specific researches to the decision-making sphere.

But we have come upon noteworthy conclusions. Perhaps most interesting and unexpected is the support for the conceptual functions of research. Our study suggests that decisionmakers are receptive to controversial research, research that makes them rethink comfortable assumptions. They consider it not unlikely that they, and others, will take such research into account in making decisions.

Notes

1. In addition to the studies reported in this volume, other efforts at quantitative investigation of research use include: Q. Lindsey and J. Lessler, *Utilization of RANN Research Results: The Program and Its Effects* (Research Triangle Park, N.C.: Research Triangle Institute, March 1976); Research Triangle Institute, *RANN Utilization Experience; Final Report to the National Science Foundation* (Washington, D.C.: NSF, June, 1975); Marvin R. Burt, Donald M. Fisk, and Harry P. Hatry, *Factors Affecting the Impact of Urban Policy Analysis: Ten Case Histories* (Washington, D.C.: The Urban Institute, July 1972); Mark van de Vall, "Utilization and Methodology of Applied Social Research: Four Complementary Models," *Journal of Applied Behavioral Science* 11, no. 1 (1975), pp. 14-38; F.W. Heiss, *Urban Research and Urban Policy-Making; An Observatory Perspective* (Boulder: Bureau of Governmental Research and Service, University of Colorado, 1975).

2. For further discussion of these hypotheses, see Carol H. Weiss, "Policy Research in the University: Practical Aid or Academic Exercise," *Policy Studies Journal* 4, no. 3 (1976), pp. 224-28, and Carol H. Weiss, "Improving the Linkage between Social Research and Public Policy," in National Academy of Sciences, *Policy Relevance: The Use and Non-Use of Social Research* (forthcoming).

3. The specific solution shown in Appendix 15B is the result of an oblique rotation, using a direct oblimin criterion, of the factors with eigenvalues greater than 1.00 emerging from a principal components factoring of a matrix of Pearson correlation coefficients where the missing values have been deleted pairwise. Indices measuring the dimensions were calculated from the factor score coefficients. Because of the use of pairwise deletion in the correlation matrix, some method was necessary for the estimation of the effects of missing values. A number of methods of weighting missing observations were tried. The factor scores from each were correlated with the original items; this matrix was compared to the primary factor structure matrix obtained in the course of the factor analysis. The method of index computation selected was that which best reproduced this factor structure matrix. It involved total estimation with missing observations assigned the mean value of the item. The factor score of an individual was declared as missing if more than half of the items with loadings greater than .40 (in the factor pattern matrix) on that factor had missing observations.

4. Four items of characteristics that appear elsewhere in the interview could not be examined because of our research strategy. For example, we could not ask about the readability of reports because we wrote all the abstracts ourselves in identical format.

5. The effects of research quality and conformity turn out to be complementary, not synergistic. One supplements the other in an additive way; the presence of one does not heighten the effect of the other. Statistically, there is no interaction effect.

6. In terms of attribution theory, this would say that they are making a *situational* attribution for their own behavior; it is circumstances that lead them to do what they do. They make *personal* attributions for the behavior of others; *they* do what they do because that is the kind of people they are. Kelly G. Shaver, *An Introduction to Attribution Processes* (Cambridge: Winthrop Publishers, 1975), pp. 81-82, 126-137.

7. For discussions of social engineering versus enlightenment functions of social research, see Morris Janowitz, *Political Conflict* (Chicago: Quandrangle, 1970), and E.T. Crawford and A.D. Biderman (eds.), *Social Scientists and International Affairs* (New York: Wiley and Sons, 1969).

8. Robert K. Merton, "Manifest and Latent Functions," in *Social Theory and Social Structure*, 1968 ed. (New York: Free Press, 1968), pp. 73-138, esp. 118-22.

9. Irwin Deutscher, "Public Issues or Private Troubles: Is Evaluation Research Sociological?" *Sociological Focus* 9, no. 3 (1976), pp. 231-37.

10. Our analysis focused on the *relationship* between ratings of usefulness and descriptive ratings of research characteristics.

Appendix 15A
Items Appearing in
Interview Schedule

Usefulness

Assuming your office had to consider the issues discussed in the study, how likely is it that you would take the study results into account?

Focusing for a moment just on the study's findings, and not considering external constraints, to what extent does the study contain *ideas or information* that can contribute to the work of your agency?

How likely do you think it is that these decisionmakers (those named by respondent as most appropriate users) would actually take the study results into account?

Focusing just on the findings, and not considering external constraints, to what extent can the *information or ideas* in the study contribute to their (those named by respondent as most appropriate users) work?

Research Characteristics

To what extent is the general topic of the study relevant to the issues your office deals with?

To what extent do you think that the findings are valid?

To what extent do the findings agree with your sense of the situation?

Please indicate the extent to which each statement applies to the study.

a. Deals with a high priority issue
b. Adds to descriptive, causal, or theoretical knowledge in the field
c. Adds to practical knowledge about the operation of policies or programs
d. Compatible with the ideas and values of the potential user
e. Analyzes the effects of factors that decisionmakers can do something about
f. Has direct implications for a course of action
g. Implies the need for major change in philosophy, organization, or services
h. Targeted—that is, focuses on a narrow set of dependent, or outcome, variables
i. Contains explicit recommendations
j. Supports a position already held by the user
k. Recommendations are supported by the data

231

l. Implications of the findings are politically acceptable
m. Consistent with a body of previous knowledge.
n. Findings can be applied within existing agencies and programs
o. Challenges existing assumptions and institutional arrangements
p. Raises new issues or offers new perspectives
q. Inexpensive to implement
r. On time for a pending decision
s. Findings are unexpected or novel
t. Provides quantitative data
u. Generalizable to equivalent populations
v. Comprehensive—that is, includes most of the potentially explanatory variables in analysis
w. Statistically sophisticated
x. Technical quality of the research is high
y. Findings are internally consistent and unambiguous
z. Objective, unbiased

Appendix 15B
Factors of Research
Characteristics

Loading	Factor I (Research Quality)
.922	Technical quality is high
.890	Statistically sophisticated
.794	Objective, unbiased
.745	Provides quantitative data
.702	Findings internally consistent, unambiguous
.625	Comprehensive set of explanatory variables
.634	Recommendations supported by data
.612	Generalizable to equivalent populations
.569	Validity of findings
.560	Adds to descriptive, causal, theoretical knowledge

Loading	Factor II (Conformity to User Expectations)
.745	Supports user position
.718	Consistent with previous knowledge
.663	Compatible with user ideas and values
.613	Agrees with respondent's sense of situation
−.550	Findings unexpected or novel (negative)

Loading	Factor III (Action Orientation)
.706	Contains explicit recommendations
.703	Manipulable independent variables
.664	Targeted—few dependent variables
.661	Direct implications for action
.605	Applicable within existing programs
.526	Adds to practical knowledge

Loading	Factor IV (Challenge to Status Quo)
.764	Challenges existing assumptions and arrangements
.738	Implies need for major change in philosophy, organization, or services
.574	Raises new issues or perspectives
−.437	Findings politically acceptable (negative)

Note: Factors are derived from 510 ratings of fifty research studies.

16 Problem Setting in Policy Research

Martin Rein
and
Donald A. Schon

There is clear evidence of the growth of policy research and of its institutionalization. At the same time, there is also clear evidence of contemporary disaffection with it. Questions about its utility are coupled with a variety of proposals for its reform.

Much of the contemporary doubt rests upon a somewhat narrow view of what policy research can or should do.[1] The dominant conception of policy research today centers on its use within a framework of decision making and problem solving. Yet, to all appearances, policy research has not been strongly instrumental in public problem solving. If we examine the current patterns of its use for power and political positioning, for legitimation of action, and for reform, we come upon a range of uses that are neither envisioned by those who espouse the problem-solving framework nor accepted fully by members of the research community.

The problem-solving framework holds three crucial assumptions that, for most policy situations, we question.

First, the image of the process of policy development is incomplete. It assumes that policy development begins with a shared articulation of the problematic situation and defines the task of research as instrumental problem solving, where solutions entail discrete policy decisions. This formulation excludes, we believe, what is perhaps the most crucial aspect of the policy process. In policy development one seldom starts from a consensual definition of the problem to be solved, and research influences the climate of opinion even more than it influences concrete decisions. Therefore, a more reflective view of the policy world would indicate:

1. Policy development is essentially about a process of *problem setting*; it is concerned with developing new purposes and new interpretations of the inchoate signs of stress in the system that derive from the past.
2. Policy development must address the management of dilemmas as well as the management of tradeoffs; all possible courses of action have mixed positive and negative values attached to them; and some conflicts of values are intractable.
3. Policymakers use research as an instrument to legitimate action in the

We wish to thank Paul Keckemeti and Harold Garfinkel for the criticism of an earlier draft of this chapter. Sheldon White has contributed significantly to several parts of the argument, and Jonathan Cole has been exceptionally helpful in surfacing the role of skepticism.

perpetual striving for consensus of belief and for organization of the fine structure of government action; policy may influence the research agenda more than research influences the direction of policy.

4. Interest groups outside of government, who also participate in policy development and implementation, also use research to further their aims, sometimes by contention and sometimes by cooperation.

If we take this larger view—that policy development is about problem setting, dilemma and tradeoff management, and consensus building *via* coalition formation—then we can find understandable and in a certain sense legitimate those uses of research data and social science theory that might otherwise seem illegitimate.

We believe that policy researchers can go further toward conflict management and goal development if they attend systematically to problem setting. Problem setting is important because the questions we ask shape the answers we get.

Although we can argue for the importance of problem setting, there are serious impediments to its inclusion in policy research. The political and administrative settings in which policy research tasks tend to be defined are conducive to the definition of policy research as problem solving. In this case, for example, policy research, whatever its espoused purpose, serves the actual function of legitimating or discrediting particular courses of action. The very uses of policy research for legitimation, political positioning, or reform along preconceived lines causes most policy research to be cast in the mold of engineering or applied science. Accordingly, the administrative machinery for commissioning research makes it difficult or impossible to treat problem setting as an object of analysis.

Proponents of rigorous methodological standards for policy research take the view that rigor is a necessary condition for relevance, if the researcher wishes his analysis to enter into policy development. However, the pursuit of methodological rigor in officially sponsored research does not by any means assure the relevance of the research to considerations of policy. And there is the further danger that a narrow interpretation of rigor will favor quantitative studies that give the illusion of scientific precision while discrediting a probing qualitative analysis of issues as "soft headed"—that is, a mere expression of the researchers' preferences not grounded in "hard data."

Despite all of the administrative and organizational deterrents to the inclusion of problem setting in government-supported policy research and despite the reinforcement of these prejudices within the social scientific community, we believe that it is useful to attempt an exploration of the problem-setting processes. It is the purpose of this chapter to open this subject for analysis and to attempt in a preliminary way to develop some of the guides and strictures that can enable analysts to make problem setting problematic rather than given.

Let us start with a situation in which the traditional ways of formulating a problem are cast in doubt either because they can no longer usefully explain what people are worried about or because they no longer serve the most passionately supported normative ideals in society. When consensus has eroded and the nature of the problem is itself in doubt, then the exploration of problem setting becomes most urgent. In this situation, policy research becomes an important instrument for creating the conditions that then make it possible for a problem-solving perspective to enter policy analysis. Policy research then becomes an instrument through which researchers try to mobilize a belief that can lead to action. In this sense, we will call our approach *value critical*. But how are problems set in this period of doubt? We believe that problem setting requires the finding, building, or selecting of a framework within which uncertain situations can be organized.

Almost all the camps of contemporary cognitive psychology, from information processing to the current developmental analysis of the construction of reality, now perceive learning and knowing as beginning with the problem of construing the initially inchoate experience field—that is, as a matter of finding formats of perception through which to organize the bombardment of sensory events into meaningful aggregates. Similar developments have occurred in the sociological tradition, where students of the sociology of knowledge have convincingly argued that science is a social construction of reality. Nevertheless, this understanding, although widely accepted among philosophers, sociologists, and cognitive psychologists, has not been translated into policy research where such perspectives are regarded as an unwarranted intrusion into scientific analysis of values and preferences. The whole enterprise of policy research is predominantly value committed, and we think it cannot be anything else.

Toward a Methodology for Problem Setting

We would like to take a first step toward the development of a framework for policy-relevant research that we believe can draw together, in a nonformalistic way, the interplay between problem setting, policy and program design, and the translation of design into action.

Our main argument is that the transition from worries to problems cannot be made without the use of frames that distinguish the significant from the trivial. But frames can imprison the analyst just as they free him for creative work. To generate problems from our worries requires that we discover the tacit frames that organize our insights and then that we challenge them. It is an exercise in reflection designed to encourage doubt about frame adequacy. As such, it is a call for organized skepticism, as well as for the conscious selection and construction of frames. While this creative skepticism is a norm in scientific inquiry, it is not institutionalized where social science is applied to questions in the public arena. In part, the desire to be legitimate, according to prevailing canons of legitimacy, has inhibited the application of this norm in the field of policy analysis.

This chapter is not another call for skepticism, but a discussion of how to be skeptical, and how to move from skepticism to the conscious selection and construction of frames.

The problem-setting process begins with a problematic situation. We experience a situation as problematic, according to John Dewey,[2] when it provokes in us a diffuse, intuited discomfort or irritation. In problematic situations, the knowledge we have accumulated does not enable us to cope with what bothers us now. We find ourselves initially without the capacity to make an orderly formulation of the problem.

Starting, as we do, with the instances in which traditional ways of formulating policy problems are cast in doubt, the predicament of the problematic situation appears more agonizing to us than it did to Dewey. Dewey saw in the quandaries and discrepancies of the cognitive process an invigorating, creative condition that could stimulate inquiry directed toward the creation of a moral, humanistic world with science at its core. We also want to capture that quality of problematic situations that takes the form of malaise and disorientation and that can be overcome only through laborious and uncertain steps.

The main task in problem setting is to work through the process by which worries, arising in problematic situations, can be converted into the orderly formulation of problems. Every student of policy research who has tried to do a study knows how frustrating this stage of inquiry can be, because of the difficulty in grasping precisely what is the problem. (This stage can be all the more frustrating when the researcher cannot, within the formal context of commissioned research, admit to the process in which he is engaged.) We believe that the discovery of the problems is perhaps the most difficult aspect of policy research. How do worries come to be problems?

In the context of public affairs, worries are often triggered by signals that are negative or are construed to be negative. Seemingly unrelated events may appear in a variety of settings. Statistical reports show an increase in an unsatisfied demand for housing. Opinion polls register discontent. In a large city, rents rise. People cannot find places to live at prices they can afford. Some units are dilapidated; others are abandoned. There is the overall environment of a housing shortage. People come to be worried about "the housing situation." The housing worries may or may not be connected to coexisting worries in other fields such as health, crime, the political process, and so forth. Depending on how such worries are aggregated into sets, various "housing problems" may be defined.

Problem setting is a judgment about the problematic situation—that is, a diagnosis that also contains the prescription of directions for action. We cannot make a judgment of this kind unless we apply a frame to a field of experience. This frame enables us to (1) highlight certain features of the situation, including certain worries that we select as symptomatic, (2) ignore, or select out, certain other features of the situation, including certain worries, as noisy and irrelevant, and (3) bind together the salient features of the situation, including the relevant worries, into a pattern that is coherent and graspable. Frames help us to organize not only the worries we address, but also those we neglect.

In this sense, the process of *framing* is complementary to a process of *naming*. We cannot frame a field of experience without also generating a context for the naming of elements within the frame. And just as frames give us a way of seeing some things and of not seeing other things, so names call our attention to certain features of elements within a frame while they invite us to ignore other features of those elements. Whatever is said of a thing, denies something else of it. So, for example, within a broad frame of economic dependency and its related difficulties, we single out the feature "single parent" and use the name "single-parent families" partly because there has been such a sharp increase, among all families with children, in the proportion of those that are single parented, and partly because single parenting is assumed to be related to economic dependency. Naming this phenomenon "single-parent families" rather than "broken homes" suggests an important shift in values and therefore in the frame for constructing the problem. Similarly, the succession of terms, such as *backward, underdeveloped,* and *developing* countries, signifies an underlying frame associated with modernization.

The complementary processes of naming and framing mediate the transition from disaggregated worries and scattered perceptions of situations toward the cognitive experience of meaning and the work of creative problem solving.

Different frames, and their associated names, may be used to integrate experiences in different ways. Thus, one housing official, facing the worries we have outlined, might construe the situation as one of tenant disaffection leading to landlord's neglect. Another might permute much the same elements and judge that there has been landlord exploitation leading to tenant neglect. The two ways of interpreting the situation reflect frames that set the stage for different ways of allocating blame (though both share the property of allocating blame to someone) and different values, perhaps even moral perspectives, for the situation.

Both of these frames for the problem are relatively small in scope and bound the problem by those worries that are most immediate and salient. A third official, working from a larger frame, might see the worries as linked to a larger institutional problem: the culture of poverty. And still a fourth might see the housing worries as tiny expressions of a much larger set of problems conveyed in classical Marxist theory: outcroppings of the general erosive alienation inherent in capitalism. A final frame might enable a housing official to insist that none of the frames listed above go to the root of the problem because they neglect economic variables such as the cost of land, labor costs, the costs of money and materials, and the like.

Frames differ in scope, in the number and variety of worries and other features of the situation they subsume, and in the degree to which they reduce collections of worries to a mode of understanding consistent with a single direction of action. But all frames used to set problems must serve both explanatory and normative functions. They must enable the inquirer to group a distributed set of worries in terms of phenomena that are sequenced according to before-and-after, then-and-now. They must allow the inquirer to order events in the field of social experience so as to permit explanation of later events in terms of earlier ones—that is, they must permit the location of events in a causal space so that questions of "Why?" and "What if . . . ?" can be addressed to actions in this space with the possibility of a determinate answer. Moreover, frames must contain a basis for action. They must permit the inquirer not only to explain the phenomena associated with his worries, but to set the directions of actions designed to reduce them. In this sense, frames must facilitate what we have called the normative leap from findings to recommendations.[3]

Where do frames come from? For most people, most of the time, frames are transmitted from one person to another. A good deal of ordinary discourse among people traffics in frames, in ways of seeing phenomena, in ideas, in conceptions of the world. It is characteristic of the overlapping cultures embedded in society that they are reservoirs of frames on which members of the culture may draw. The frames available in cultural reservoirs change over time, however, according to rules that are poorly understood. At various times, in various cultures, particular ways of framing experience become powerful— become, in effect, ideas in good currency.[4]

The need for new frames arises frequently in the policy world when old frames seem to have lost their utility and having moved out of good currency, no longer seem to provide a consensual basis for action. This situation may happen because standards of explanation shift, so that old frames no longer seem to explain events as well as they once did; or because situations change, so that earlier ways of framing come to seem unacceptable as explanations or as normative guides for action. In such cases, we move toward the selection or construction of new frames. Although we discuss this process as an intellectual one, let us emphasize again that a new frame may emerge, after the fact, as the rationalization of a political act—that is, we may do something new, and then ask: "How did we get here?" "How may we justify what we have done?" In such an instance, action may give rise to the frame.

Generative Metaphor

Whatever their particular origins may be, the frames (whose application to experience sets policy problems) contain generative metaphors that enable us to reason from the familiar to the unfamiliar. Familiar concepts are brought to unfamiliar situations and in the process transform the familiar, providing a way of organizing and understanding it, while they are themselves transformed.

Thus, the housing official we have been following might frame his worries in terms of a metaphor of disease and pathology. He might think in terms of "decaying housing stock," which he contrasts with "healthy stock." He might then search for means to "arrest decay" and to "protect healthy stock," and these notions might lead him to think in terms of rehabilitating old stock and in terms of the insulation of healthy neighborhoods from decaying ones.

That we are dealing here with a metaphor becomes clear when we consider that houses are not literally either healthy of diseased. Indeed, one man's "decay" may be another man's old world charm. That we are dealing with an operational, rather than a decorative metaphor, becomes clear if we observe that the housing official pays attention to just those phenomena that fit his metaphor and ignores the rest, and if we observe that the remedies he espouses, and considers obvious, are those that flow from the metaphor and would not seem obvious (indeed, might seem wrong) if considered from the point of view of a different metaphor. That we are dealing with a generative metaphor becomes clear if we observe that the metaphor sets the direction of remedial action in the very process by which it selects out events and explains them. Once we have been able to see houses as diseased or healthy, a whole set of prescriptions present themselves for action.

A great deal of contemporary policy tends to organize events in terms of a health metaphor in which worries are interpreted as outcroppings of social pathology. Thus, the housing stock may be seen as decayed: "sick" families may be seen as requiring both isolation and special treatment in public housing projects that may be seen, alternately, as hospitals or as dumping grounds; and finally, neighborhoods may be the elements chosen as sick or healthy, and may be so regarded depending on whether or not they have been scattered and isolated as a consequence of physical developments such as urban renewal. Each of these ways of bringing the health metaphor to the housing situation tends to give rise to a different order of explanation and to a different set of prescriptions.

Metaphors enable us to gain, and to convey, essential insights into patterns of phenomena and to tease out lessons. Generative metaphors provide a basis for making the normative leap by projecting onto unfamiliar situations familiar notions that are already evaluated. Because we believe that it is better to be healthy than diseased, the health metaphor is generative of directions of solution for the problem of housing.

Different kinds of metaphors are generative in different ways. For example, some metaphors permit us to frame problematic situations in terms of departures from a prototypical idea. The aim is to identify a correctable flaw, to cause the abnormal to revert to the normal. We move from a worry to a problem in this way when we can isolate the flaw that, in our minds, produces the departure from the ideal prototype.

In this manner, a housing worry becomes a housing problem when we can identify that single-parent families lack access to the credit market, which thus inhibits the capacity of that market mechanism to work as it should. Accordingly, the worry about the failure to attract investment in the ghetto is explained in terms of this "flaw" in the market mechanism. But the "flaw" so isolated is not coextensive with the set of all possible flaws that might have produced the same outcome. What other "flaws" can help us understand the situation? How do they overlap?

Similarly, the prototypical ideal may be identified with a representation of the situation "as it used to be." Neighborhoods "used to be" integrated and well cemented; now, due to the intrusions of urban renewal, they have come to be characterized by scatter and mutual isolation. Physicians used to have close personal relationships with their patients; now, because of the alienating effects of medical specialization, physicians are distant from their patients; the essential conditions of trust and closeness have been destroyed. The "problem" is how best to return the situation to the status quo ante.

Again, the generative metaphor may be one of "need." Here, the analyst will see the situation as one in which essential needs remain unmet; remedy will consist of devising ways to meet such needs. For example, people may be taken to "need" decent housing, according to certain standards of decency. Remedy may then take the form not only of measures to increase the supply of decent housing but of measures, such as rigorously enforced building codes, that restrict the supply of housing that is not decent.

Or the generative metaphor may be one of battle and victory. If it is possible in the situation to identify villains, victims, and heroes, then the problem setting may be construed in terms of doing battle with the villains and winning.

These types of metaphors do not exhaust the set. There may be many such metaphors, although, we believe, only a limited number of them will tend to be powerful enough for action within a given culture at a particular time.

We do not mean to imply that we must start with a generative metaphor already in hand and then move with it from worries to problems. It is often only in the course of inquiry that we come upon the metaphors that enable us to set the problem. Furthermore, it is not uncommon to find that insight into the metaphor that integrates our understanding comes only at the end of our inquiry, rather than at the beginning. Indeed, we may move through the whole process without gaining consciousness of the metaphor that guides our inquiry.

But this lack of awareness is a source of concern. The generative metaphors contained in the frames by which we set our problems may carry with them consequences we do not intend: prices we do not wish to pay. Thus, the "obviousness" of the explanations associated with such terms as *flaws, disease, needs,* and *battles* disappears the moment we subject them to conscious scrutiny; and the solutions that seemed to flow from them so obviously cease to appear obvious at all. However, we cannot assess the prices paid for our metaphors, nor can we compare them to options, until we have become aware of them.

Our frames, along with their generative metaphors, tend to be tacit for us at the beginning of inquiry. Although values influence what we are prepared to accept as a fact, or as a solution, we are not usually aware of our values or beliefs. How can we learn what it is that we value and believe at the very early stages of inquiry? Our fundamental commitment is to creative skepticism in problem setting. We must surface and criticize our tacit frames. We must, in order to do this, entertain multiple frames for the organization of our experience. Through the critical comparison, selection, and integration of frames, and through a reflective awareness of the stands we wish to take, we can move to more nearly adequate problem setting. But before we can subject our framework to skeptical review, we need to make explicit the tacit frames we use to organize experience.

Story Telling

Story telling is at once a medium for problem setting and a way of discovering the tacit frames that underlie our problem settings.

We use the term *story telling* because the logical structure developed in this mode of analysis is much the same as that of the story. It contains "... a sequence of events, each of them leading to the next, and, like the story-teller ... he presents the story in terms of the behavior of a few major 'characters'. The succession of events is made to appear to be caused, at each step, by the actions of the characters; and the entire story is made to unfold according to some 'inner necessity'."[5] This account captures much of what is central to our idea of policy analysis as story telling, although it gives too much attention to the role of key characters and presents a deterministic view of events.

The main advantage of the story is that it uncovers the theoretical orientation of the storyteller and what he takes as important. This permits him to ask whether the same facts can be integrated around a different story line. What has he left out of his account? What new pieces of evidence must he gather if he wished to modify his story?

Story telling also lends itself to empirical support by the canons of good historiography—that is to say, we can criticize a story in terms of its truth value: Did the sequence of events occur as explained? Although we are interested in a correct diagnosis, not just a persuasive one, it is much more difficult to validate the interpretation of why the sequence of events occurred. Aside from the obvious edict that causally related events must occur in a time sequencing where consequences follow antecedent events, judging the interpretation of a story and the lesson to be learned from it is much more difficult. Nevertheless, stories do permit partial objective social assessment and this allows a scientific debate to take place.

Perhaps a concrete example would be useful to illustrate the themes we have been discussing. Consider the situation in the field of social services for children. We start with a diffuse worry that things are not going well. The holding power of social agencies is weak, they seem unable to keep their clients for more than a short period of time. The outcome of their effort seems to have only doubtful utility. Lack of confidence in the effectiveness of social agencies is accompanied by a rising concern about neglect and abuse of children and the feeling that opportunities for advancement are not being exploited, as the educational attainment of children measured by national achievement tests seems to be declining. This scenario of worries is not uncommon. What is the problem?

One widely held view about the problem is that services are fragmented, poorly coordinated, so the varied needs of the same child cannot be met. The metaphor is contained in concept of fragmented services that suggests that broken crockery and social services have a shared pattern. Each was once whole and at one time was broken into fragments. Just as we can recement the shattered pieces of pottery so, too, can we coordinate or integrate fragmented social service programs. There is a very strong normative implication that fragments should be reintegrated and organized as wholes. The metaphor provides an interpretation about what is the problem and what future course of action should be taken in general. The story of how fragmented social services affect the difficulties in the development of children is not regarded as an idiosyncratic story because it can be generalized to many situations. The story of fragmented social services thus provides us with a plausible understanding of social processes and an imperative for action.

There are, of course, alternative interpretations. We can, for example, argue that the villain of the piece is not poor coordination but the poor quality of services. Coordination according to this view is wrongheaded because an integrated pattern cannot be stronger than its constituent parts. Here the central metaphor is "upgrading" rather than "recementing."

Maps, Theories, and Models

Maps, theories, and models may be understood as analytic devices that permit examination of the elements and relations in a story. In this sense, they are also vehicles for increased awareness of the tacit frames on which our problem setting rests. But maps, theories, and models may also be understood as steps toward increased formalization of problem setting. Then we may conceive of the problem-setting process as moving from the diffuse detection of a worry, to the telling of a story about the problematic situation, to the construction of a theory that makes explicit the causal linkages suggested in the story, to the formulation of a model that displays the hierarchical interrelationships of the essential elements of the theory.

Problem setting does not often neatly fit this developmental picture, but the picture is useful, nonetheless, as a kind of ideal type in terms of which we can better understand the complexities of the actual process.

Mapping

We describe mapping as a first order attempt at the formalization of the story. A map rigorously identifies the variables that are operative in the situation, but it is loose about the dynamics of their interaction—that is to say, in a map we must specify the contours or the streets or the points of demarcation. Map making forces a commitment to these strategic variables and places them in context by specifying their relative values. Maps are indispensable for organizing conduct; they are the basic factor in learning about reality. Maps are what enables a person to move from a random, unfamiliar, informationless situation, in which he is paralyzed, to situations he can master. Mapping provides an orderly arrangement of landmarks and is a crucial step in a more formal attempt to organize evidence.

Although a map is sometimes less persuasive and more difficult to interpret to a community of policymakers than stories, partly because it doesn't tell them what to do, it is not entirely bereft of action implications. For example, we can impose a set of rules that say that when one sees such and such a landmark, then one acts in the following manner: turns right, or left, or perhaps stands still. When we impose a purpose on these visual patterns located in a space, such as a destination, then a map becomes a crucial tool for action, because it serves as an aid for helping us to get where we want to go.

Once we establish a map, we can then question whether we have selected the correct route, or whether we might prefer a different destination. Have we cluttered the map with irrelevant details or have we failed to add crucial landmarks, perhaps in the way people see the world in which they live? The map provides a representation of the way we structure in space our selective perceptions of reality.

Theories and Models

Models and theories are different from stories in that they attempt to provide a simplified picture of reality; they are different from maps in that they not only identify strategic variables, but specify how they dynamically relate to each other. Some models seek only to provide an accounting or description on how the variance of complex events can be partitioned. Here a model is like a map, because it seeks to identify what are the crucial landmarks in charting a relatively unexplored terrain.

Stories, maps, and models are three interrelated ways of translating worries into problems. Each provides a different way to surface beliefs so they can be subjected to organized skepticism. They differ largely in terms of the degree of formalism of the key variables and their interrelationships rather than in the extent to which they rely upon explicatory metaphors to diagnose and by implication to prescribe a course of action. Many sophisticated theories are unadorned metaphors. For example, the theory of wage contours draws heavily on a mapping metaphor to describe the ripple effect of wage settlements on the same industry. For example, wage levels for automobile workers are high in Detroit (the center of the industry) and low in the South. There are theories of labor market queues that suggest that members of labor markets form a single line and those at the end of the lines do worse than those at the beginning; hence, the best way to improve the position of those at the end of the line is to alter their position within the queue by training. Other theories hold that labor markets are segmented and those caught in the secondary labor market are entrapped with little chance of getting out and that changing the characterization of workers will have little impact on their mobility between segments.

There is no sharp, rigid demarcation between stories, maps, theories, and models. Each is an attempt to arrive at an understanding about the nature of the problem. These media can reinforce each other. For example, a theory of genetic endowment or environmental determinism can be called upon in telling a story about service failures and individual malintegration. Sometimes the theory is tacit and a model uncovers the framework that is implicit in a story that is widely accepted.

Strategies of Problem Setting

Within the basic outline of naming and framing, of generative metaphors, and of stories, maps, theories and models, there remains considerable space for free movement in which inquirers may employ different strategies for the passage from worries to problems. Some of the more prominent of these are described below.

Disaggregating Worries

This approach proceeds on the assumption that worries are not of the same set; they must consequently be further subdivided into their component parts. Conceptual respecification of the same phenomenon from different perspectives provides us with a shifting angle of vision from which new insights can be drawn.

Single parenting is, for example, not a uniform condition: One way to disaggregate the phenomenon is in terms of the circumstances that created the single-parented situation. Thus, we find that some single-parent situations come about because of widowhood, others because the mother is unmarried, others because of divorce or separation. Each of these situations is quite different in terms of the rate of transition from a single-parent status into a married-couple status. Thus, widows are least likely to remarry, while unmarried women are likely to marry. It may be reasonable to characterize unmarried parenting as a traumatic situation, but of short duration; whereas widowhood is likely to remain a persistent difficulty.

Most attempts at developing typologies that are based on disaggregation often imply, for policy purposes, that a single strategy of intervention will not suffice. There is not one problem but many problems, each having different roots and different consequences and hence must be treated differently in turn. This aspect of the strategy of problem setting is not essential, but the logic of disaggregation invariably drives one to this perspective.

Aggregating Worries

The passage from worry to problem may take the form of a broadening of frame for construction of the problem so that worries not usually clustered are brought together. For example, concerns about shortages of decent housing may expand to include concerns about child health and well-being, about economic independence and upward mobility, about jobs and career development. This process is what has happened, for example, with the introduction of the term *housing services*. The physical house now comes to seem simply an element in an array of services that touch on nearly all aspects of human life. The "housing problem" has been remapped so that its scope becomes very nearly coincident with the growth and development of families. Within this frame, attention focuses now on self-help housing as a pivotal intervention aimed at achieving independent family growth and development.

Just as the strategy of disaggregation contains the assumption that "there are many problems," here we have the assumption that many problems ought really to be made into one.

Working Back from Action

According to this strategy, one discovers what is problematic by eliciting implications of a problem definition for action. One engages in thought experiments. What if this were the problem, where would it lead me in terms of the kind of action I might seek to take? If it leads in a direction that I do not wish to go, because of my beliefs about what I judge to be undesirable, then I must reformulate the problem.

Various philosophical writings have described this approach to problem setting. For example, John Dewey, in a discussion of the standards that are used in making value judgments, explains: "We do not know what we are really after until a course of action is mentally worked out."[6] In other words, we truly know what we want only when the consequences of pursuing our ends are more fully evident. John Rawls discusses a similar strategy and calls it "reflective equilibrium."[7]

This way of approaching worries and transforming them into problem sets is very common. For example, a researcher might say he rejects the problem definitions that see the causal agents as largely resting in the victims themselves (the culture of poverty) and fail to take proper account of the role of institutions in bringing about unwanted social conditions. The assumption is that what is unpalatable cannot be true. Accordingly, if an urban problem is defined in terms of the intergenerational transmission of deprivation, then the problem must be misspecified, because it leads to a theory of causality and a policy of intervention that must be rejected on normative grounds. Problem specification is not purely a trial-and-error process. We often have strong value preferences; and these shape not only the way in which problems are set, but what we are prepared to accept as fact.

Many people have noted that we tend not to discover errors that confirm our predispositions. When we find what we want—when we discover a problem that requires an action that we find congenial—then curiosity tends to abate. A more skeptical approach would question a problem setting precisely because we find it congenial. We would ask just the questions that we are apt to regard as unaskable and that question what we desire most. Such a process asks not that we foresake our values but that we subject them to inquiry.

Criteria for Problem Setting

With strategies for problem setting, as with all of the processes we have so far discussed, there is a fundamental and unavoidable question of evaluation. Under what conditions ought we to say that a strategy is effective because it leads to the adequate formulation of a problem? What are the criteria for a good story? Under what circumstances may we say that one generative metaphor is better than another? What features of a frame make it adequate for problem setting?

The criteria for defining adequacy go deeply into the axioms on which social scientific inquiry rests. The adequacy of the problem formulation can be judged by two quite different standards. Consider, first, the *principle of consistency*. To what extent does the formulation of the problem draw together a large number of facts and relate them into a consistent framework? A good problem is one that subsumes a large possible set of worries into a network of plausible causation (which Popper calls "the stage of conjecture"). Here, "plausibility" designates not only consistency of propositions within the problem formulation itself, but consistency of that formulation with other sets of beliefs held by the inquirer.

There is, however, a second principle for judging the adequacy of problems; namely, to what extent can my formulation of the problem be put in jeopardy by empirical investigation? Here the *principle of testability* governs problem adequacy—that is, the theory or model contained in the problem setting should be subject to empirical test; it should be capable of disconfirmation.

Ideally, these two principles should be mutually reinforcing and thus provide no conflict. A good problem is one that meets simultaneously the tests of plausibility and testability. Unfortunately, in practice, these two governing principles often conflict. For example, Freudian interpretations of problems are extremely plausible within the framework of their own assumptions; so too are Marxian interpretations. But these plausible arguments lack the kind of scientific specification that really permits them to be subject to refutation by appeal to observation. Neither of these approaches lends itself to the social experimentation that permits one to so arrange things that, whether one likes it or not, whether one wants to believe or not, one's problem set is subjected to refutation. By the criterion of testability, problems are gambles—risk-taking ventures in which we make an informed guess—but we must be prepared to be judged wrong by the evidence.

If we are forever challenging the ambiguities of conventional wisdom with respect to how problems are formulated, we will discover that much of our definitions rest on ambiguities and inconsistencies. To consistently challenge the official language can, from the point of view of action, be extremely disruptive. Of course, the great art is not only to challenge an established formulation of a problem but to transform it, or to substitute a different one that explains as much as the first as well as that which had remained unexplained.

Piven and Cloward have attempted to reformulate the problem of welfare in the United States by arguing that welfare is not a response to distress but to disorder. It follows that if public largess is to be liberalized, it can only do so not by establishing the need for aid, but by mobilizing discontent so that society will respond to the disorder that political activity has generated. In principle, this theory that society can be terrorized into being good is both plausible and testable. Yet, even if we can identify empirical examples where relief is a response to distress rather than disorder, the plausibility of the theory may not be challenged, because of the difficulties in establishing the line of causality and in understanding why events occurred as they did.

Perhaps the central dilemma in problem setting is that there is such a widely diverse range of generative metaphors that identify what is the problem, how the problematic situation came to be as it is, and how it might be set right. The principles of consistency and testability provide only partial guidance in selecting among different problem frames. Aside from these, there are three other criteria that at least implicitly enter in the judgment of problem adequacy.

First is the question of the normative implications of the problem frame. Does the frame lead to a morally acceptable position? How conflicts between what is truthful and what is desirable are resolved is a fascinating question.

Secondly, frames differ in terms of their utility for action regardless of their normative implication. Here the imperative is that frames should lead to action, and while action should be broadly consistent with personal values, we often find it necessary to settle for much less, because we assign an even higher priority to the need to act: "Don't just stand there, do something." Of course, it is impossible to do nothing, because inaction is itself a form of action. The principles of testability and of utility for action may be closely interrelated. We might insist, for example, that the metaphor of fragmentation of services be subjected to rigorous evaluation by a social experiment. Accordingly, we would then require a much more fine-grained interpretation about the causal nexus of events and of their relations to desirable outcomes. We would need, then, to develop more formal procedures for refutation by moving from a story to a map, and then to a theory or model. If, however, there are formidable practical and political difficulties of achieving the coordination of agencies required for a social experiment, then the problem setting is for all practical purposes untestable.

Finally, there are those who are less attracted to value or action imperatives and are more concerned with the "beauty" that is inherent in the problem frame as revealed by the grace, subtlety, elegance, or interest with which the elements of the theory or story are put together.

In other words, there are different weighting schemes for judging the adequacy of a problem frame. We may judge such a frame by its plausibility and consistency, by its capacity to lead to action, by its value implications, by its "beauty," and finally, by its testability—its openness to learning through the correction of thought by experience.[8]

To make problem setting central to policy analysis is to expose latent ethical, political, aesthetic, and scientific differences, and this makes the task of relating thought and action more difficult. Nevertheless, we believe that in the long run, alternative problem frames facilitate a dialectic between perspectives and thus make it more possible to spell out and manage the dilemmas which are inherent in social policies. Not because such an exposure will lead them to disappear or to be finally resolved by an overarching criterion to which all would appeal. Rather, analysis may contribute to reducing symbolic posturing and hence to a more direct confrontation with things as they are, in their true complexity. The need to reenter a problematic situation—to see it from different perspectives and to develop different theories about why things happen and what can be done—is felt to be most urgent when theory is not settled and where policy is uncertain. Of course, continued questioning and doubt and uncertainty can be disruptive as well as integrative, if they undermine faith in action and faith in the capacity to build a collective community of inquirers who can engage in a good dialectic over time. If conscious attention to problem setting makes us lose confidence in action and cooperative inquiry, then it can produce a negative effect. But this, in our opinion, it need not do.

The argument we have been developing does not attempt to displace a problem-solving framework but rather to subsume it within a larger view of policy research. Problem solving is a special case of policy research and should not be equated, therefore, with the entire field of inquiry.

Notes

1. See Martin Rein and Sheldon White, "Belief and Doubt in Policy Research," *Policy Analysis* (forthcoming).

2. John Dewey, *Logic: The Theory of Inquiry* (New York 1938).

3. Martin Rein, "The Fact-Value Dilemma," Working Paper No. 28, Joint Center for Urban Studies of M.I.T. and Harvard University, Cambridge, Mass., September 1974.

4. See Donald A. Schon, *Beyond the Stable State* (New York: Random House, 1971), for a discussion of ideas in good currency.

5. Sidney Shoeffler, *The Failure of Economics: A Diagnostic Study* (Cambridge, Mass.: Harvard University Press, 1955), p. 150.

6. John Dewey, *Human Nature and Conduct: An Introduction to Social Psychology* (New York: Modern Library, 1930), p. 36.

7. John Rawls, *A Theory of Justice* (Cambridge, Mass.: Harvard University Press, 1973), p. 20.

8. That truth is not the only way to evaluate the quality of speculation is, of course, not a new idea. Lave and March in an interesting discussion of the issue argue that one never fully resolves the conflict between truth, beauty, and justice as criteria for judging theories and ideas. Charles Lave and James C. March, *The Social Science* (New York: Harper & Row, 1975), Chapter 3, pp. 51-78.

Index

Academic style of information processing, 186
Acquisition function, 168, 170
Action orientation, 218-219, 220, 221, 222, 223-224, 225, 233, 250
Adversary system, 117
Advisers, 131-135
Advocacy style of information processing, 186-187
Aggregation, 247
Alcohol, Drug Abuse, and Mental Health Administration, 215
Alkin, Marvin C., 11, 141
Analytic techniques, 72, 73-74, 75, 78, 89, 128-130, 133, 134, 135, 194; factor analysis, 217-221, 229n; maps, theories, and models, 244-246
Analytical sociology, 55, 56, 57, 58
Anthropology, 78, 128, 129, 133, 134
Armor, David, 74, 79
Attitude measures, 75-77
Attribution theory, 230n
Austria, 165-166, 169

Bankruptcy Act, 119
"Beauty," 250, 251n
Beveridge, William, 44
Bill of Rights, 119, 120
Blackmun, Harry A., 119
Bowles, Sam, 73, 74
Brandeis, Louis D., 110-111, 113, 116
Brewer, David J., 111
Brookings Institution, 23, 104
Brown, Henry B., 112
Brown v. *Board of Education*, 67, 69, 71, 111-115, 118
Buckley, James, 101-102, 106
Burtt, Edwin A., 57

Califano, Joseph, 107n
Caplan, N., 171, 208, 209, 213
Cardozo, Benjamin N., 110, 116
Carnegie Corporation, 8
Census function, 166-167, 170
Challenge factor, 219-220, 221, 222, 224-226, 233
Cherns, A.B., 37, 45, 50
Civil Rights Commission, 70, 74-75
Civil service, 41-43
Clark, Kenneth B. and Mamie, 114
Clinical style of information processing, 186
Cohen, David, 141
Coleman, J.S., 79

Coleman Report, 67, 69-70, 72, 73-74
Community control, 70-71, 202
Conceptual utilization, 15-17, 19, 200-201, 203-204, 206, 209, 227, 228, 246
Conformity factor, 219, 220, 221, 222, 225, 230n, 233
Congressional Budget Office, 104, 105-106
Congressional Research Service, 104-105
Consensual objectives, 29-35, 236, 237, 240
Consistency, principle of, 248-250
Continuous National Survey, 199-209
Controlled experiments, 46-47
Cowhig, James D., 53n

Davidoff, Paul, 120
Decision-driven model, 12
Decision-making: defined, 214; executive, 183-196; judicial, 109-121; legislative, 99-107; long-term/short-term, 202-205
Decision-making roles of social science, 171-172
Democratic institutions, 47-48
Deutscher, Irwin, 227
Dewey, John, 238, 248
Disaggregation, 246-247
Discipline-oriented: advisers, 131-132; research, 127
Disconfirmation, 249
Discursive concept, 179-180
Dissensus, 32-33, 35n
Donnison, David, 14
Donoughue, Bernard, 47
Downey, K.J., 172
Dror, Yehezkel, 100, 107n

Economics, 32, 38, 41, 44, 51n, 74, 128, 129, 133, 134, 165, 169, 184, 239
Education, 56, 60, 165, 187, 191, 202. *See also* "Experimental Educational Project"; School desegregation
Energy-related policy, 205-207
Engineering functions, 22n, 26-27, 35n, 88, 179, 226, 230n, 236. *See also* Instrumental utilization
Enlightenment functions, 17, 18, 19, 22n, 25, 26-27, 88, 179, 226, 227, 230n. *See also* Conceptual utilization
Equality of Education Opportunity Survey. *See* Coleman Report
Etzioni, Amitai, 17, 52n
Evaluation of problem adequacy, 248-251
Evaluation research, utilization of, 141-161
Evans, John W., 21n, 141

253

About the Contributors

Michael J. Bucuvalas is a research staff member at the Columbia University Bureau of Applied Social Research and a Ph.D. candidate in the Columbia Department of Political Science. Prior to the present project on the Usability of Social Research, he was affiliated with a B.A.S.R. evaluation of the administrative decentralization of New York City municipal services.

Nathan Caplan is a social psychologist and a program director in the Center for Research on Utilization of Scientific Knowledge, Institute for Social Research, University of Michigan. He has also conducted research on the role of values, political ideology, and biases inherent in social science methodology on the determination of problem definitions and social problem solving models. More recently he has researched the use of social science research among upper level government officials. He has been a member of a number of governmental policy-related advisory panels.

David K. Cohen is IBM Visiting Professor at Yale University's Institution for Social and Policy Studies (1976-77) as well as a professor at Harvard's Graduate School of Education. His research interests include: the relations between social science, social policy, and the work of practitioners; the politics of education; the social functions of innovation; and the expressive and symbolic content of public action.

Daniel Dreyfus graduated from the Meguro High School in Tokyo, Japan and has bachelor and master degrees in engineering and the Ph.D. from American University in political science. Dr. Dreyfus was employed as a refinery construction engineer for Texaco; as a remote-site planning engineer for the Alaska District, U.S. Army Corps of Engineers. Since February 1968, he has been on the professional staff of the Senate Committee on Interior and Insular Affairs where he is presently the Deputy Staff Director for Legislation.

Karin D. Knorr studied sociology, anthropology, linguistics and philosophy of science in Vienna. Assistant Professor at the Institute for Advanced Studies in Vienna, she has lectured there and at the University of Vienna and on topics of sociology of science and methodology since 1972. Major research interests focus on the question of utilization of knowledge, and especially social science knowledge, and on the analysis of scientific discourse and argumentation with a view to scientific development.

Eleanor Farrar McGowan is Research Associate at the Center for Educational Policy Research at the Harvard Graduate School of Education and a Senior

Associate at the Huron Institute. Ms. McGowan is conducting an implementation and policy study of a major educational R&D/federal program, and has also done research on the implementation of the education voucher demonstration. She has carried out studies of other innovations at the college and non-college level, and studies of organizational change in non-profit agencies.

Renate Mayntz received the B.A. from Wellesley College and the Ph.D. in sociology from the Free University in Berlin. Before going to the University of Cologne, where she is a professor and Director of the Institut für Angewandte Sozialforschung, Dr. Mayntz held chairs at the Free University in Berlin and the Hochschule für Verwaltungswissenschaften in Speyer. She has taught at Columbia University and the New School for Social Research in New York, at the University of Edinburgh and at FLACSO (Facultad Latinoamericana de Ciencias Sociales), Santiago de Chile.

Michael Q. Patton is Director of the Minnesota Center for Social Research, University of Minnesota, and Director of the Evaluation Methodology Training Program at the University. He received the B.A. from the University of Cincinnati and the M.S. and Ph.D. (1973) from the University of Wisconsin, all in sociology. He was a Peace Corp volunteer in Upper Volta. Dr. Patton's current research interests include utilization and application of social science knowledge, development and application of evaluation methods, and the implementation and effectiveness of innovative teaching methods.

His co-authors, Kathryn M. Guthrie, Patricia Smith Grimes, Barbara Dickey French, Nancy J. Brennan, and Dale A. Blyth, are advanced graduate student trainees in the NIMH-supported evaluation methodology training program at the University of Minnesota. Guthrie is in the Department of Speech-Communication, Grimes in the School of Public Affairs, French in the Department of Educational Psychology, Brennan in the School of Social Work, and Blyth in the Department of Sociology.

Martin Rein, Professor of Urban Studies and Planning at M.I.T., is author and co-author of many books dealing with the problems of poverty, income redistribution, and social policy. He has had continuing interest in the questions surrounding the utilization of social science knowledge in policy implementation and professional practice. His chapter in this volume was written while he was a Fellow at the Center for Advanced Studies in Behavioral Sciences.

Robert F. Rich is Assistant Professor of Politics and Public Affairs at Princeton University. He has conducted utilization studies concentrating on U.S. Foreign Service Reporting and the practices of National Science Foundation/RANN division program managers. Currently, he is Principal Investigator on a N.S.F. project focusing on the utilization of technology assessments by policy-makers in and out of government. In addition, he is conducting experiments on strategies for promoting utilization of scientific knowledge by policy-makers.

Richard Rose has been Professor of Politics at the University of Strathclyde, Glasgow, since 1966. He is author and editor of more than 15 books in the field of comparative politics, and has been Secretary of the Committee on Political Sociology, IPSA/ISA since 1960. Professor Rose is convenor of a work group on comparative public policy, holding meetings in Europe and America.

Paul L. Rosen has taught sociology at New York University and is Associate Professor of Political Science at Carleton University, Ottawa, Canada. He is engaged in a study of the political and legal theory of disobedience.

Donald A. Schon is Ford Professor in the Department of Urban Studies and Planning and the Division for Study and Research in Education at M.I.T. As an industrial consultant, a government administrator, and a president of OSTI (a non-profit social research and consulting organization), Dr. Schon has worked as researcher and practitioner on the problem of organizational learning and professional effectiveness. Dr. Schon was invited in 1970 to deliver the Reith Lectures on the BBC.

L.J. Sharpe, B.Sc. (Econ.), M.A. (Oxon.), graduated from the London School of Economics in 1957. He held a Fulbright and English Speaking Union Fellowship at Indiana University 1957-58. He taught at the London School of Economics 1961-65 and has been a Fellow of Nuffield College, Oxford since 1965. He was Research Director of the Royal Commission on Local Government in England 1966-69.

Pio D. Uliassi is Senior Program Officer, Office of External Research, Department of State. With State since 1957, he has done research on such topics as West European Communist movements and political union and integration, and has managed and coordinated Department-financed research.

Michael Useem received the Ph.D. from Harvard University (1970) and is Associate Professor of Sociology, Boston University. He recently completed a study on the structure and impact of federal support for social science. His current research includes a study on the internal organization of the upper class and an investigation of the audience for the arts in America.

Janet A. Weiss is a graduate student in the Department of Psychology and Social Relations, Harvard University, and expects to receive a Ph.D. in social psychology in 1977. Her current research is focused on human judgment and decision-making and she is interested in the role of social science in decisions made by public policy makers.

About the Editor

Carol H. Weiss is Senior Research Associate at Columbia University's Bureau of Applied Social Research. Her current research interests include the processes of public policy-making, the uses of social research in policy-making at federal, state, and local levels, and the effects of social science on the formulation of political agendas. She has served as consultant to such agencies as the National Institute of Mental Health, the National Center for Health Services Research and Development, the Assistant Secretary for Planning and Evaluation of the Dept. of Health, Education, and Welfare, the National Science Foundation, the General Accounting Office, the Dept. of Housing and Urban Development, and the National Academy of Sciences. She is the author of *Evaluation Research*, Prentice-Hall, 1972 and *Evaluating Action Programs*, Allyn and Bacon, 1972.